BILL
BELICHICK
★ ★ ★ ★ ★ ★ ★ **VS.** ★ ★ ★ ★ ★ ★ ★ ★ ★
THE NFL

THE CASE FOR **THE NFL'S GREATEST COACH**

ERIK FRENZ

TRIUMPH
B O O K S

Library of Congress Cataloging-in-Publication Data

Names: Frenz, Erik
Title: Bill Belichick vs. the NFL : the case for the NFL's greatest coach / Erik Frenz.
Description: Chicago, Illinois : Triumph Books LLC, [2016]
Identifiers: LCCN 2016022906 | ISBN 9781629373119
Subjects: LCSH: Belichick, Bill. | Football coaches—United States—Biography. | New England Patriots (Football team)—History. | Football coaches—United States—Rating of.
Classification: LCC GV939.B45 F74 2016 | DDC 796.332092 [B]—dc23
LC record available at https://lccn.loc.gov/2016022906

This book is available in quantity at special discounts for your group or organization. For further information, contact:

Triumph Books LLC
814 North Franklin Street
Chicago, Illinois 60610
(312) 337-0747
www.triumphbooks.com

Printed in U.S.A.
ISBN: 978-1-62937-311-9
Design by Patricia Frey

To Mom, Dad, and Alison.

★ ★ ★

Contents

Foreword

I first met Bill Belichick in 1982 when I was 23 years old and a long shot to make the New York Giants football team as a free agent. Bill was only six years older, but three things were immediately apparent: he was intense, he was incredibly detail oriented, and he had a gift for teaching. Bill coached the special teams and linebackers, and I knew right away that this guy was going to be a terrific coach.

Since joining NFL Network in 2005, I have closely followed his career and further realized what a special coach he is. How special? Well, in this book, *Bill Belichick vs. the NFL*, Erik Frenz makes a compelling argument that Bill Belichick is the greatest NFL coach of all time. To make his case, Frenz tackles the statistical variations between Belichick and most of the great coaches throughout NFL history while being fair and measured in the differences in coaching at different times in NFL history.

The conversation weaves in and out between George Halas, Paul Brown, Vince Lombardi, Chuck Noll, Bill Walsh, Bill Parcells, and Tom Coughlin, among other bright, inventive, and successful coaches. Can anyone match the longevity of Halas, who coached for 40 years? Was Brown the best coach of all time? Perhaps he was the most innovative. How about the iconic Lombardi, for whom the Super Bowl trophy is named? Noll and the Pittsburgh Steelers were a machine in the 1970s with a multitude of NFL Hall of Famers to prove it. The myriad branches of Walsh's coaching tree remain successful, while Belichick coached alongside Parcells and Coughlin.

Though Frenz takes great pains to pay respect to these great coaches while profiling their backgrounds and respective places in NFL history, his overriding theme is that not only do the numbers support his claim, but also the continued evolution of Belichick as a coach and his significant impact on the game make him the best ever. During his 16 years guiding the New England Patriots, Belichick has won 73 percent of his 256 regular-season games, 13 AFC East titles, four Super Bowls, and reached double-digit victories in 13 consecutive seasons. Frenz details Belichick's transition from a defensive mastermind to an offensive-minded head coach whose teams routinely average close to 30 points per game while rarely turning the ball over.

Bill's genius is that he fully understands what each player on his roster can do, and he puts him in the best position to execute. When you combine that with an uncanny ability to gameplan every opponent and to be more prepared than any team I have ever seen, it's hard to argue that Belichick shouldn't be on the short list for every football fan.

This book is like a great barroom conversation. Each reader will come to their own conclusions as to the greatest NFL coach of all time. All I know is that Bill Belichick has to be a very prominent name in that conversation.

—Mike Mayock
NFL Network analyst

★ ★ ★

Introduction

It's one thing to make a case for a player as the best of all time. His impact can be quantified by his performance on the field. Quantifying a coach, however, is tricky.

The win-loss record has to be part of the discussion and so do championships at the division, conference, and league level, but there's no practical way to measure how much of an impact the strategies have on each play of each game. Some coaches have won more games, more NFL championships, and/or more division titles than other coaches, but it would be inaccurate to plug those numbers into an equation for the best head coach of all time.

The years have changed the game. Today's coaches deal with a completely different set of circumstances—from rules that have altered the playing of the game to offseason free agency, which have changed the team-building standard. Who knows how successful any of these coaches would have been in another era? That being said, Bill Belichick's run of success in this era measures up to the success of any coach before him in his own era.

Over the years the NFL has done everything in its power to eliminate the ability for one team to remain at the top for an extended period of time. These rules are also designed to help teams at the bottom get better. Free agency and the draft are the two main weapons of this parity; the best teams can't keep everyone, and the worst teams get the first choice of new, young players to add to the roster.

The Patriots have defied the unwritten laws of parity since 2000 with 209 combined regular-season and postseason wins, 78 combined losses, 13 AFC East championships, six AFC championships, and four Super Bowls. Each of those marks is more than any other team in that time. Belichick wasn't supposed to be this successful, but he has overcome stacked odds to achieve that success. In a sense it truly has been Bill Belichick vs. the NFL.

★ ★ ★

I was six in 1992, when I saw football for the very first time on the television downstairs in my childhood home in Maine. By the time I was a senior in college, I already had witnessed two NFL dynasties: the golden days of the Dallas Cowboys from 1992–95 and the New England Patriots' out-of-nowhere 2001–04 run. Those two dynasties were separated by just six years. Eight of my first 14 years as a football fan were heavily dominated by two teams.

I thought that's the way it was supposed to be. Up until recently, I was right.

The Patriots' dominance is remarkable, if not unbridled, in the free agency era. It's an era that forces teams to constantly change their nucleus. In that respect Belichick is the perfect coach for this day and age. Year to year and even week to week, Belichick is willing to adapt his philosophy to do what is best for his team to win. He is able to stay ahead of the curve by going against the grain of the NFL. "One of the things we've tried to do is be a little bit of an outlier in some respects," Belichick said as the keynote speaker at 2016 Salesforce World Tour. "When I came to the Patriots in 2000 as the head coach, we played a 3-4 defense and we only had two teams in the NFL, us and the Pittsburgh Steelers, who played a 3-4. We had quite a bit of success, won three Super Bowls in four years, and by 2005 half the league was playing a 3-4 defense. So when I came here trying to find a nose tackle like Ted Washington, it was easy because no one else wanted him. Five years later, if we were looking for a nose tackle, there were probably five other teams in the draft ahead of us. We've kind of had to find different players, different schemes, whether it be tight end-based offenses or whether it be going from an odd to an even front defensively, whatever it happened to be, trying to find different ways to capitalize on the talent that's available. Otherwise, we're going to get like the fifth, sixth, seventh best guy at whatever the position is. So we've tried to take more of our way in areas that are less populated."

The league forces teams to constantly change their rosters, so Belichick is constantly evolving to account for those changes. Who knows how successful he could have been if he never had to worry about expiring contracts? Vince Lombardi never had to worry about free agency when it came to Hall of Famers like running back Paul Hornung, linebacker Ray Nitschke, and quarterback Bart Starr, who played every down of their careers for the Green Bay Packers during Lombardi's time as the coach.

Maybe the Patriots would never have missed a step from 2005–13 if they didn't have to move on from so many of their key players due to contracts and salaries. Maybe, with a veteran-laden group, they would have still taken steps back. What makes it interesting, though, is that Belichick doesn't often lose big-name players to expiring contracts. Yes, it's happened on occasion; kicker Adam Vinatieri, cornerback Asante Samuel, and wide receiver Wes Welker can attest to that. There are far more examples, however, of Belichick cutting ties while it still can benefit the Patriots in some way. Take, for example, the Patriots' trades of wide receiver Deion Branch (2006), defensive end Richard Seymour (2009), wide receiver Randy Moss (2010), left guard Logan Mankins (2014), and most recently, defensive end Chandler Jones (2016). Belichick has taken free agency, which is supposed to be a means of taking the best teams down a peg, and has turned it into a means of maintaining prolonged success.

★ ★ ★

One of my favorite football books is *The Essential Smart Football* by Chris B. Brown. In the first chapter, Brown says, "New ideas in football tend to arise as potential solutions to specific problems." That sentence in a nutshell encapsulates Belichick's career. The Patriots head coach is always adapting from one year to another and also within each year.

Coaches have been innovating and adapting since the introduction of the forward pass in the early 1900s. But what's remarkable is the frequency and quickness with which Belichick adapts. If he notices a weakness in his own team, he tries to find a way to correct it either schematically or through coaching. If he notices a strength, he finds ways to emphasize things that are working well. These strengths and weaknesses change each year as the roster changes, and Belichick is right there to adapt and accommodate the yearly turnover on his roster.

Make no mistake: Tom Brady has helped put concealer on some of the team's biggest blemishes over the years. But if we penalized every great coach for having a great player that has helped him to success, there would be no great coaches left. When the Patriots have been their best, it isn't because of the Brady show. It's because the Patriots have been talented enough at the top of the roster and deep enough at the bottom and because Belichick and his coaching staff have found ways to get the most out of all 53 players on the roster.

He's always very quick to pass the credit to the players when his team wins and to accept the blame when his team loses, but whether he likes it or not, he is synonymous with his team's success, and their run of dominance since 2000 will always be attributed in large part to him.

With that in mind, there's still a part of Belichick's legacy that remains to be written: the part where we find out whether the Patriots will stay afloat without the best quarterback the team—and possibly the league—has ever seen. You won't find anyone who anticipates the Patriots getting better when Brady is no longer behind center, but imagine what it would do for Belichick's legacy if his team remains the AFC's standard-bearer.

CHAPTER 1

★ ★ ★

The Making of a Legendary Coach

One does not simply walk into the NFL and become a legendary head coach. Bill Belichick built his legacy brick by brick and he didn't start when he showed up in Foxborough, Massachusetts, to become the Patriots head coach. In fact, Bill was born into football as the son of Steve Belichick, who coached in various roles across college football for more than 40 years from 1946–89. Steve spent most of his days as a scout and coach for the United States Naval Academy. Bill immediately took an interest and became something of a child prodigy as a coach.

His attention to detail was evident right from the get-go. "I never pushed Bill," Steve said, according to ESPN. "He was just always so interested…and so attentive to detail. He went to prep school at the Phillips Academy, where the Bushes went, because he once heard me advising recruits that they needed an extra year at prep school. Then Bill told me he wanted to go to college in New England, and I said, 'You've never even been to New England.' Bill said, 'Yeah, but I've done some studying and found there are more good schools in New England than anywhere else and I want to see them.' So we spent two weeks seeing them."

Bill ended up at Wesleyan, in Middletown, Connecticut, where he played tight end and center in football and where he also took interest in lacrosse and squash. In 1975—the same year Belichick finished his economics degree—he began his

NFL career as an assistant to Baltimore Colts head coach Ted Marchibroda. He was making $25 a week to study the opponent's offensive tendencies by drawing play diagrams on note cards, punching holes in the cards to denote categories such as first and 10, gains of more than four yards, screen passes, defensive blitzes, etc., and then sliding an ice pick through the holes to sort through the cards. "I learned probably more football in that room—it was a cinderblock closet, really—but I probably learned more football in that room than anyplace else I've ever been," Bill said. "It was like a graduate course in football."

Belichick's next resume builders followed. He was an assistant special teams coach with the Detroit Lions in 1976 and he added tight ends and wide receivers to his list of hats in '77. From there, he took another job as an assistant special teams coach and a defensive assistant with the Denver Broncos in '78. The next stop was with the New York Giants, but Belichick didn't start off with the defensive coordinator job that eventually put him on the map. Initially, his move to the Giants was lateral. He took a small promotion to become a special teams coach, shedding the "assistant" label from his title while maintaining his role as a defensive assistant.

In his third year with the Giants, Belichick added linebacker coach to his resume. He maintained his role as special teams coach and linebackers coach from 1980–84, during which time the Giants linebackers were feared, earning the

★　★　★　★　★　★　★

"By the time [Bill] was nine, he would sit with his father as Steve went through the film of Navy's next opponent's recent games. When he was 10, Bill had first crack at the films, breaking down each play by down and distance, the hash mark the ball was on, and a diagram of the opponent's defense. Every Thursday, Ernie Jorge, Navy's assistant coach in charge of the offensive game plan, sent Bill a copy of all the plays the Mids would be using in their next game. He sent it over in an envelope marked 'Bill's Ready List.' Even before he was a teenager, Bill Belichick was fluent in the language of schemes and formations."

—Leonardo Shapiro, *The Washington Post*

2

nickname "The Crunch Bunch" for a group that featured Lawrence Taylor, Harry Carson, Brian Kelley, and Brad Van Pelt. Taylor and Carson would eventually be named to the Hall of Fame, Van Pelt was named to five Pro Bowls, and from the year of 1980–84, the four linebackers were named to a combined nine Pro Bowls (four for Taylor, four for Carson, one for Van Pelt). The Crunch Bunch last played together in 1983, but the Giants' defensive reign of dominance was not over. The Crunch Bunch gave way to the Big Blue Wrecking Crew, right around the time Belichick was named defensive coordinator in 1985—just a couple years after Bill Parcells took over as head coach from Ray Perkins.

It wasn't long before Belichick's 3-4 defense was wrecking everything in sight. They were the No. 5 scoring defense in the NFL in Belichick's first year as coordinator and No. 2 in his second year. They held Joe Montana's San Francisco 49ers to three points in a 49–3 rout in the first round of the playoffs, followed by a 17–0 shutout of the dominant Washington Redskins, and then a 39–20 bucking of the Denver Broncos in Super Bowl XXI. Belichick's first taste of Super Bowl glory was quickly followed by his first taste of a Super Bowl hangover, but the Giants rebounded in the following years and ranked in the top 10 in scoring from 1988–90.

And that's when Belichick had the finest single-game performance of his young coaching career. The year was 1990, the game was Super Bowl XXV, the opponent was the Buffalo Bills. Led by quarterback Jim Kelly, running back Thurman Thomas, wide receiver Andre Reed, and others, the Bills offense was a scoring juggernaut with 95 points in their previous two playoff games.

That was before they ran into Belichick and the Wrecking Crew. The Giants held the Bills to 19 points—just the fifth time all season the Bills had been held below 24 points on offense—and they did it with the first example of Belichick's signature pick-your-poison approach.

Over the years, Belichick has developed a reputation for eliminating an opponent's greatest strength and forcing the opponent to win through unconventional means. The Giants sought to disrupt the Bills passing attack with aggressive coverage against the wide receivers, knocking them off the line and off their routes. This aggressive plan focused on the passing game but opened up opportunities for the running game. As a result the Bills ran the ball 25 times for 166 yards and two touchdowns, but Kelly was just 18-of-30 for 212 yards on the day.

The Giants began the game with just two defensive linemen on the field, but despite a defensive scheme that was designed to slow down the passing game, the Bills kept trying to pass the ball, as that had been their bread and butter all season. By the time they adjusted, it was too late. Belichick's Super Bowl XXV defensive gameplan landed in the Hall of Fame. And in a league that has trended toward the passing game in recent years, there are elements of his gameplan that have become commonplace in defensive strategies across the NFL.

★ ★ ★

It should come as no surprise that Belichick earned his first head coaching job hot off the heels of his now legendary defensive gameplan. While the Giants were running roughshod over the NFL in 1990, the Cleveland Browns were in the midst of a lost season in which they fired their head coach, Bud Carson, just nine games into the season and just a year and a half after he took over for former Browns head coach Marty Schottenheimer.

In 1991 Belichick took over a team that had won just three games the year prior to his arrival, and success didn't follow him from New York to Cleveland. The Browns won six games his first year and seven games each of his next two years.

One thing he did take with him, however, was his grisly demeanor. He didn't exactly endear himself to the local media with his tendency to avoid revealing anything resembling information, which made it all the easier for the media to rail against his decision to jettison popular quarterback Bernie Kosar in the middle of the 1993 season in favor of Vinny Testaverde.

The media began singing a different tune in 1994, when Belichick coached the Browns to an 11–5 record and their first playoff appearance since 1989. Belichick's defensive genius began to show through, as the Browns were the league's No. 1 scoring defense. He earned his first career playoff victory against his mentor, Bill Parcells, and the New England Patriots. That was the high point of Belichick's Browns career. It was all downhill from there.

"Bill Belichick will be my head coach in 1996." The Browns were 4–5 when Browns owner Art Modell gave Belichick that endorsement. The Browns went on to lose six of their next seven games from that point. How quickly things change. Modell had made the declaration after announcing he had made deals to move the team to Baltimore, but things went downhill well before that point.

★ ★ ★ ★ ★ ★ ★

"The Browns were [Belichick's] training camp, his boot camp for success. There were mistakes he made here on players, personnel, staff, public relations. But he's the master of adjustments. He learned how to do it right by everything he did wrong here."

—Mary Kay Cabot, *The Cleveland Plain Dealer*

Belichick wanted to add a new dimension to the offense to tilt matchups in his favor and so he implored Browns owner Art Modell to sign talented-but-divisive wide receiver Andre Rison to a $17 million contract, which forced Modell to borrow money from five banks. The move didn't pan out like Belichick hoped, thanks to a combination of underperformance, barbs thrown back and forth between Rison and Modell in the media, and Rison's self-vilification. (He infamously said, "Baltimore, here we come," in an expletive-laden tirade following the Browns' Week 12 loss to the Green Bay Packers.)

Belichick had also made another controversial decision at quarterback, when he benched veteran Testaverde for rookie Eric Zeier, who finished the season with 50.9 percent completions, four touchdowns, nine interceptions, and a 51.9 passer rating. Belichick was fired after that season, but even in a "five-year reign of error," as dubbed by Browns media, the surly head coach had laid the foundation for his next coaching gig through his mistakes.

Of course, after his failure with the Browns, other teams were hesitant to pick up what Belichick was putting down. So, Belichick linked up with his old friend, Bill Parcells, for another run at a championship with the New England Patriots. Belichick joined the Patriots as an assistant head coach and as defensive backs coach, helping the team get to Super Bowl XXXI in the 1996–97 season. The Patriots' pass defense gave up yards in bunches that year with the third highest total against them, but they allowed just 17 passing touchdowns (sixth fewest) and intercepted 23 passes (fourth most).

Belichick then took over as New York Jets head coach for the first time, while the Patriots and Jets worked out compensation for Parcells' services. Those were some successful Jets teams, and they never posted a losing record under Parcells. They even went 12–4 in 1998 and made a trip to the AFC Championship Game.

But following the 1999 season, when Belichick was named Parcells' successor, the Jets and their head coach were about to make headlines for a bizarre press conference and a now-famous note scrawled on a napkin.

CHAPTER 2

★ ★ ★

2000: Breaking Ground

"I resign as HC of the NYJ."

You won't find a more famous combination of seven words/abbreviations to ever be scrawled on a napkin in NFL history. That short phrase spelled the end of Belichick's time in New York, but it did not yet denote the beginning of Belichick's empire in New England. Only after several lawsuits and a trade of a first-round pick did Belichick officially complete his journey up I-95 from New York to Foxborough.

Coming to New England was not the end goal of Belichick's resignation press conference with the Jets. "I didn't resign to get to this spot," he said on a conference call shortly after his arrival in New England. "I resigned because I wasn't comfortable with the situation with the Jets." Belichick was looking at two situations: one under a familiar owner in Robert Kraft where he would be given dual duties as head coach and general manager, another under a changing ownership group with the Jets, where he would have his mentor Parcells looming over him in an ominous position of authority.

The Patriots were a good team when Bill Belichick arrived. They were just waiting for the right coach. In 2000 Belichick inherited a team that was already stocked with eight first-round picks and seven second-round picks. They were a young team. Of the 65 players that suited up for New England in 2000, 39 were age 26 years or younger, 19 were above that age, and only seven were 30 or older.

The nucleus was in place with Kevin Faulk, Troy Brown, Damien Woody, Willie McGinest, Tedy Bruschi, Ty Law, Lawyer Milloy, and Ted Johnson. Each of these players would go on to contribute to one, two, or all three of the Patriots' championships from 2001–04. Those pieces were all acquired in the space of seven years from the beginning of Bill Parcells' tenure as Patriots head coach in '93 to the end of Pete Carroll's tenure in '99. But most of them were dug up during the Parcells era with only a few good picks scattered in between the egregious draft flops of the Carroll-Bobby Grier regime.

That nucleus would remain the nucleus for a long time to come, but why—with so many talented players—were the Patriots falling further and further away from their goals with each passing year?

To understand the Patriots' rise to prominence after Belichick's arrival, it helps to first have an understanding of what they were before they became the model organization for the NFL. In the space of four years from Parcells' departure in 1996 to Carroll's ouster in 1999, the Patriots went from a Super Bowl contender

Patriots owner Bob Kraft (right) announces the hiring of Bill Belichick on January 27, 2000. (AP Images)

to a playoff pretender. The Patriots started 6–2 in Carroll's final year leading the organization but finished with a 2–6 slide that left the team out of the postseason for the first time in four years. After finishing 11–5 in '96, the Patriots finished with one fewer win and one extra loss each season for the next three years to go 10–6 in '97, 9–7 in '98, and finally 8–8 in '99. "In that third year, I know we only went 8–8," former Patriots linebacker Tedy Bruschi said in a conference call prior to Super Bowl XLIX. "But I thought I saw coach Pete Carroll, saw him harden a little bit. It's a different deal out here in New England. And his mentality in the way he handles things was so different than Coach Parcells. And I thought we had some players that were much older and a lot of players that were very young that only knew one way, and that was the Parcells way, old-school Jersey, if you will. And then coming in, new-school California. But I think that just that team was in a place where they weren't ready to accept what Pete was trying to give. And whether that's them being in the wrong place in their career, not at the right time…or maybe just being stubborn and too set in their ways, but those combination of things could be a factor in terms of it not working out."

But this was a sudden symptom of a long-term diagnosis, a gradual slide from the verge of championships to the brink of irrelevance.

The 2001 season is the official dawn of the Patriots dynasty; the 2000 season, though, was where it all began. Any Patriots fans who are old enough to remember can tell you exactly where they were when Jets linebacker Mo Lewis delivered the hit heard 'round the world that sent Drew Bledsoe to the bench. What they might not be able to tell you, though, is why Tom Brady was the one who took over at quarterback in the moment that changed the course of NFL history forever.

The Patriots didn't necessarily need a quarterback of any variety, even a backup, headed into the 2000 NFL Draft. They carried four quarterbacks into the 2000 season: Brady, Bledsoe, John Friesz, and Michael Bishop. Was Brady dead weight? Yes. Would it stay that way? Obviously not.

The 2000 roster needed an extra running back, defensive lineman, or linebacker more than it needed a fourth quarterback. To Belichick, those were all worthy sacrifices to make to keep Brady on the roster. And if they'd gone about it any other way, Brady might have been scooped up by some other team off waivers and never played a down for the Patriots. "It really doesn't matter whether the guy is on the practice squad or on the 53-man roster. If he's inactive, he's not going to play in the game," Belichick said during training camp in 2012. "Then the question is as an organization: which players do you want to protect? You can protect the ones on the 53. To some degree, you can't protect the ones on the practice squad. So in that particular case, that's why we didn't put Brady on the practice squad—because we wanted to make sure that we had him, not so much for that year, but for the following year."

A fourth quarterback wasn't the reason the Patriots lost their first four games, including two against division rivals. A fourth quarterback wasn't the reason the Patriots lost 11 games that year, but that fourth quarterback was arguably the biggest reason the Patriots won 10 or more games in 14 of the next 15 seasons and counting.

Brady wouldn't stay fourth on the depth chart for long, but his opportunity only came because Belichick saw in 2000 what he hoped could pay off in 2001 and beyond. But Brady's addition to the roster was just one of many factors that made the 2000 season so important in building for the future of the franchise. To borrow from his old mentor, Bill Parcells, Belichick was just starting to cook the dinner and still needed to shop for the groceries. In order to do so, however, he first had to find out exactly what he had in the cupboard.

Patriots 2000 Draft Picks

Round	Pick	Player	Position	Games played w/ Patriots
2	46	Adrian Klemm	OG	26
3	76	J.R. Redmond	RB	33
4	127	Greg Randall	OT	35
5	141	Dave Stachelski	TE	0
5	161	Jeff Marriott	DT	0
6	187	Antwan Harris	DB	52
6	199	Tom Brady	QB	225*
6	201	David Nugent	DE	15
7	226	Casey Tisdale	LB	0
7	239	Patrick Pass	FB	78

*=still with Patriots

From the end of 1999 to the beginning of 2000, the Patriots made 28 changes to the 53-man roster (including those on the practice squad and reserve lists). From the beginning of 2000 to the beginning of 2001, the Patriots made 28 more changes to the roster. In the first two offseasons of the Belichick era, the Patriots almost completely turned over their 53-man roster; only 16 players on the 1999 roster were a part of the 2001 Super Bowl champions.

Don't blame Belichick for walking into a kitchen where the previous cook had left him some top-shelf ingredients to work with. After all, Belichick eventually made a better dinner out of those groceries than his predecessors. Belichick isn't the first coach to ever acquire a team that had a lot of talent; he's just the only one lately who's maximized that talent into three Super Bowl championships.

It all started with whittling down the roster, trimming the fat to find the best players to build the team around. Personnel changes were just the tip of the iceberg, though. Any new head coach makes changes to the roster and to the schemes. Instead of Carroll's preferred Air Coryell offense predicated on vertical passing, Belichick switched to the Erhardt-Perkins offense to help with both the versatility and simplicity of his offensive scheme by relying on concepts more than individual assignments.

Defensively, Belichick was switching from the 4-3 front to his preferred 3-4. Fortunately, he had some players (McGinest, Johnson, and Bruschi in particular) who could play in either system. The versatility allowed Belichick to switch between the two schemes as he tried to put players in the best position to succeed.

But Belichick wasn't just changing the schemes or the personnel; he was changing the culture. Gone were the days of laid-back Carroll breathing cool, mellow California air into the frigid atmosphere of Foxborough, Massachusetts. Here were the days of Belichick, whose frosty demeanor matched perfectly with rigid guidelines.

Ever since Day One, Belichick has never been afraid to tell it like it is with the cold, hard truth. "We've got too many people who are overweight, too many guys who are out of shape, and too many guys who just haven't paid the price they need to pay at this time of the season," he said during training camp in 2000 after cutting backup tackle Ed Ellis for failing his physical and banning four players from a practice. "You can't win with 40 good players while the other team has 53."

1999 Patriots on 2001 Super Bowl Roster

QB Drew Bledsoe	LB Tedy Bruschi
WR Troy Brown	LB Ted Johnson
WR Terry Glenn	LB Andy Katzenmoyer
RB Kevin Faulk	CB Ty Law
TE Rod Rutledge	CB Tebucky Jones
C Damien Woody	SS Lawyer Milloy
DE Willie McGinest	P Lee Johnson
DE Brandon Mitchell	K Adam Vinatieri

He knew what worked and he wasn't afraid to go against the grain to that end. "I've been with some very successful franchises," he said. "The Giants, the Jets, and with those teams we had some very successful systems. And not just X's and O's, with everything, including conditioning. So I am trying to do here what we did with those franchises. I'm telling the players, 'This works. It's proven. So let's follow it.'"

Even in the early days, though, Belichick was changing. Yes, he was still the same hard-working, disciplined, strategic coach he had been in New York, but he wasn't the same churlish, crusty, impersonal coach who was chased out of Cleveland. He was becoming more personable, though he hadn't lost the disposition that's become his calling card.

Belichick earned the respect of his players that year while operating almost diametrically opposed to the previous regime. "You can tell he is a hard worker," defensive back Lawyer Milloy said in 2000. "And we needed a chewing out. I respect a coach who can walk up to you and say, 'You're not cutting it.'" Belichick uttered some iteration of that phrase many times to many players in molding the Patriots into his vision.

CHAPTER 3

★ ★ ★

2001: The Dawn of a Dynasty

Let's dispel the notion that the Patriots' 2001 season began the moment Jets linebacker Mo Lewis laid out Drew Bledsoe and ushered in the Tom Brady era.

The foundation for the Patriots' first Super Bowl championship season was laid in the year prior, when Belichick evaluated the roster he had been handed and found the nucleus of the team. The framework was built in the 2001 offseason when the Patriots made a litany of under-the-radar free-agent signings. Linebackers Mike Vrabel, Roman Phifer, Larry Izzo, and Bryan Cox, along with defensive lineman Anthony Pleasant, running back Antowain Smith, and wide receiver David Patten, were all among those signed to the Patriots roster in the 2001 offseason. Each of those players made big contributions to the Patriots' Super Bowl run. Pleasant ranked second on the team with six sacks; Vrabel, Phifer, and Cox saw plenty of action at linebacker; Smith finished with 1,157 rushing yards (12th most in the NFL) and 12 rushing touchdowns (tied for second-most); Patten finished second on the team in receptions (51), receiving yards (749), and touchdown catches (four).

Some of those players (Vrabel, Patten, Phifer, and Smith) would contribute to multiple Super Bowls, but the Patriots weren't done adding to their roster.

Next came the addition of two future All Pros in the draft: defensive end Richard Seymour in the first round and left tackle Matt Light in the second.

That's a total of eight starters the Patriots found in one offseason, more than one-third of a 22-man starting lineup. It's important to remember that Belichick inherited some talented players; it's even more important to remember the impact of the events that transpired in Week 2 against the Jets; but it's easy to see how the Patriots turned things around so quickly: Belichick was adding championship players to his roster at an eye-popping rate.

In adding those players, the Patriots had to drop some of the dead weight—both figuratively and literally. Some players were out of shape, others were not a good fit to the team schematically, others did not meet Belichick's high standards of football intelligence.

In any case, what better way to symbolize this than by bringing an anchor and putting it right in the middle of the locker room? "'You see that anchor downstairs?'" Brady recalls Belichick saying, in the NFL Films documentary on the 2001 Patriots. "'That signifies all the dead weight we've been dragging around for the last year.'"

Thanks to all those moves, by the beginning of the 2001 season, his vision was already beginning to become reality, but it did not come together the way

Patriots 2001 Draft Picks

Round	Pick	Player	Position	Games played w/ Patriots
1	6	Richard Seymour	DE	111
2	48	Matt Light	OT	155
3	86	Brock Williams	DB	0
4	96	Kenyatta Jones	OT	5
4	119	Jabari Holloway	TE	0
5	163	Hakim Akbar	LB	6
6	180	Arther Love	TE	0
6	200	Leonard Myers	DB	15
7	216	Owen Pochman	K	0
7	239	T.J. Turner	LB	2

Belichick pictured in the first two weeks of the season when the Patriots were 0–2. Neither the offense nor the defense consistently held up its end of the bargain; namely, the defense collapsed in a 23–17 Week 1 loss to the Cincinnati Bengals, and the offense ran into a wall in a 10–3 loss to the New York Jets in Week 2.

No one remembers the first two games for anything but the hit heard 'round the world. Lewis' hit on Bledsoe ushered in the Brady era and is a moment that lives on in Patriots lore. In the moment, though, I doubt if there was anyone who was excited about the change. Yes, the Patriots' offense had struggled in its first two games. Yes, Bledsoe had thrown two interceptions against the Jets that day. But Bledsoe was the face of the franchise from 1993–2001 in much the same way Brady has been for more than a decade. No one was eager to see how a second-year quarterback, the 199th overall pick of the year before, would fare in replacing an eight-year veteran.

If Belichick was going to avoid starting his Patriots career with back-to-back losing seasons, mimicking the start to his disappointing stay in Cleveland, he would have to do it with an inexperienced quarterback and they would have to start with a win against gunslinging quarterback Peyton Manning and the Indianapolis Colts' high-powered offense. With 44 points on the board, you'd think the offense found its groove that week. It was actually the defense that ruled the day with four turnovers against Manning and the Colts (one fumble recovery and three interceptions, two of which were returned for touchdowns). Brady was efficient, but with 23 pass attempts and 39 rush attempts, the Patriots were in a ball-control mode offense to take advantage of their sterling defensive performance while also protecting their fresh-faced quarterback.

These weren't wholesale changes being made on the fly. Some of these modifications were already in motion. The Patriots wanted a calculated pass attack with a smashmouth rushing attack, which they implemented with both Bledsoe and Brady at quarterback. By the time the future Super Bowl champion quarterback took the helm, Belichick had already implemented schemes that benefited his whole team more than just one player.

But things got worse before they got better. They were curb-stomped in their third loss, 30–10 to the Miami Dolphins. The first of many tough trips to Miami for Belichick left the Patriots at 1–3, looking up at three of their division rivals: the Dolphins (3–1), Jets (2–2), and Colts (2–2). It was one of the uglier losses the

Patriots had suffered under Belichick up to that point—which is saying a lot for a team that (at the time) had lost 14 out of 20 games since Belichick's arrival. But it also gave birth to a motivational tactic that sparked a turnaround.

When the team returned from Miami, Belichick had dug a hole in a corner of the practice field. He took the game ball from the loss, put it in the ground, and covered it in dirt. In the years to follow, other coaches would borrow from this eloquent yet gritty message: the game was over, and it was time to move on.

★ ★ ★

In Week 5 of the 2001 season, we finally saw a glimpse of what Brady could become—and of what the Patriots could be under Belichick's tutelage. Against the San Diego Chargers, the Patriots put the load on Brady's shoulders for the first time in his career, and the young quarterback delivered with 33 completions on 54 pass attempts for 364 yards and two scores. But most of Brady's best work was when the Patriots were facing a 26–16 deficit with less than nine minutes to go in the fourth quarter.

After a field goal drive, Brady had the first "clutch" moment of his career when he went 5-of-8 and led the team downfield 60 yards for a game-tying touchdown. He had his second clutch moment when he led a drive that began with a 37-yard defensive pass interference penalty and ended with a 44-yard field goal. Brady completed all three of his pass attempts in between to cap off a brilliant 29–26 comeback win.

Following that heart-stopper, the Patriots headed on the road for a three-game trip. The first of those road games was a second meeting with the Colts, which ended with a second resounding Patriots win and with the offense playing a much bigger role than it did the first time around. Brady threw three touchdown passes, but the star of the game was David Patten.

Belichick sought to catch the division-rival Colts off guard with something they hadn't seen, which led to Patten becoming the first player since 1979 with a passing touchdown, a rushing touchdown, and a receiving touchdown in the same game. Each of those scores was on the opening play of the drive. Patten capitalized on good field position with a 29-yard touchdown run on a reverse on the Patriots' first play from scrimmage, he was on the receiving end of a 91-yard touchdown pass, and he connected with Troy Brown on a double-pass for a 60-yard score on the Patriots' very next possession.

Belichick pulled more wrinkles out from his sleeves (which had not yet been cut to three-quarter length) against the Atlanta Falcons when he called one of the most aggressive defensive games of his career. There were plenty of exotic pressure schemes and defensive back blitzes, and the Patriots defense brought down the Falcons quarterbacks Chris Chandler and Michael Vick nine times.

A 10-point win against the Buffalo Bills put a cap on an impressive five-game stretch in which the Patriots won four games, including two out of three consecutive road games, to get to 5–4 ahead of their biggest test of the season and a turning point in the Patriots dynasty.

★ ★ ★

The St. Louis Rams were aiming for the Promised Land once again. Led by upstart quarterback Kurt Warner, the Rams offense, dubbed "The Greatest Show on Turf," had already become the first NFL offense to score 500 points or more on more than one occasion, and St. Louis had done it back-to-back seasons from 1999 to 2000.

The Rams were on their way to uncharted territory on the stat sheet, and their certain return to the Super Bowl in 2001 was to put a ribbon on an historic three-year run. But the Patriots weren't resigned to roll over for the juggernaut. "This is the Greatest Show on Turf coming in," safety Lawyer Milloy said in the NFL Films documentary of the Patriots' 2001 season. "This is the team that everybody labeled the Super Bowl champion before the season. All the publications had them winning the Super Bowl."

Who wouldn't want to prove themselves against that team? Who wouldn't use it as a measuring stick? And when the final whistle blew, the measuring stick didn't put the Patriots too far off of this seemingly unstoppable force. The Patriots' 23–16 loss was as close to a "moral victory" as you'll find in the NFL. "If this is the next Super Bowl champions, hey, they're not that much better than us," kicker Adam Vinatieri recalled feeling after that game.

The Patriots weren't the only ones that felt that way; Rams head coach Mike Martz told his men in the locker room that they had "just beaten a Super Bowl-caliber team."

The Patriots might have looked and smelled like a Super Bowl-caliber team, but at 5–5, there was no guarantee that they would even be a playoff team, let alone a championship contender. But Belichick made a decision that week that would rock New England to its core and would change the direction of the Patriots franchise forever.

On November 22, 2001, Belichick took the podium for a Thursday press conference and announced that he had named Tom Brady the starting quarterback for the rest of the season. "That's what Mr. Kraft is paying me to do, and that's what I'm going to do. I'm going to make the decisions that I think are the best for the football team. T-E-A-M as in team," he told assembled media that fateful day.

That four-letter emphasis was important with regard to Bledsoe, who felt spurned by a promise made by Belichick the week before: that the veteran, $100 million quarterback would have a chance to compete with Brady to be the quarterback when he was healthy enough to do so. Given his team's 5–3 record with Brady and the positive momentum they had built, Belichick felt that giving Bledsoe a chance—and taking a chance that his team's chemistry and rhythm would be thrown off—was not a chance worth taking. Whether Belichick had made the right choice or not was hotly debated, but no one could know at the time that it all hinged on how his team finished the season. In the meantime, no criticism was spared for Belichick's handling of the situation—from a media base, which had fallen in love with Bledsoe over the years.

This wasn't the first time Belichick had spurned a locally beloved quarterback in favor of an unknown youngster (see Kosar, Bernie), but this time, it was handled much better publicly. "Maybe last week, maybe there was a little gap in the understanding of what an opportunity would be," Belichick admitted. "Maybe I shouldn't have made the commitment to Drew."

Belichick's decision had the potential to backfire in a major way. The shine had already begun to wear off Brady's star by the time Belichick chose the former sixth-round pick over the former No. 1 overall pick. Brady was 34-of-48 for 292 yards, two touchdowns, three interceptions, and a 74.3 passer rating in the two games prior to Belichick's decision. Things could have gone south for the Patriots very quickly from that point.

But they didn't. Belichickian foresight strikes again.

Belichick showed his team a clip of the Breeder's Cup and stopped it roughly three-quarters of the way through the race. After asking his team who they thought would win, he retorted, "Who cares? It's not over yet." At 5–5 the Patriots' season wasn't over yet either. And Belichick had just shown them concrete proof that they could still make a push and finish the season strong.

The Dolphins and Jets held a clear advantage over the Patriots in the hunt for the AFC East title with both teams sporting matching 7–3 records after 10 games. The Dolphins went 4–2, and the Jets went 3–3 in the final six games of the season; the Patriots closed out with six straight wins and handed each of the other two teams a loss.

Brady was hardly responsible for those wins, as the Patriots defense continued to pulverize opponents and did not allow more than 17 points in any of their final six games. The defense allowed fewer than 50 percent of completions on passing attempts, gave up three passing touchdowns, forced 11 interceptions, and allowed just one rushing touchdown in those final six games. It also forced at least two turnovers in five of those six games.

The defense had rounded into their best form of the season. This is another theme we will see a lot from Belichick and his team. The Patriots were a combined 72–18 (.800) in the final six games of the 2001–15 seasons. The next closest team was the Steelers at 63–27 (.700). Belichick's teams haven't always played their best football at the beginning of the season, but they've almost always gotten better as the season wore on. That trend began in 2001.

★ ★ ★

Whether you remember the 2001 divisional round for the snowy conditions on the field, the Tuck Rule, Vinatieri's pair of improbable field goals, or a combination of all three (probably the latter), you should always remember this game as the improbable beginning of the Patriots dynasty. The Patriots' first playoff game of the postseason against the Oakland Raiders was perhaps the most memorable game in Patriots history. As of the end of the 2015 season, the Patriots have played 254 games since that day, and they could play 254 more that won't be as memorable as this one was.

But at first, the game looked like it would be a snoozefest. The Raiders took a 7–0 lead into halftime after a first half that saw 11 punts, an interception, and a turnover on downs.

The Patriots made some adjustments in the second half, including—surprisingly—a heavier focus on the passing game. Brady had 13 pass attempts for 74 yards in the first half and 39 attempts for 238 yards in the second half and overtime. The Patriots ran the ball 16 times for 44 yards in the first half and 14 times for 24 yards in the second half and overtime.

Meanwhile, the defense clamped down to hold Rich Gannon to 7-of-17 passing for 72 yards in the second half after allowing him to go 10-of-14 for 87 yards in the first half. Belichick had already earned his reputation as a gameplan-oriented head coach, confusing his opponents by giving them myriad looks on defense. Raiders head coach Jon Gruden referred to the way that they used a different defensive scheme in seemingly every game to keep his opponents guessing as "Beli-checkers."

The Patriots continued their streak of allowing 17 points or fewer with three more such performances in the playoffs, That streak began with the Raiders and the fourth-ranked scoring offense in the NFL. But all those plaudits and statistics were thrown out the window when referee Walt Coleman went under the hood to review what appeared to be a late, game-ending fumble by Brady with the Patriots facing a 13–10 deficit.

Football fans were about to get very familiar with Rule 3, Section 22, Article 2 in the NFL rulebook. The "Tuck Rule," now no longer in the league lexicon, stated the following: "When [an offensive] player is holding the ball to pass it forward, any intentional forward movement of his arm starts a forward pass, even if the player loses possession of the ball as he is attempting to tuck it back toward his body. Also, if the player has tucked the ball into his body and then loses possession, it is a fumble."

By the letter of the rule, Coleman made the right call. Watching it in real time? The Patriots' season was over. "After reviewing the play, the quarterback's arm was going forward," Coleman said. "It's an incomplete pass." An eruption of elation soared into the air at Foxboro Stadium, and the Patriots had new life. Brady was clearly never thinking about attempting a pass when he pump-faked, but it no longer mattered.

What happened next would set the tone for the Patriots dynasty: a close win, thanks to a clutch kick (or two) from Vinatieri. The Patriots moved the ball 14 yards to set up a 45-yard field goal try into the wind in driving snow. Vinatieri said if he had 100 attempts, he would have made, "10, maybe."

And he wasn't even done. The Patriots got the ball to start overtime, and Brady promptly completed six straight passes for 36 yards, and the Patriots ran the ball on seven of their next nine plays to move the ball to the 5-yard line and set up another 23-yard field goal for Vinatieri. After the first kick, this one must have been a breeze.

But as much as the singular moments of the game, this game should be remembered as an excellent coaching job by Belichick. His defensive scheme held the Raiders offense in check, and the adjustments on offense helped the Patriots move the ball in key moments to set up those field goals.

No one gave the Patriots much of a chance to beat the Steelers in the AFC Championship Game. The line of 10 points indicated this would be a decisive Pittsburgh victory. But the Steelers would become the second offense to run into the Patriots' buzzsaw defense in the playoffs. The Steelers made a game of it in the second half, but their first nine possessions amounted to just three points, as they punted five times and had an interception, a fumble, and a blocked field goal.

But although Belichick had put his quarterback controversy to bed two months before this game, the position would once again be thrown into flux when Brady suffered a high-ankle sprain in the second quarter after a low hit by a Steelers defender. Turnabout had seemingly become fair play, as the backup quarterback was tasked with taking over for an injured starter. The quarterbacks changed, but the gameplan stayed the same. Belichick wanted to air it out against the Steelers defense, where he felt he had an advantage if he could spread the defense out and neutralize the pass rush, as opposed to running the ball into the teeth of a vicious front seven.

Bledsoe completed 10-of-21 passes for 102 yards and a touchdown, guiding the Patriots to victory and he shined so bright in that game that there were immediate questions as to whether it would be the former franchise quarterback or the current one to take the reins in the Super Bowl. Ultimately, there was never much of a question: Brady was the one who got them there. If he was healthy enough, he would play.

★ ★ ★

No one expected there to be a rematch in the Super Bowl, but even fewer expected the rematch to be anything but a blowout. Las Vegas betting odds viewed the Rams as 14-point favorites—a curious line, considering the close contest between these two teams just two months prior. There was one factor that Vegas didn't give enough weight: Belichick as a genius defensive strategist.

Up until that point, teams had played scared against the Rams. Belichick didn't want his team to just let the Rams offense get in rhythm. He wanted to dictate the tempo the other way.

The Patriots came up with a gameplan that would define their defense during the dynasty of 2001–04. Right from the beginning, the Patriots hit the Rams hard on every play. They bumped the Rams receivers at the line of scrimmage, disrupting the timing between Rams quarterback Kurt Warner and his pass catchers. They also hit running back Marshall Faulk on almost every play whether he was running, blocking, or coming out of the backfield as a receiver.

Poking another hole in the theory that Belichick only benefited from the hard work of Bill Parcells before him, many of Belichick's additions to the roster were the ones making the biggest plays in the biggest game of the year. Seymour, a 2001 first-round pick, had a sack of Warner; veteran free agent Vrabel had pressure on Warner, which led to the lasting image of Ty Law streaking down the field with an interception, waving to the fans as he ran it back for a touchdown; Patten created an immortal Super Bowl image when he caught a leaping touchdown at the end of the first half; and veteran running back Smith averaged 5.1 yards per carry with 18 carries for 92 yards on the night.

The strategy led to a 17–3 lead headed into the fourth quarter and would have gone up 24–3 on a 97-yard fumble recovery touchdown by Tebucky Jones, but a defensive holding call on Willie McGinest (one of what probably should have been many) brought the ball back to the 1-yard line, and the Rams scored a touchdown two plays later to make it 17–10.

The Rams then got the ball with less than two minutes to go, completed three passes for 55 yards in the space of 14 seconds, and got in the end zone for Warner's first touchdown pass of the night. That tied the game at 17. "You have to just run the clock out, you have to play for over time," announcer John Madden said.

Madden wasn't alone in thinking the Patriots would and should take a conservative approach to the final seconds of regulation. With 1:21 left in the game and no timeouts remaining, no one was thinking that the Rams had given Brady too much time—except maybe Belichick and Charlie Weis, who were ready to move down the field to at least try for the game-winning field goal.

Excluding two spikes to stop the clock, Brady was 5-of-6 for 53 yards on the final drive to set up Vinatieri's game-winning 48-yard field goal as time expired to cap off the biggest upset in Super Bowl history. Belichick had already redeemed himself from his Cleveland days, and he had only just begun to scratch the surface of what he would accomplish as "HC of the NEP."

CHAPTER 4

★ ★ ★

Bill Belichick
vs. Bill Parcells

No single individual has had his hand in more successful franchises than Bill Parcells.

Parcells has led four teams to the playoffs as a head coach and is one of only six men to take two teams to the Super Bowl. The New York Giants, New England Patriots, New York Jets, and Dallas Cowboys all made the playoffs under his watch. The year before he took over, those teams were all among the worst in their division, sometimes among the worst in the league.

The Giants were 23–34 in four years under Ray Perkins before Parcells took over and they were 4–5 in a strike-shortened 1982 season before Parcells was named head coach in '83. By '84 the Giants were in the playoffs. By the end of the '86 season, the Giants were hoisting the first of two Lombardi Trophies over their heads.

Fast forward to '93, when Parcells took over a Patriots team that won eight games in their previous two years under Dick MacPherson and held the draft's No. 1 pick after a 2–14 '92 season. In '94 the Patriots went to the playoffs for the first time since the Giants' first Super Bowl win. In '96 they were in the Super Bowl.

Parcells' Quick Turnarounds as Head Coach

Team	Year before Parcells	Years until playoffs
New York Giants	4–5	2
New England Patriots	2–14	2
New York Jets	1–15	2
Dallas Cowboys	5–11	1

Just a few months later, Parcells moved on to his next rebuilding project with the 1–15 Jets in '97. Parcells immediately improved the Jets' win-loss record by eight games. In '98 the Jets were in the AFC Championship Game. In 2003 Parcells took over a 5–11 Cowboys team and took them to the playoffs in his first year on the job. Everywhere Parcells went, he brought success with him.

The legacies of Bill Belichick and Bill Parcells intersect at so many key plot points. It's hard to distinguish at times. Belichick is often credited with the defensive gameplan that held the Buffalo Bills' high-powered offense in check when the Giants won Super Bowl XXV with Parcells as head coach. Parcells, on the other hand, is credited with creating the core of the Patriots' dynasty.

★ ★ ★ ★ ★ ★ ★

"Pretty much every [team he joined] was not doing well when he got there. Either they were the bottom or close to it. He made them all pretty competitive in a very short amount of time…Two Super Bowls in New York, and that franchise really hadn't done a lot in a while…A lot of respect for Bill, learned a lot from him, glad I had the opportunity to work with him and work for him. Patriots was definitely an example of a team that was pretty much rock bottom when he got here, rejuvenated the franchise…I personally value his friendship and have a lot of respect for him as a person and as a football coach/ football person. It's not just coaching; it's beyond that with him."

—Bill Belichick on Bill Parcells

Each man deserves his own legacy. Belichick proved in his first stop with the Cleveland Browns that without Parcells he wasn't quite ready to lead an entire organization on his own. Belichick also removed any doubt that he could build his own Super Bowl winner when his 2014 championship team contained exactly zero Parcells players.

Belichick's stats are better than Parcells'. Part of that is because of the Tom Brady factor, but the other part has to be Belichick's coaching. The coaching pendulum swung back and forth—from a hard-line head coach in Parcells to an easygoing leader in Pete Carroll and back to a more no-nonsense coach in Belichick.

Each coach is his own man, but unsurprisingly, it's easy to spot the ways in which Parcells has influenced Belichick. You can almost hear Belichick's voice when reading Parcells quotes. "It's not who plays the best; it's who's willing to do it the longest," Parcells told *Sports Illustrated*. "It's a marathon, not a sprint," he told *Newsday*.

Patriots owner Robert Kraft, who hired both men as head coaches, saw how similar Belichick was to Parcells, especially at first and especially with his tone. "He used to be a junior Parcells," Kraft told *SI*. "He walked around saying things like, 'This team's worse than I thought,' or, 'We can't win with this.' I told him to cut it out. Who needs that? Talk to me about what we can do to make it better. And he did."

Parcells and Belichick had a close but sometimes contentious relationship, and the falling out over Belichick resigning as "HC of the NYJ" sparked even more

Tale of the Tape

Coach	Bill Belichick	Bill Parcells
Years as a head coach	21	19
Career W–L	223–113	172–130–1
Ratio	.664	.569
Playoff trips	14	10
Playoff W–L	23–10	11–8
Division championships	13	5
Super Bowl wins	4	2

animosity in an already bitter Patriots-Jets rivalry. Their relationship has warmed since then, and the two speak glowingly about each other in the media, but for as much success as the two coaches have enjoyed individually, much of it is shared.

Without Belichick's defensive gameplans, Parcells might never have won his two Super Bowls. Without Parcells laying the groundwork for the Patriots dynasty, Belichick may never have righted the ship in New England. But for all the similarities and intersections between Parcells and Belichick, the two have strikingly different legacies. Parcells' legacy is as a rebuilder; he has proven that he can turn a franchise around time after time. Belichick's legacy is endurance; he has proven that he can make one team competitive over a long stretch of time.

During Super Bowl XXV, in which New York Giants defensive coordinator Bill Belichick thwarted a potent Buffalo Bills attack, Belichick stands next to one of his mentors, Giants head coach Bill Parcells. (AP Images)

Bill Belichick vs. Bill Parcells, Head to Head

Year	Teams	Score	Winner	Belichick's Record
1993	Browns vs. Patriots	20–17	Parcells	0–1
1994	Browns vs. Patriots	13–6	Belichick	1–1
1994*	Browns vs. Patriots	20–13	Belichick	2–1
1995	Browns vs. Patriots	17–14	Parcells	2–2
2003	Patriots vs. Cowboys	12–0	Belichick	3–2

*= denotes playoff game

On the whole, Belichick has achieved more success than Parcells, but that's to be expected—given the fact that Parcells was continuously coaching bad teams for a year or two before his team would break through to the postseason. Parcells also proved that he could have sustained success with the Giants from 1984–90, a stretch during which the Giants had just one losing season. In total, Parcells' teams finished with a losing record in just five of his 19 seasons as a head coach. Not bad, considering all four of the teams he coached had a losing record the year before he arrived.

And yet, they were successful in different ways for the same reasons. Both coaches mastered the art of striking balance between finding players that fit their system and also adjusting the system to fit their best players. They both subscribed to the idea of neutralizing an opponent's strength and exposing their weakness on the way to victory. And five years after Belichick retires, they'll both have busts in Canton at the Pro Football Hall of Fame.

CHAPTER 5

★ ★ ★

2002: Hung Over

Super Bowl hangovers come in all shapes and sizes. Sometimes, it's injuries. Sometimes, it's key players leaving the fold after getting big paydays. Sometimes, it's just a team coming back to Earth.

Bill Belichick wisely kept the nucleus of his team together in 2002; Bryan Cox was the only key departure that offseason. The veteran linebacker was one-and-done with the Patriots—as was his post-Patriots career. He played for the New Orleans Saints one more year before retiring.

The Patriots also added several talented players through the 2002 draft, including tight end Daniel Graham, wide receiver Deion Branch, defensive end Jarvis Green, and wide receiver David Givens. This quartet of young players would play key roles in the orchestration of two championship runs, but they were just tuning up as rookies in 2002.

With the core of the team in place, and with young talent added to the roster, the Patriots were poised to compete once again in 2002. So, what happened?

They opened up the season with three straight wins and back-to-back blowouts.

They smothered the Pittsburgh Steelers on opening night in the team's first banner-raising game ever. New England held a 30–7 lead until the final play of the game, when quarterback Kordell Stewart picked up a rushing touchdown to help save face after turning the ball over four times on his own. (The Steelers had five turnovers as a team.)

Belichick made it two straight over the New York Jets with a 44–7 win at the Meadowlands. The game was scoreless in the opening quarter, but the Patriots put up 27 unanswered points to start the scoring and 17 unanswered to finish the game. The Patriots bottled up running back Curtis Martin. He had four carries for five yards during one of his worst days as a pro.

The Patriots' defense was once again stout, building off its positive momentum from the second half of the 2001 season. In two games the Patriots had allowed 21 points, 106 rushing yards, and 377 passing yards combined. The offense was once again efficient, putting up 74 points and 775 yards of total offense (549 passing, 226 rushing). Both units were about to go into the tank for awhile.

The Patriots won their third game of the season over the Kansas City Chiefs in overtime to start the season 3–0. The first close game of the year was the Patriots' first sign of trouble, especially considering the opponent. The Chiefs were 6–10 the previous year and finished 8–8 in 2002. New England held a 31–17 lead in the fourth quarter before the Chiefs outscored the Patriots 21–7 in the final 10 minutes of the game. The Chiefs went to the air 13 times in those final 10 minutes with nine completions for 92 yards and a touchdown. They also ran the ball 12 times for 83 yards and two touchdowns. Those 25 plays accumulated 175 yards. Tom Brady led the team on a 53-yard field goal drive that ended with a 35-yard game-winner by Adam Vinatieri to seal a 41–38 overtime win, but the Patriots displayed some weaknesses, which would be exploited.

Four straight losses. It's only happened three times in Bill Belichick's tenure. From 2002 to 2015, there have been 227 losing streaks of four games or longer, and only one of which was by the Patriots. Dating back to 2001, the Patriots had built an 11-game streak of allowing 17 points or fewer to their opponents. Beginning with their win against the Chiefs, they went on a five-game streak of allowing 21 points or more.

Belichick has always had his reputation of taking away an opponent's best offensive weapon, even going back to his days as a defensive coordinator for the New York Giants. But that wasn't the case in 2002, especially when that team's best player was a running back.

In Week 4 San Diego Chargers running back LaDainian Tomlinson had a career day against Belichick's defense with 27 carries for 217 yards and two touchdowns. That rushing total still stands as the fourth highest by a single player

Patriots 2002 Draft Picks

Round	Pick	Player	Position	Games played w/ Patriots
1	21	Daniel Graham	TE	63
2	65	Deion Branch	WR	89
4	117	Rohan Davey	QB	4
4	126	Jarvis Green	DE	121
7	237	Antwoine Womack	RB	0
7	253	David Givens	WR	53

against the Patriots in history and the second highest by a single player against the Patriots under Belichick.

In Week 5 Miami Dolphins running back Ricky Williams carried the ball 36 times for 105 yards, and while the 2.9 yards-per-carry average is very low, Williams' role helped the Dolphins hang onto the ball for 39:59. With so few scoring opportunities, the Patriots couldn't afford one turnover in that game—much less three of them. Brady's two interceptions and one fumble proved the difference in a 26–13 loss.

The turnovers continued against the Green Bay Packers at Gillette Stadium with four giveaways. The Patriots struck in the first six minutes of the second quarter and in the final six minutes but allowed four unanswered touchdowns in between en route to a 28–10 loss. Another big-name running back came up with a big game against the Patriots defense. This time it was Packers running back Ahman Green, gaining 136 yards and a touchdown on 31 carries. Rare was the day when Brett Favre would have fewer pass attempts than the team would have rush attempts, but against the Patriots that gameplan made perfect sense.

There was hope that a week off would help, but the Patriots dropped their fourth straight game of the season in a homestand against the Denver Broncos. The Patriots won the turnover battle 2–0, but they were outgained 179–351, and the Broncos converted eight of their 13 third downs while the Patriots converted just three of their 12 third downs. And it was another game with another big outing for a running back, as Clinton Portis racked up 111 yards on 26 carries and tacked on two touchdowns.

This four-game losing streak might have derailed the Patriots' season before the midway point, but it also served as a lesson. Through the 2015 season, Belichick's Patriots have not suffered a four-dame losing streak since. Things weren't about to get easier, though, with three straight road games ahead on the schedule.

A 3–4 record was not uncharted territory for Belichick; his team had won the Super Bowl the year before despite having the same record through seven games.

But things would have to change if his team was going to compete for a playoff spot in 2002, much less the Lombardi Trophy. There were three main factors contributing to his team's downfall and Super Bowl hangover. The foremost was the dip in production from Brady.

Belichick had helped make an efficient quarterback out of Brady in 2001 and early in 2002, but that four-game losing streak saw Brady complete just 58.6 percent of his throws with six touchdowns, seven interceptions, and a 69.1 passer rating. The next six games, Brady hit 64.4 percent of his passes with 11 touchdowns, two interceptions, and a 98.6 passer rating. The revival of the passing game was one of the biggest reasons for the Patriots' change of fortune in that stretch, as the Patriots won five of their next six games despite similar failings in other areas.

In their first two games of the season, the Patriots allowed an average of 53 rushing yards per game. In their next five games, they allowed an average of 178 rushing yards per game. During the upcoming 5–1 stretch, though, Belichick's defense allowed 100 yards per game—better than before but still with room for improvement.

The same could be said of the rush attack, which averaged 79 rushing yards per game during the team's four-game losing streak. Antowain Smith and Kevin Faulk created a brief spark and pummeled the Buffalo Bills into submission with 163 rushing yards and two rushing touchdowns between them. But with 82, 48, and 80 rushing yards in their next three games, the rush attack was far from a renaissance.

By the time this six-game stretch was at its end, the Patriots were 8–5 and in the mix for a playoff spot, as they were tied with the Dolphins atop the AFC East. The Patriots' Week 14 win against the Bills had put their division rival at 6–7, while the Jets sported a 7–6 record and were nipping at the heels of the division leaders.

With three games left, the Patriots didn't quite have the feel of last year's championship team, but they still had the chance to go on a run. But it went right back to the same three problems that had plagued the team all season long up to that point: inconsistency in the passing game, no respectable running game, and an inability to stop the opponent from running the ball.

It started when the Patriots went on a road trip to take on the Jeff Fisher's Tennessee Titans. Fisher had always tried to establish an effective ground game, but there wasn't much "trying" involved as the Titans had success running the ball every which way against the Patriots for 48 carries, 238 yards, and two touchdowns with 49 yards and both scores on runs by quarterback Steve McNair. The Patriots held running back Eddie George to 101 yards on 31 carries (3.3 yards per carry), but the Titans' ability to keep the ball moving on the ground allowed them to milk 41:30 off the clock in time of possession more than doubling New England's time with the ball.

Old nemesis Martin was the next running back up and he, too, piled up more than 100 rushing yards—106 on 26 carries, to be exact—but this time it was the passing game that let the Patriots down. Brady barely completed half of his passes, going 19-of-37 for 133 yards with one touchdown and one interception. On the flip side, Chad Pennington was ripping the Patriots' secondary apart with completions on 70 percent of his throws and touchdown passes to wide receivers Laveranues Coles, Santana Moss, and Wayne Chrebet.

With that loss, the Patriots' playoff fate was stripped from their hands, and chances of a Super Bowl repeat dwindled to almost nothing. And if they were to have any prayer of making the playoffs, Belichick would have to turn his team around with a win over a team that had beaten them soundly earlier in the year: the Dolphins.

They didn't necessarily exorcise their demons—Williams had an even better game this time around with 31 carries for 185 yards and two scores—but they did exact some revenge by knocking the Dolphins out of the playoffs with a 27–24 win at Gillette Stadium. Vinatieri kicked four field goals, and the Patriots scored the game's final 14 points in the fourth quarter and overtime.

Had the Patriots won that game against the Jets and then the Dolphins, they would have won the division. Instead, they watched the playoffs at home for the second time in Belichick's three years as their head coach. Repeating as champion is hard to do, but this would not be the Patriots' last chance to do so.

CHAPTER 6

★ ★ ★

Bill Belichick vs. Tony Dungy

After being fired by the Tampa Bay Buccaneers, Tony Dungy's legacy was shaping up to be a lot like Peyton Manning's, as they joined forces with the Indianapolis Colts in 2002. Headed into his first year as the Colts head coach, Dungy's playoff record stood at 2–4 with just one trip to a conference championship and no trips to the Super Bowl. And like Manning, Dungy had proven to be proficient at his craft despite the postseason futility. He built a talented defense that never finished outside the top 10 in scoring and only finished outside the top 10 in total defense in his first year as a head coach (They ranked 11th.)

Yes, he inherited Hall of Fame talents like defensive tackle Warren Sapp and outside linebacker Derrick Brooks with the Buccaneers and defensive ends Dwight Freeney and Robert Mathis with the Colts, but he added plenty of his own pieces to the puzzle with both teams. And though Dungy had plenty of talented players on those teams, his scheme brought out the best in almost all of them. In his time with the Buccaneers, coaching alongside Monte Kiffin, Dungy popularized the Tampa-2 defense—a variation on the Cover-2 scheme, which borrows from Dungy's time with the Pittsburgh Steelers in the mid-70s. "My philosophy is really out of the 1975 Pittsburgh Steelers playbook," Dungy said during media interviews at Super Bowl XLI. "That is why I have to laugh when

I hear 'Tampa-2.' Chuck Noll and Bud Carson, that is where it came from. I changed very little."

Whatever you call it, Tampa-2 is a zone defense with two safeties in deep coverage, and each is responsible for half the width of the field. The cornerbacks jam the wide receivers at the line of scrimmage to throw them off their route, the outside linebackers patrol the short zones, and the middle linebacker is responsible for the middle of the field. The concept is to keep everything in front so that the offense is forced to execute long drives where they move the ball five yards at a time. Once the offense completes a short pass, the defense is in position to swarm the ballcarrier because their eyes will all be on the play as it develops.

It was Dungy's work on the defensive side that earned him the job with the Colts. The year before he took over, the Colts ranked second worst in the league in total defense and fourth worst in scoring defense. In his first year, the Colts finished seventh and eighth, respectively. Of course, the Colts had their ups and downs on defense with Dungy at the helm. They were a top 10 scoring defense on four separate occasions and finished outside the top half of the league three times in Dungy's seven-year Colts career. On the whole, he took a team on the cusp of greatness and turned them into a powerhouse.

Bill Belichick vs. Tony Dungy, Head To Head

Year	Teams	Score	Winner	Belichick's Record
2003	Patriots vs. Colts	38–34	Belichick	1–0
2003*	Patriots vs. Colts	24–14	Belichick	2–0
2004	Patriots vs. Colts	27–24	Belichick	3–0
2004*	Patriots vs. Colts	20–3	Belichick	4–0
2005	Patriots vs. Colts	40–21	Dungy	4–1
2006	Patriots vs. Colts	27–20	Dungy	4–2
2006*	Patriots vs. Colts	38–34	Dungy	4–3
2007	Patriots vs. Colts	24–20	Belichick	5–3
2008	Patriots vs. Colts	18–15	Dungy	5–4

*= denotes playoff game

Tony Dungy shakes the hand of Bill Belichick, who holds a 5–4 career record against Dungy, after the Patriots defeated the Colts 24–20 during a match-up of undefeated teams during the 2007 season. (AP Images)

Sometimes, it felt as though Bill Belichick and Tony Dungy were merely spectators to the eternal feud between Tom Brady and Peyton Manning. History judges the quarterbacks based on their performance in these games without giving credit to the coach whose gameplan slowed the other down or assigning blame to the coach whose gameplan simply couldn't hold the other back.

The Patriots offense hardly ever missed a beat against the Colts' Tampa-2, as Brady picked them apart, and the Patriots scored 21 points or more in six out of nine games. Belichick's defensive scheme held Dungy's offense in check in early meetings between the two coaches, holding the Colts below 20 points in two of the first four meetings, but Dungy's offense cracked the code in later matchups with 21 points or more in three straight games. And it was almost always close. Only two of the nine games were decided by more than 10 points. Most of their meetings came down to the final seconds with one team making a play to win it.

From 2002 to 2008, Dungy and Belichick accounted for six out of 14 trips to the AFC Championship Game. On three occasions the winner of their regular-season showdown was the winner of the postseason showdown and was the AFC's eventual representative in the Super Bowl.

Brady and Manning might be the default figureheads of the rivalry, but so many other players played roles in those games. From Ty Law's eight interceptions off Manning to Dwight Freeney's four sacks of Brady to countless clutch catches by Marvin Harrison, Reggie Wayne, Troy Brown, and Wes Welker, it was often the rest of the team that made the difference more than the quarterbacks.

The Patriots launched past the Colts in 2003 and 2004 thanks to a running attack that plowed over a Colts defense predicated on speed, not size. Likewise, it was the Colts defense finally clamping down on Brady with fierce pressure that launched Indianapolis to Super Bowl XLI. These matchups always brought out the best in both the players and the coaches on both sides.

You can't divide the story of Manning from the story of Dungy. Both achieved greatness in the form of a Super Bowl championship, but their postseason slip-ups leave room to wonder what might have been. The regular-season meetings were always so close between the Patriots and Colts, and the implications of those

Tale of the Tape

Coach	Bill Belichick	Tony Dungy
Years as a head coach	21	13
Career W–L	223–113	139–69
Ratio	.664	.668
Playoff trips	14	11
Playoff W–L	23–10	9–10
Division championships	13	6
Super Bowl wins	4	1

regular-season meetings are impossible to ignore. If any of those Gillette Stadium nightmares had taken place at the RCA Dome or Lucas Oil Stadium instead, the Colts might very well have been the dynasty that the Patriots became.

In the regular season, Dungy's win-loss ratio surpassed Belichick's. In the play-offs, Belichick has been superior, as Dungy's record dragged well below .500 for much of his career until that four-game Super Bowl run. The former Steelers defensive back-turned-coaching savant, Dungy had opportunities to forge his own legacy even before arriving on the scene in Indianapolis with a Buccaneers defense that sparked a movement lasting a decade. The Tampa-2 defined the mid-2000s, well after Dungy had uprooted from the southeast to the midwest. "I'll bet you 30 out of 32 teams in the league play it," Jim Schwartz, then the Tennessee Titans defensive coordinator, said of the Tampa-2 scheme. So, while Dungy might not have the hardware that Belichick has on his shelf, it's fair to say he left an indelible mark on the league.

CHAPTER 7

★ ★ ★

2003: They Hate Their Coach

As the 2002 season unfolded, it was fair to wonder if Bill Belichick would be a one-hit wonder as a coach. The team showed fight, but it didn't perform up to the Super Bowl expectations set the year prior. In the long run, the 2002 season was proven to be the anomaly, and the 2003 season would begin a return to normalcy.

But they could not get there without a lot of work from Belichick to improve the defense in the run-up to his fourth season as head coach. There were aspects on offense that needed improvement—namely the running game. The Patriots didn't make many moves there, only adding center Dan Koppen in the fifth round. Eventually, Koppen would force incumbent center Damien Woody over to guard, and the move would stabilize the offensive line and add some toughness to the running game. Nearly all of the high-profile additions were on defense: the biggest were linebacker Rosevelt Colvin, safety Rodney Harrison, rookie first-round defensive lineman Ty Warren, and fourth-round cornerback Asante Samuel.

Warren came in off the bench as a rookie, helping out in run defense and moving all over the line. Samuel was a cornerback in nickel and dime packages. Colvin was coming off back-to-back seasons with 10.5 sacks and at least 60 tackles, and his seven-year, $30 million contract was the third-biggest contract for

Patriots 2003 Draft Picks

Round	Pick	Player	Position	Games played w/ Patriots
1	13	Ty Warren	DE	106
2	36	Eugene Wilson	DB	62
2	45	Bethel Johnson	WR	7
4	117	Dan Klecko	DT	29
4	120	Asante Samuel	CB	75
5	164	Dan Koppen	C	121
6	201	Kliff Kingsbury	QB	0
7	234	Spencer Nead	FB	0
7	239	Tully Banta-Cain	LB	85*
7	243	Ethan Kelley	DT	1

* = two separate stints with Patriots

a linebacker ever. With Warren and Colvin, Belichick continued building toward a defense that could shapeshift between a base 3-4 and 4-3 front.

With a backlog of big, athletic defensive linemen and linebackers in the front seven, the Patriots could change their game plan to beat a specific opponent. Perhaps the most notable addition, though, was Harrison at safety. The former San Diego Chargers defensive back came via free agency and had been nagged by injuries in the previous four years, missing 15 of a possible 64 games. Belichick was fond of his style and signed him to a six-year, $15 million contract that made him one of the top 10 highest paid safeties in the league. More than his athletic attributes, his best asset was his physical demeanor. He attacked and set a tone for the defense with big hits and an aggressive style.

He was a leader in a physical aspect but a mental one as well. "Leadership is something that's not feigned. Either you have it or you don't have it," former offensive coordinator Charlie Weis said in the 2003 *America's Game* documentary. "Rodney obviously had leadership. It didn't take but a short time for the team to recognize and to look to him for guidance."

It's hard to imagine that there was room for any more leaders with a defense that included Ty Law, Lawyer Milloy, Willie McGinest, Tedy Bruschi, Ted Johnson, and Richard Seymour. Soon, one of those leaders would be making his controversial exit.

★ ★ ★

The Patriots released Lawyer Milloy. Those five simple words spawned a week of discussion, which eventually led to four weeks of consternation.

Belichick called it the hardest situation that he's had to go through in terms of releasing a player, "here or anywhere else." That's just a glimpse of what Milloy meant to the Patriots. And it's not hard to understand why it was so difficult for Belichick to make that decision. After all, Milloy had heavily endorsed Belichick as the next head coach of the Patriots when the position became open in 2000.

At the time, it was a shock. In retrospect, it was the birth of a pattern. Over the years, Belichick has built a reputation of making high-profile, highly controversial personnel moves just days before the beginning of the regular season. He traded Seymour days before the 2009 season began and did the same with Logan Mankins shortly before the 2013 season.

The first such instance came from out of nowhere and sent shockwaves through New England. "This is a player and person I have immense respect for, and he meant a lot to this team and organization," Belichick said. "Unfortunately, he's a casualty of the system. The timing is not good. We tried to find a way to make it work. In the end, we weren't able to get to that point."

Milloy was signed to a seven-year, $35 million contract in 1999 and he had a $5.856 million cap number in 2003. The Patriots wanted to reduce the cap hit; Milloy didn't want to take a pay cut. The two sides were at an impasse.

The news hit the players hard. "Everyone was hurt and stunned by it," Harrison said in the NFL Films documentary. "I thought it was going to be Lawyer and myself as the safeties back there. I was looking forward to that. That was one of the reasons why I signed with New England."

Bruschi was rarely the kind of player to come out in criticism of Belichick. Maybe more in his media days, but certainly not as a member of the organization. That's why his words then carry so much significance. "Has it ever been this quiet in here [the Patriots locker room]? I don't think it has," Bruschi said to media the day after the move. "I think 'shocked' is the word...You sort of just shake your head and ask yourself, 'Why?'"

Such moves by Belichick were often seen as cold decisions, but oftentimes, they would prove to be calculated ones. They were cold because many of the players were veterans with value both at their position and in the locker room. They were calculated because those players usually didn't go on to have great success once they took an exit off Route 1 in Foxborough, Massachusetts. Milloy would go on to play eight more years after being released by the Patriots, but he never reached the same level during his run in New England.

At this point, though, Milloy's release was a shock, and the Patriots didn't just shrug it off. It was one of the first times he had to keep his team focused amid controversy. In Week 1, it was clear they failed to do that. AFC East foe and Week 1 opponent, the Buffalo Bills, signed Milloy.

The scoreboard after playing the Bills, who also had Drew Bledsoe at quarterback, said it all. The Patriots played like a team that had been told before the game that they would lose 31–0. "I want to say this very clearly: they hate their coach," said ESPN analyst and former Denver Broncos linebacker Tom Jackson. "And their season could be over, depending on how quickly they can get over this emotional devastation they suffered because of Lawyer Milloy."

That's a strong proclamation on both counts. The first—about the Patriots hating Belichick—was by far the more egregious comment. Harrison said it was "one of the stupidest things" he'd ever heard, and Belichick said he was "not going to dignify the comments with any type of response."

The second proclamation, about the Patriots season being over, was just plain ignorant on Jackson's part. This is a team that had fought back from an 0–2 record to win the Super Bowl just two years prior and had fought back from 3–4 to finish 9–7 the next year. As we'll see, this definitely would not be the last time a Belichick team would be buried and eulogized before the beginning of October. But with 15 games left to play, the season was far from over, no matter what Jackson or anyone else said.

That was the message from Belichick to his team after that game.

The 2002 season started strong and finished cold. The 2003 season took the exact opposite trajectory with a sluggish start and a mad dash to the finish line.

★ ★ ★

Nose, meet grindstone.

If Belichick's team was going to get off the schneid, it would have to do so against a seasoned coach in Andy Reid and the Philadelphia Eagles. The Eagles were also coming off a shutout home loss to the Tampa Bay Buccaneers and were looking for a redemption win of their own. The Patriots would have none of it.

The running game was a non-factor for both offenses—the Eagles by design (16 rush attempts for 100 yards), the Patriots by force (30 rush attempts for 62 yards)—and it was the stark difference in the team's ability to take advantage of match-ups in the passing game that created the end result, a 31–10 win for the Patriots.

One one hand, you had the Patriots. The offensive line kept Tom Brady upright (with the exception of two sacks), and he completed 30 of his 44 passes for 255 yards and three scores. Brady completed at least one pass to 10 different receivers and multiple passes to eight different receivers. It was a very controlled but effective game plan in the passing game.

On the other hand, the Eagles were in disarray; quarterback Donovan McNabb was under pressure all day and was sacked a whopping eight times. The Patriots didn't send any exotic rush packages after McNabb but simply generated a good rush with their defensive line and the occasional linebacker blitz. McNabb did escape the pocket to rush five times for 54 yards, but he was harassed in the pocket and completed 18 of his 46 throws for 186 yards and two interceptions.

With eight sacks, six turnovers, and just one offensive touchdown against them, this was the kind of game that would ordinarily get the swagger back in a team; but after a close-fought home win over the New York Jets, the Patriots were back at .500 after a Week 4 loss to the Washington Redskins. "We were very frustrated because we felt that we had lost to an inferior team," Weis said. "Here we are, are we going to be an up-and-down team, are we going to be inconsistent like we were in 2002? As disappointed as we were after the Buffalo loss, the Washington loss got the team saying, 'That's the end of this losing stuff.'"

That was, indeed, the end of that "losing stuff"—for more than a full calendar year. The Patriots weren't just on a mission to win games. They were out to prove they could win by any means necessary.

They won shootouts, such as the 38–30 victory against the Tennessee Titans in Week 5. They won defensive slugfests, such as their 9–3 Week 8 win against the Cleveland Browns. The gameplan changed week to week and it was clear through the final score as well as the on-field strategy.

This philosophy on football required the Patriots players and coaches to be ready for anything. Belichick wanted his team to master situational football—the practice of being prepared for any of the millions of variations on different scenarios that could come up within a game. The most unique example of situational football would occur in Week 9 against the Denver Broncos. Trailing 24–23 with 2:51 left and three timeouts, the Patriots had the ball at their 1-yard line facing fourth and 10. They lined up for a punt, but Belichick had the snapper intentionally snap the ball out of back of the end zone for a safety.

The Broncos got two points and the ball back.

Wait, what? How is this a wise strategy?

The question you ask reading this to yourself is the same question the Patriots players were asking on the sidelines. But by giving the Broncos the ball back instead of punting out of the end zone, the Patriots were giving themselves an opportunity at better field position. Belichick trusted his defense to get stops, and with three timeouts, his offense could still get the ball back in better field position with plenty of time to win.

And how did it all unfold? Exactly as Belichick thought. The Broncos went three-and-out, the Patriots burned two of their three timeouts, and they got the ball back at their own 42-yard line—an upgrade in field position of 41 yards. The Patriots only needed to move the ball 30 yards at most to be in safe range for Adam Vinatieri, but that was never even an issue. Brady completed four passes for 58 yards and the game-winning score to David Givens with 36 seconds remaining.

And it was all because Belichick took a unique approach to a common situation, and his players were ready for it. With the win Belichick moved to 2–2 all-time with the Patriots against Mike Shanahan and the Broncos and he did it by outsmarting Shanahan—a two-time Super Bowl champion in his own right—in his own house.

By the time Peyton Manning and Brady were doing battle for the third time, Belichick was getting ready for his fifth matchup with the former No. 1 overall pick. But this was the first matchup between Belichick and veteran coach Tony

Dungy. A former Super Bowl champion safety with the Pittsburgh Steelers, Dungy took over as Colts head coach in 2002 after being fired by the Tampa Bay Buccaneers. His mission was to implement those same Tampa-2 zone schemes, which had been so effective with the Bucs.

This was also the first match-up that actually felt like it meant something. The Patriots were not a competitive team in 2000, and the Colts weren't competitive in 2001, so while history views the '01 match-ups through a grandiose lens as the first match-ups between Brady and Manning, they didn't have that big-game feel at the time. This one had that feel before the opening kickoff. The two 9–2 teams were on a collision course for the AFC Championship Game, and this was going to decide which team would have home-field advantage in that game.

At first, it looked like New England had the better gameplan. The Patriots built a 17–0 lead before the Colts even got on the board and they held a 31–10 lead in the middle of the third quarter. But Manning got into rhythm in the second half and did what he usually does: throw a bunch of touchdowns. Within six minutes of game clock (from 1:20 left in the third quarter to 10:21 left in the fourth quarter), Manning threw three touchdowns: 13 yards to Reggie Wayne, 26 yards to Marvin Harrison, and six yards to Troy Walters.

Both teams did a fine job of shutting down the run. A grand total of 52 rushes for 154 yards (just shy of three yards per carry) and two touchdowns were accumulated between the two teams. This game had been put in the hands of the two quarterbacks. But several running plays would determine the nail-biting finish.

The first of those plays came with 3:53 left in the fourth quarter with the Patriots holding a 38–31 lead and trying to ice the game. Kevin Faulk fumbled the ball, giving the Colts great field position for a game-tying touchdown. Three straight incomplete passes forced a field goal and a 38–34 score. The Patriots went to the air on the next drive but had to punt after four plays and picking up just one first down. Ken Walter's punt netted just 18 yards, and the Colts had the ball at the Patriots' 48-yard line.

Taking their time, the Colts wanted to score the game-winning touchdown without giving Brady enough time to manage an end-of-game situation. The Patriots had no timeouts left, so the Colts kept the ball in-bounds to milk the clock. That's when a few more running plays, and a few more situations, became critical. As the Colts were trying to punch the ball in at the goal line, McGinest went to the ground when his left foot got caught in the turf, causing a knee sprain. Law was also limping around, getting attention from the staff.

"Again, situational football," McGinest said on the 2003 *America's Game* documentary. "If you have an injury, get down. If you know the Indianapolis Colts, if they see a player hobbling off the field, they'll hurry up to the line, they'll snap the ball, and we didn't want that to happen."

Dungy was furious on the Colts sideline, accusing the Patriots of intentionally going to the ground to slow down the Colts' hurry-up, no-huddle offense. Whether he was right or wrong didn't matter because there was no rule against the strategy at the time. The Patriots were aware of situations down to the last detail, and this was simply a way of implementing it in their own favor.

Now with the ball at the 9-yard line, the Colts immediately went to the ground game for a 7-yard carry by Edgerrin James. They had first and goal at the 2-yard line but were stonewalled on two runs that gained only a yard. Manning threw an incomplete pass, and McGinest stormed back onto the field for the final play. He would prove to be the determining factor, making a 1-yard tackle for loss.

The Patriots players were proud after such a big, emotional win over a conference rival. Belichick went back to work eager to correct the mistakes that led to the game being so close in the first place. The Patriots ended the season the opposite of the way they started it. Instead of being shut out on the road, they blew out the Bills at home 31–0. How poetic.

And with that, the Patriots had their retribution and were on to the playoffs, where they would face a pair of familiar foes and a pair of NFL co-MVPs in Titans quarterback Steve McNair and Colts quarterback Peyton Manning.

The first, against the Titans, was one of the coldest games in NFL history with temperatures as low as 4 degrees, but the Patriots needed their kicker and defense to have ice water in their veins down the stretch. The Patriots took over the ball on the Titans' 40-yard line with 6:40 left and a chance to put the game away with a touchdown. The offense moved the ball just 13 yards, though, and so Vinatieri—who missed a 44-yard field goal try earlier—needed to make a 46-yarder to give the Patriots a lead. His try was true, and then it was up to the defense.

"It was our season," Harrison said. "We had let them go downfield, and enough was enough. We challenged them. We stepped up and said if they're going to beat us, they're going to beat us. You can't let him sit back there and sling the ball. We decided to try something different and give him a different look."

The Titans couldn't beat them; wide receiver Drew Bennett dropped a fourth-down pass, and the game was over.

Then came the rematch with Manning, and just as had been predicted, the winner of the regular-season game had the home-field advantage in the playoff meeting. This was the true beginning of Gillette Stadium as Manning's house of horrors. The Patriots beat up on Manning with four sacks and frustrated him with four picks. Law had three interceptions.

It was a similar defensive gameplan to the physical one that thwarted the St. Louis Rams and the "Greatest Show on Turf" in the Super Bowl two years prior. The Patriots defensive backs were aggressive with the Colts receivers at the line of scrimmage, disrupting the timing between Manning and his pass catchers. After the game Colts players and coaches began complaining that the Patriots had been perhaps too aggressive and outside the boundaries of acceptable contact by a defensive player on a receiver. The Competition Committee met shortly after the conference championship games to discuss a new focus and stronger emphasis on penalty flags for defensive holding, illegal contact, and pass interference.

The emphasis, the Competition Committee claimed, was in response to a dip in passing yardage. It could not be seen as coincidence, though, that two coaches who had been bludgeoned by Belichick's defensive strategy—Dungy and Rams head coach Mike Martz—both sat on the subcommittee that recommended the heightened enforcement of those penalties. Colts president Bill Polian also sat on the Competition Committee. Belichick's strategies were so effective that they quite literally changed the game, but the Patriots were not the only team that used such a strategy to their benefit on championship weekend, and they were about to meet that other team in the Super Bowl.

As could be expected, two physical defensive teams came out with an attitude of wanting to dictate the tempo and tone of the biggest match-up of the year. Where the Patriots had dealt with two top-notch quarterbacks in their first two playoff games, they were looking at a dominant running game in Super Bowl XXXVIII. But against the Patriots defense, which ranked fourth in the league against the run in 2003, the Carolina Panthers neither wanted nor pretended to want to establish the run with just 16 carries in the game.

Typically, a back-and-forth game is one where the two teams take turns scoring. In the Super Bowl, the back-and-forth feel of the game also applied to the pace with long droughts of dominant defense followed by a frenzy of fireworks. In the final 3:05 of the first half, the score went from donuts on both sides to a 14–10 Patriots advantage headed into the locker room. Neither team scored in the third quarter until the game turned into a shootout in the final 15 minutes.

From that point on, neither defense could get a stop. It was one big play after another, with 11 plays of 20 yards or more in the game (10 in the second half and one with seconds left in the first half). The Panthers even had the longest play from scrimmage in Super Bowl history when quarterback Jake Delhomme hit wide receiver Muhsin Muhammad for an 85-yard score.

This time around, Vinatieri's game-winning field goal was no sure thing. The clutch kicker had already missed two field goals—one that was blocked, one that was simply off-target. But in the same situation as two years earlier, Vinatieri delivered the same result: a field goal right down the middle as time expired.

In four years as Patriots head coach, Belichick had already led the team to two times as many Super Bowls as it had been to before he arrived. He had also matched the total Super Bowl wins of his mentor Bill Parcells but also of legendary coaches such as Mike Shanahan, Don Shula, and Tom Landry. To say Belichick's Patriots career was off to an incredible start would be an understatement.

CHAPTER 8

★ ★ ★

Bill Belichick vs. Vince Lombardi

Perhaps the one element of Vince Lombardi's coaching career that is most impressive is what the Green Bay Packers had been prior to his arrival. In short: not good.

In fact, in the 11 years before Lombardi's arrival, the Packers were a combined 37–93–2. In the nine years after his arrival, they were a combined 98–30–4 (including playoffs). During those previous 11 years, one of the NFL's most dominant teams had been the New York Giants—with Lombardi as their offensive coordinator from 1954–58. Lombardi coached alongside defensive coordinator and future Dallas Cowboys coach Tom Landry, and together, the two helped the Giants to an NFL championship in '56.

He became a commodity to NFL owners and joined the Packers as head coach in 1959.

The success was almost instantaneous. Lombardi took a roster full of talented players who simply weren't being utilized appropriately and turned them into a competitive team the very next year. They finished the '59 season with a 7–5 record, wrapping up his first season with a four-game winning streak.

In his second year, he had the Packers in the NFL championship. In his third and fourth years, they won it. In his seventh, eighth, and ninth years on the job, they won it again, making him the third and last head coach to ever win three straight NFL Championships (along with Guy Chamberlin from 1922–24 and Curly Lambeau from 1929–31). An eye for talent, a tireless work ethic, and one simple but effective play call were his tickets to success in Green Bay.

Vince Lombardi coached 11 players to the Hall of Fame in his time with the Packers. He added plenty of his own talent to the Packers roster, acquiring five future Hall of Famers to the roster, but he also inherited a team that already featured six eventual Canton inductees on its payroll during a 1–10–1 season in 1958.

The players already in the fold were fullback Jim Taylor, linebacker Ray Nitschke, running back Paul Hornung, quarterback Bart Starr, offensive tackle Forrest Gregg, and center Jim Ringo. Talk about untapped potential. All six of those players were starters for the '61 and '62 NFL champion Packers, and all but Ringo were still a part of the '65 NFL champions and the first Super Bowl champions in '66.

The "Lombardi Sweep" (known in the playbook as "49 Sweep") was the tool that brought those Hall of Fame talents together on offense. When you watch the Lombardi Sweep, it looks like a simple run play based on ruthless, aimless aggression with Packers linemen running all over the place and knocking everyone to the ground to clear the path for the running back.

Beneath the surface, though, there is an elegance to the gruff. Everybody had an important assignment. Every assignment needed to be carried out in order for the play to succeed.

Taylor, Hornung, Gregg, and Ringo were just the Hall of Fame players who had key roles in the play, but everyone from tight end Ron Kramer to guards Fuzzy Thurston and Jerry Kramer to split end (now known as wide receiver) Boyd Dowler had a key role.

One of the most memorable videos that exists of Lombardi is him at a chalkboard describing the play: "What we're trying to get is a seal here and a seal here and run this play in…the…alley." The two guards pull to the outside, typically the strong side (toward the tight end). The fullback and right tackle take care of any defenders pursuing from the backside of the play. The tight end blocks the outside linebacker directly in front of him, and the guards are free to block downfield to create a big hole. It's a simple enough play—but when executed right and

Following the Super Bowl XXXIX victory against the Philadelphia Eagles, Bill Belichick raises the trophy named after legendary coach Vince Lombardi. (AP Images)

Tale of the Tape

Coach	Bill Belichick	Vince Lombardi
Years as a head coach	21	10
Career W–L	223–113	96–34
Ratio	.664	.738
Playoff trips	14	6
Playoff W–L	23–10	9–1
Division championships	13	6
NFL championships/Super Bowl wins	4	5

with dominant players, it's almost impossible to stop even when you know it's coming (which the Packers' opponents did).

In his book *Blood, Sweat and Chalk*, Tim Layden calls the Lombardi Sweep "the chalkboard emblem of the first dynasty of the modern NFL." In some ways, it's even more than that. It's also emblematic of Lombardi's coaching style at its core. It's based off of physical prowess, teamwork, and perfection through practice.

There are a lot of people who will never fully embrace Bill Belichick as the greatest head coach of all time, and Lombardi is the reason why. They're not renaming the Lombardi Trophy anytime soon, but if they did, Belichick would have to be a candidate for the new namesake of the NFL's biggest prize. Belichick's early run of success in the playoffs left him with some eerily similar numbers. Lombardi won an NFL record nine straight playoff games as a head coach—a record that was not broken until Belichick won 10 straight from 2001–05.

Belichick remains behind Lombardi in total NFL championships, though, and the Packers legend's unprecedented run of three straight championships (NFL championship in 1965, Super Bowl champions in '66 and '67) may never be matched. Lombardi retired from the Packers after the Super Bowl II title before joining the Washington Redskins in 1969. He passed away in 1970.

On one hand, you could argue that free agency has prevented Belichick (or any team for that matter) from enjoying the kind of consistent success that Lombardi achieved in the '60s. On the other hand, while the Patriots certainly have lost good players to free agency, they've lost many others to Father Time—and some of their personnel moves (think Richard Seymour, Randy Moss, Logan Mankins trades) were timed perfectly. The Packers had their pillars on the roster, and those pillars stuck around until very near the end of Lombardi's time as their head coach. Belichick has had to make alterations to his roster while finding ways to stay at the top.

That's just one way in which their legacies—while similar in their dominance—vary greatly. Belichick's legacy is as a chameleon, always changing what he does on both offense and defense to stay ahead of the curve. Lombardi's legacy is as a vine, staying firm to his principles while growing and dominating the league. Belichick has been dominant because he's been able to adapt to changes in the NFL. Lombardi was dominant because his scheme and players were so dominant. He rebuffed every team's attempts at adapting to stop them.

CHAPTER 9

★ ★ ★

Bill Belichick vs. John Madden

Boom!

Those born after 1980 know John Madden more for his video games—as well as his broadcasting work CBS, Fox, ABC, and NBC and appearances on ads—than they do for his Hall of Fame coaching career. Coaching, in its purest form, is teaching. It would make sense, then, that at least one of the greatest head coaches of all time would have a degree in education.

As it turns out, many of the coaches in this book earned an education degree of some kind (either bachelor's or master's). Vince Lombardi, Chuck Noll, Pete Carroll, Paul Brown, and Tom Coughlin all earned education degrees, while Bill Parcells, Bill Walsh, Joe Gibbs, and Don Shula earned physical education degrees. Like Madden, those coaches all enjoyed fruitful careers by applying the skills they learned in school to a personal passion. Madden turned to coaching after suffering a career-ending knee injury, which occurred after being drafted by the Philadelphia Eagles in the 21st round (244th overall) in 1958.

From there, Madden worked his way up through the college ranks as a coach before finding his way back to the NFL. Al Davis hired Madden as the linebacker coach for the Oakland Raiders in 1967. Two years later, when John Rauch stepped down as Raiders head coach, Madden was named the successor. The switch gave birth to one of the most dominant franchises of the decade, as the Raiders would go on to win 103 games during Madden's tenure as head coach from 1969–78. That's the third most wins of any team and only two wins behind the first-place Dallas Cowboys for that time frame.

Madden's early success was not a huge surprise. The Raiders had lost a combined three regular-season games in the previous two seasons, they had been to two straight conference championship games, and they had been to a Super Bowl. He took over a roster with six players who were already bound for the Hall of Fame: wide receiver Fred Biletnikoff, offensive tackle Art Shell, guard Gene Upshaw, center Jim Otto, cornerback Willie Brown, and kicker George Blanda. He would go on to coach six more Hall of Fame players for at least one year: offensive tackle Bob Brown, tight end Dave Casper, linebacker Ted Hendricks, offensive tackle Ron Mix, punter Ray Guy, and quarterback Ken Stabler. Madden and Davis consistently built some of the most talented teams in the NFL.

Davis is known as the overlord of the Raiders, presiding over all coaching and personnel decisions, and usually gets more of the credit for the roster moves. Davis was the head of football operations (essentially a general manager) in Madden's first three years, but the future owner of the team only earned his near-absolute power over the Raiders' personnel moves in 1972 after Madden had been the coach for three years. Aside from Casper and Hendricks, all of the Raiders' Hall of Fame players under Madden had been added to the roster before Davis' power play.

In Madden's first three years, the Raiders were a combined 28–9–5 (.757 win-loss ratio) in the regular season with two trips to the playoffs and a 2–2 postseason record. In the next seven years, the Raiders were 75–23–1 (.765 win-loss ratio) in the regular season with six trips to the playoffs, a 7–5 playoff record, and a Super Bowl victory.

★　★　★

Bill Belichick and Madden could relate on some of the low points and high points of their coaching careers. Madden knew a thing or two about being on the wrong end of a mind-blowing, unlikely catch in a big game. His Raiders were on the wrong end of the Immaculate Reception in a playoff loss to the Pittsburgh Steelers

Tale of the Tape

Coach	Bill Belichick	John Madden
Years as a head coach	21	10
Career W–L	223–113	103–32
Ratio	.664	.759
Playoff trips	14	8
Playoff W–L	23–10	9–7
Division championships	13	7
Super Bowl wins	4	1

in 1972; Belichick's 2007 Patriots, of course, infamously remember David Tyree and the Helmet Catch.

Madden also knew something about being the beneficiary of a controversial call that propelled his team to an eventual Super Bowl win. In 1976 Madden's Raiders earned a playoff victory against the Patriots thanks in part to a (debatable) call against Patriots defensive tackle Ray Hamilton for roughing the passer. The play occurred on third and 18, and the penalty gave the Raiders a fresh set of downs on their way to the eventual game-winning touchdown. The Patriots, on the flip side, kicked off their 2001–04 dynasty with the Tuck Rule in a full-circle moment of sports karma—in a playoff game against the Raiders.

Despite some similarities in their stories, the two have very different legacies. Belichick earned championship after championship early in his career, and although his team suffered through a decade-long drought of Lombardi Trophies, there was never any doubt that Belichick could win the big one. There was some doubt with Madden, on the other hand, when his team made five trips to the AFC Championship Game in a seven-year span—and lost all of them.

There were some heartbreakers, like in 1969 when the Raiders finished the regular season at 12–1–1 before losing the final AFL Championship Game to the Kansas City Chiefs; the Immaculate Reception in '72; and in '74, when they knocked off Don Shula's two-time defending Super Bowl champion Miami Dolphins in the first round of the playoffs, only to be knocked off by the Steelers the very next week; and in '75, when they were 11–3 in the regular season before again losing to Pittsburgh in the playoffs. Madden had to dust himself off time after time before eventually reaching the pinnacle of his career.

Madden was the only coach in NFL history to reach the conference championship game five consecutive years—until last year, when Belichick joined Madden on that exclusive list.

In that sense, both coaches share one particular common thread: consistent winning seasons and playoff appearances under their watch. Madden's .759 win-loss rate is the second-best for any head coach with at least 50 career games.

CHAPTER 10

★ ★ ★

2004: Three Out of Four Ain't Bad

The 2004 season was not only an opportunity for the Patriots to prove their greatness. They had already done that in two of the previous three seasons. This year was bigger. The Patriots had a chance to go down in history as one of the best organizations over any period of time. The word "dynasty" had been thrown around well before the Patriots took the field in 2004, as everyone saw the opportunity that was ahead of them. Before 2004, there were only six teams in NFL history to repeat as Super Bowl champions, and only one other team (the 1992–95 Dallas Cowboys) had ever won three Super Bowls in a four-year stretch.

In 2001 the Patriots came from out of nowhere. By the time the 2004 season began, they were a juggernaut. In order to enter the prestigious group of repeat champions, the Patriots would have to climb the mountain as the front-runner with a giant bull's eye on their backs.

They could not afford to hang back and watch everyone else climb that mountain while they hit a plateau. That meant the Patriots would have to improve their running game, which was one of the 10 worst in the league in 2003. Antowain Smith, who bludgeoned opponents into submission for the Patriots from 2001–03, had declined dramatically since joining the Patriots. He was replaced by running back Corey Dillon, a troubled but talented runner in his days with the Cincinnati Bengals.

In order to avoid a plateau, the Patriots also would have to stay ahead of the curve in replenishing their defense, which was loaded with veterans. Perhaps the biggest addition of the offseason (figuratively and literally) was the defensive tackle out of Miami, Vince Wilfork, who had the build of a true nose tackle to plug in the middle of Belichick's 3-4. In addition to finding the right players outside the organization to add to the roster, the Patriots also had to improve from within.

Belichick and his staff did a great job of helping young players develop. Tight end Daniel Graham, wide receiver David Givens, cornerback Asante Samuel, and others took steps forward, developing into full-time starters after spending the previous year as part of a rotation. Even Tom Brady continued to improve. He completed a higher percentage of his throws, averaged nearly a yard more per pass attempt, and threw more touchdown passes in 2004 than the year before despite attempting fewer passes.

In the end it turned out that season wasn't as much about players developing during the offseason but more about players stepping up at a moment's notice. Headed into training camp, the Patriots had a wealth of depth at wide receiver but were thin at cornerback. Belichick has always valued versatility in his players,

Patriots 2004 Draft Picks

Round	Pick	Player	Position	Games played w/ Patriots
1	21	Vince Wilfork	NT	158
1	32	Ben Watson	TE	71
2	63	Marquise Hill	DE	13
3	95	Guss Scott	DB	6
4	113	Dexter Reid	DB	2
4	128	Cedric Cobbs	RB	3
5	164	P.K. Sam	WR	2
7	233	Christian Morton	DB	0

and the ability to play multiple roles has helped players make the team each year on his watch. This year that would be taken to a new level. He and then-defensive backs coach Eric Mangini worked together to help wide receiver Troy Brown prepare to be an emergency defensive back. Little did anyone know, Belichickian foresight was about to strike again.

The Patriots narrowly escaped opening night with a 27–24 win against the Indianapolis Colts in a rematch of the AFC Championship the previous year. Concerned with keeping Colts pass-rushers Dwight Freeney and Raheem Brock at bay with quick passes, Brady completed 26-of-38 passes for 335 yards, three touchdowns, and one interception while being sacked just twice.

It was a back-and-forth game early with the Colts taking a 17–13 lead to the locker room, but the Patriots scored on back-to-back drives and took a 10-point lead. The Colts rallied back and had a chance to tie the game, but Belichick moved to 2–0 against Colts head coach Tony Dungy thanks to a shanked 48-yard field goal by Colts kicker Mike Vanderjagt.

But trouble did not wait long to rear its head. In the Patriots' second game of the season, Belichick lost one of his best wide receivers to injury. Deion Branch had become a favorite target of Brady, but the former Louisville pass catcher had fallen victim to an illegal block at the knees during a return of a Brady interception. The knee injury would force Branch out for nine games.

Whatever adjustments the Patriots made after the fact worked even better. The Patriots gained 300 total yards or more in five of their first six games, four out of five without Branch. Whether it was a product of injury, gameplan, or Brady's maturation, it became clear that there was a new directive: find the open man and spread the ball around to different receivers. In the first six games, Givens caught 24 passes, David Patten caught 20, Graham caught 18, and Kevin Faulk caught 11.

Those players had one thing in common: at least two years of experience in New England. The Patriots offensive system, known as the Erhardt-Perkins offense, is set around a couple of basic principles.

- Play designs that are based on concepts, rather than routes, which make the plays repeatable in different offensive formations.
- Sight-adjustments for receivers, which allow them to get open against different defensive play calls and schemes.

Both of these principles revolve around experience with the system and with the quarterback. But Brady, too, was more experienced in the offense. He knew where to look for open receivers against certain looks. He knew how to make adjustments at the line of scrimmage to get into a play that would work against whatever he suspected the defense might do.

It was a perfect storm on defense, too. Belichick's defense was athletic, but physical. Though experienced, they were not on the decline. And above all else, they were versatile. They executed a different gameplan every week, doing

Tom Brady talks with Indianapolis Colts quarterback Peyton Manning after the Patriots defeated the Colts 27–24 in the opening game of the 2004 season. (AP Images)

whatever necessary to take away an opponent's best offensive weapon, eliminating the haymaker and forcing the offense to beat them with a series of left jabs.

Both sides were playing at an elite level in the first six games, during which time Belichick and the Patriots set the record for most consecutive wins. With 15 straight wins to end the 2003 season and six straight to start 2004, the Patriots' 21 straight wins (regular season and playoffs) remain the most by any team. But the juggernaut was about to get its first taste of adversity.

★ ★ ★

It was fitting from a Patriots perspective that their first loss in 21 games took place on Halloween. This was an absolute horror show for the entire team. The Pittsburgh Steelers handed the Patriots their first loss of the season, a 34–20 result that was far worse than the numbers on the scoreboard. As a team, the Patriots' five rushing yards was and remains the second lowest ever in team history; they turned the ball over four times (all by Brady), and New England possessed the ball for 17:02 on the clock.

Steelers quarterback Ben Roethlisberger looked less like a rookie and more like a game-managing veteran against the Patriots secondary, completing 18 of his 24 passes for 196 yards and two touchdowns. Running back Duce Staley looked less like a journeyman and more like a future Hall of Famer with 25 carries for 125 yards and only 10 carries of fewer than four yards.

The Patriots struck first with a 43-yard Adam Vinatieri field goal, but that treat gave way to a series of tricks. The Steelers offense scored on three of their first seven drives (and once on an interception return) while the Patriots had a turnover on three of their first seven drives.

Miami in 2001, Washington in 2003, Pittsburgh in 2004—the Patriots had what you could call a signature loss in each of their first three Super Bowl championship seasons. That signature loss would be defined as a beatdown of epic proportions. Their only choice would be to put it behind them quickly. "[On] some teams that can turn into a two- or three-game losing streak if you don't turn it around mentally," linebacker Tedy Bruschi said in the *America's Game* documentary on the 2004 Super Bowl champions.

The Patriots wanted another shot at the Steelers. In order to get it, they had to play their best football from now until the end of the season. To the surprise of no one, the loss sparked another big winning streak. The Patriots somehow played even better in the six games after that loss than the six games before it. They won their first six games by a combined 58 points, an average of almost 10 points per game. They won their next six games by a combined 104 points, an average of more than 17 points per game. Their average margin of victory increased by a touchdown.

It was also during this time that Belichick's foresight would pay off. Veteran All-Pro cornerback Ty Law broke his foot in the Patriots' loss to Pittsburgh, which summoned the need for Brown to serve as an emergency cornerback against the St. Louis Rams in Week 9. Two plays into the game, Samuel went down with an injury, and the Patriots' worst-case scenario was now a reality. "You've got to be kidding me," Belichick said of the injury. "We talked about this as an emergency. Well, now, the emergency is with 59 minutes left to go in the game."

Brown fared well enough for a wide receiver in his first game action at cornerback. Were it not for that success, Brown might have never had a chance to become the most fun piece of New England sports trivia by being the only man to ever catch a touchdown pass and an interception from Drew Bledsoe.

With duct tape and glue holding together their secondary, the Patriots defense still presented a brick wall for opponents to run into. From Weeks 9 to 14, the Patriots allowed 15.5 points per game, 217 pass yards per game, and 78 rush yards per game while forcing an average of three turnovers per game. These offenses weren't pushovers either. Three of the six were top-10 scoring offenses. But even though the Patriots measured up against the best the NFL had to offer, they were still capable of being caught off guard by some of the worst the NFL had to offer.

The Patriots and Steelers each had one loss, and in order to earn home-field advantage, neither team had any margin for error. The Patriots found that out the hard way against the Miami Dolphins in prime time on *Monday Night Football* in Week 15. New England at 12–1 was aiming to win each of its remaining three games and hoping for the Steelers to suffer at least one loss. The Patriots held an 11-point lead, 28–17, with 3:59 left in the game and managed to lose. Belichick had almost no words after the game. The Dolphins got exactly what they needed: a quick touchdown drive, a quick turnover, and another quick touchdown. But, obviously, it wasn't that simple.

The real story was the lack of discipline and football awareness shown by the Patriots in those final four minutes. A pass-interference penalty by Rodney Harrison in the end zone gave the Dolphins the ball at the 1-yard line. The Dolphins were driving, and there's no guarantee the Patriots would have held them out of the end zone without Harrison's penalty, but the Dolphins capitalized on a rare Patriots mistake.

On the ensuing kickoff, Patten ran out of bounds before the two-minute warning. The warning, plus three timeouts, gave the Dolphins plenty of time to pull off a huge upset. There's no guarantee Brady wouldn't still have thrown an interception while falling to his back just a few plays later, but without those two brain farts, who knows what the outcome would have been?

From an 11-point lead with four minutes left to a stunning defeat to a clearly inferior team. This was a nearly two-year low point for the Patriots. "That's a situation we're usually pretty good in," he said. "We weren't tonight…I'm disappointed in that. I don't know how else to put it to you." But with back-to-back wins to close out the season, the Patriots put themselves into another situation they're pretty good in: at home in the playoffs.

★ ★ ★

"Just like last year." Whoever the Patriots fan was who hollered those four words at Peyton Manning as he walked out the tunnel onto the field at Gillette Stadium, he might have to consider taking up a future as a fortune-teller in Salem.

Manning's stats against the Patriots in the 2003 AFC Championship game were bad: 23-of-47, 237 yards, one touchdown, four interceptions, a 35.5 passer rating, and four sacks. His stats in the 2004 divisional round game were nearly as bad: 27-of-42, 238 yards, no touchdowns, one interception, a 69.3 passer rating, and one sack.

But the conversation around Manning and the Colts that year was historic. Manning threw for a league-record 49 touchdown passes. They had the league's highest-scoring offense that year and the fourth highest scoring offense ever. In 2003 the Patriots held the Colts to 14 points. In 2004 the Colts didn't even make it into the end zone, scoring just three points.

How were the Patriots even more fired up for this game than they had been the year before? Thank Belichick, the motivator. "I got a call from somebody that said, 'You know, coach, I don't know if you'd really be interested in knowing this or not, but the Colts have called the Steelers and they're looking for an extra 1,500 tickets for the AFC Championship Game next week when they go to Pittsburgh,'" Belichick said in *America's Game*. "When I told the team that, they didn't really say anything, but you could see the hair stand up on the back of their neck a little bit."

"If we needed any motivation at all," Bruschi said, "that gave it to us."

By the time that clock struck 0:00, the narrative was written. The Patriots owned the Colts. Belichick owned both Manning and Dungy, against whom he was now 4–0.

And this time, the narrative was written despite the best efforts of Dungy, Bill Polian, and the Competition Committee. They did it without the seemingly pushing-the-envelope style of defense. In fact, although the defense played another stifling game, it was the offense that stepped up in critical situations. A controlled passing game (Brady completed 18-of-27 passes for 144 yards and one touchdown, pedestrian numbers by any stretch) was bolstered by a bruising running game. Dillon rushed 23 times for 144 yards, and the Patriots as a team ran the ball 39 times for 210 yards and a touchdown.

The Patriots punted on their first two drives and five times total, but they put together three key, long drives that kept the Colts offense off the field. Those drives lasted 16 plays and 9:07, traveling 78 yards for a field goal; 15 plays and 8:16, traveling 87 yards for a touchdown; and 14 plays and 7:24, traveling 94 yards for a touchdown. The Patriots held the ball for 37:43, leaving Manning almost no time to work his magic.

History was repeated in the 2004 playoffs. The divisional round was an opportunity for the Patriots to repeat history with another physical beatdown of the Colts. The AFC Championship Game was not only an opportunity for the Patriots to redeem history from their midseason curb-stomping at the hands of the Steelers, but also to repeat history by advancing to the Super Bowl with a win at Heinz Field, as they had done in the 2001 season.

And redeem, they did. Not only did the Patriots thrash Pittsburgh in their own building, but they did it in much the same way as the Steelers had done to New England almost three months earlier. It was early turnovers that doomed the Patriots against the Steelers in Week 9. The Patriots capitalized on early turnovers in the AFC title game. A couple quick scores put the Patriots on their heels the first time around. The Patriots made the big plays early against the Steelers in the playoffs to get a leg up on their opponent.

Roethlisberger's first pass was intercepted by safety Eugene Wilson on a carom, and the Patriots caught the Steelers defense off guard with a 14-yard end-around by Branch on their opening play. The drive stalled out, and the Patriots kicked a field goal, but their defense was not done creating turnovers—in fact, they'd just started. Jerome Bettis carried the ball on fourth and 1, but was stripped by linebacker Rosevelt Colvin, and the ball was recovered by Mike Vrabel.

It was just Bettis' second fumble of the year. And it was costly. Branch's big day as a big-play machine continued with a spectacular 60-yard over-the-shoulder touchdown catch in stride, in which he was nearly tripped up but kept his footing for the score. The Steelers had turned the ball over twice in the first 11 minutes of the game, but that was just the beginning of their nightmare. Their seven drives consisted of three turnovers, three punts, and a field goal.

And thanks to another big play from Branch—this time, a 45-yard catch in the second quarter—the Patriots now took a 17–3 lead in the second quarter. But that lead wouldn't last long; it would instead become a 24–3 lead when Roethlisberger was intercepted by Harrison, who returned the pick 87 yards for a score.

And the route was on.

The two teams traded blows in the second half, but the outcome was always in hand. The Steelers pulled back within 14 points on two separate occasions, but the Patriots responded each time with a score of their own on their way to a 41–27 victory. Belichick moved to 3–1 against Steelers head coach Bill Cowher with the win, and moved to 9–1 all-time as a playoff head coach, matching Vince Lombardi's record.

★ ★ ★

Before the Patriots even took the field for Super Bowl XXXIX, they were as motivated as they had ever been for any game under Belichick. That's because the Patriots head coach had made sure they were fired up by telling them all about the Philadelphia Eagles' Super Bowl parade route. "I'm talking about the Philadelphia parade after the game, alright? It's 11:00, in case any of you want to attend that," he said in *America's Game*. "It's gonna go from Broad Street, up to

Washington Avenue, past City Hall, then down the Benjamin Franklin Parkway, and will end up at the art museum…Schools are going to be open, okay? And the Eagles are going to be in double decker buses."

Super Bowl XXXIX was a fitting finish to the dynasty because it was all about a vintage performance by the Patriots defense. In order to earn their third Lombardi Trophy in four years, the Patriots defense would have to find a way to put the brakes on an Eagles offense that ranked in the top 10 in points, yards, turnovers, and passing, as Terrell Owens had joined the team to spark the offense. The Patriots were having none of it. Three plays into the game, Eagles quarterback Donovan McNabb was sacked by Willie McGinest, and the ball was knocked out, but Eagles head coach Andy Reid challenged the ruling, and replay showed that McNabb was down before fumbling.

The tone, however, had been set. The Eagles went three-and-out on their first two drives, and McNabb had another turnover that was called back. It didn't matter, though, because McNabb saved his first turnover of the game for the very next play, when he threw an interception into the waiting arms of Harrison in the end zone.

The Eagles' next possession was more of the same, as Randall Gay forced a fumble on L.J. Smith, which was recovered by the Patriots. The gameplan was nothing we hadn't seen from the Patriots all season—a swarming front seven that created pressure on McNabb, forcing him to move in the pocket and make throws on the run with a secondary that played smart and physical in coverage and attacked the football. It was the recipe that helped them win their previous two Super Bowls and it would once again lift them to victory in 2004—if they could only play complementary football.

But time and time again, the offense could not capitalize on opportunities given to it by the defense. The "Brady bunch" went three-and-out on three of its first four possessions and four-and-out on the other.

The Eagles scored first before the Patriots could finally find it in them to put points on the board—but not without some more help from the Eagles, when Philadelphia punter Dirk Johnson had a terrible punt that traveled just 29 yards and ended with the Patriots possessing the ball at the Eagles' 37-yard line.

Up to that point, the Patriots had taken a balanced approach on offense (13 called pass plays, eight called runs on their first four drives). Who knows if it was the situation (4:25 left in the half with all three timeouts) that led to the Patriots coming out guns blazing on the next drive, but Belichick and Charlie Weis started calling one pass play after another. The Patriots spread them out with multiple receivers and three, four, and sometimes five skill players lined up out wide. Running backs, tight ends, and wide receivers alike got in on the action.

Seven plays later (six passes, one run), Givens hauled in a touchdown catch to make it 7–7. Reid has developed a reputation for bad clock management; this game reinforced that. The Eagles got the ball at the 19-yard line with 1:03 left and three timeouts. Running back Brian Westbrook was tackled for a three-yard loss. Philadelphia didn't have any timeouts, but the Patriots actually bailed the Eagles out by calling a timeout of their own, and McNabb responded by completing a 10-yard pass to Todd Pinkston. The clock wound down from 43 seconds to 17. Still no timeouts were called.

A 15-yard completion to Pinkston took place with 10 seconds left, and the Eagles' first timeout came at their own 41-yard line. With any sense of urgency, maybe the Eagles could have scored. But it no longer mattered because Reid had potentially cost his team points with bad decisions, and there was no retrieving those lost points.

After receiving the opening kickoff of the second half, the Patriots went right back to the air with seven pass plays and two runs on their way to another touchdown and a 14–7 lead.

The Eagles had been held in check, the offense was finding its rhythm, and it looked like a third Super Bowl victory might be in the works. Then, the Eagles showed everyone why they were such a great offense all season when McNabb went into the shotgun and went to work with eight pass attempts, seven of them completed for 63 yards and the tying score.

Now it began to look like we had a second rendition of Super Bowl XXXVIII with two offenses that were dormant for most of the game showing up with fireworks in fits and spurts.

The Patriots answered right back with a nine-play, 66-yard drive, but this time there was a little less emphasis on the passing game. Brady completed all four of his passes for 37 yards, but Dillon and Faulk provided their combo of thunder and lightning on five carries for 34 yards.

After another three-and-out, the Patriots were in protect-the-lead mode, running the ball on five of their seven plays on the next drive. This time Vinatieri's winning field goal would be a low-pressure, 22-yard kick with 8:43 left in the fourth quarter. After trading empty possessions, the Eagles got the ball with 5:40 left and two timeouts. This is where Belichick's superior coaching became so vital.

The Eagles did move the ball 79 yards in 3:45 for a touchdown, but they had only left themselves 1:47 to get the ball back (either on an onside kick or a defensive stop), move the ball into field-goal range, and either kick the tying field goal or clinch the game with a touchdown. They used none of their timeouts on offense, though, and spent entirely too long getting to the line for their next play. They were disorganized. There was confusion as to which receivers should be on the field with Pinkston injured and with Owens at less than 100 percent. (After breaking his leg, Owens made a miraculous recovery to play in the Super Bowl.) "We were trying to hurry up," Reid said after the game.

Whatever it was they were trying to do didn't work. The Patriots recovered the onside kick and they went three-and-out on the next possession with the Eagles burning their last two timeouts to prevent the Patriots from draining the clock. Then, Josh Miller's 32-yard punt pinned the Eagles at the 4-yard line, and the Eagles had no chance.

It was a defining Super Bowl victory for the Patriots, as it gave them the right to call themselves a dynasty, one of only two "true" dynasties in NFL history. It was also one of the finest big-game examples of Belichick's coaching prowess.

CHAPTER 11

★ ★ ★

Bill Belichick vs. Jimmy Johnson

Tom Landry and Don Shula. Those are the two head coaches who preceded Jimmy Johnson in his time with the Dallas Cowboys and Miami Dolphins, respectively. Johnson's abbreviated head coaching career did not last nearly as long as either Landry's 33-year career or Shula's 29-year career, but the coach of the 1987 national champion Miami Hurricanes won as many Super Bowls in his nine-year NFL career as his two predecessors.

His 80 wins rank just 60th all time. His teams won the division as many times as they won the Super Bowl. He sits just 16 games above .500. His playoff win rate of .692 bears striking resemblance to Belichick's .697 rate, though he coached just 40 percent of the playoff games that Belichick has coached in his career. His only two losing seasons were in his first two years as Cowboys head coach after inheriting a team that went 3–13 the year before his arrival and hadn't had a winning season in three straight years.

He joined a team with the No. 1 pick and just a handful of talented players: namely running back Herschel Walker and wide receiver Michael Irvin, with whom Johnson was familiar from their days together at Miami. Just several years later, he left behind a team that had won multiple Super Bowls and was loaded for two more runs at the Lombardi Trophy in his absence.

In following Landry, Johnson was able to carve out his own legacy. In following Shula, he was not as successful. The Dolphins were a talented team when Johnson took over in 1996. They had been to the playoffs in four out of the previous six years and won 10 or more games in three of those years. Best of all, they had Dan Marino. The record-setting quarterback was nearing the end of his illustrious career, but after the way Johnson surrounded quarterback Troy Aikman with talent in Dallas, it was expected that Johnson would have the same effect in Miami. Since his retirement, Johnson has admitted that winning in Dallas was easier than winning in Miami because of free agency, which did not begin until 1992, the Cowboys' first year as Super Bowl champions. Johnson did help revamp the Miami defense, bringing in talent like Jason Taylor, Zach Thomas, Patrick Surtain, and Sam Madison. He did not enjoy the same success on the offensive side.

The Dolphins made it to the playoffs in three of Johnson's four years with the team and never had a losing season, but they never achieved anything close to the glory of the Cowboys dynasty. The brevity of Johnson's career works against him as well but only in the volume of what he accomplished. His career is akin to Barry Sanders, Terrell Davis, Patrick Willis, and other greats who had a short-and-sweet NFL stint.

But consider this: if you extrapolate Johnson's stats into a tenure as long as Bill Belichick has coached, he would have a 21–9 career playoff record and would have at least flirted with a fifth Super Bowl win. (Mathematically, he would have won 4.667 Super Bowls in a 21-year coaching career.)

Imagine how much further he could have taken the Cowboys were it not for his eroded relationship with Cowboys owner Jerry Jones, a former teammate of Johnson's at Arkansas. When Jones bought the team in 1989, one of his first moves as owner was firing Tom Landry and replacing him with Johnson. Johnson had full power over personnel matters, but by 1992 Jones wanted more of a hand in those decisions. Johnson refused, and after the team's first Super Bowl win under the new regime, Jones famously said that anyone could have coached the Cowboys to a Super Bowl win.

Shortly after the Cowboys' next Super Bowl win—the next year—Jones and Johnson decided to part ways in lieu of Johnson's pursuit of an unprecedented third straight Super Bowl victory. Many think the Cowboys would have achieved

Tale of the Tape

Coach	Bill Belichick	Jimmy Johnson
Years as a head coach	21	9
Career W–L	223–113	80–64
Ratio	.664	.556
Playoff trips	14	6
Playoff W–L	23–10	9–4
Division championships	13	2
Super Bowl wins	4	2

that goal. Heck, Irvin thinks they would have won five straight. Were it not for such a short career, Johnson could have accomplished much more.

Johnson's impact on the game has stretched far beyond his coaching days. Nowadays, coaches and personnel men from up and down the college and professional ranks are taking the trip down to South Florida, seeking Johnson's input. Belichick has regularly been among the people to make the trip, roughly every other year since Johnson's retirement in 1999. "The first year Bill came, he wanted to talk about drafting players, evaluating talent," Johnson told the *Sun-Sentinel*. "He had all my draft picks on a piece of paper. Some I didn't remember. He said, 'They didn't make your team, but they made other teams.' The concern he had is he didn't want to waste picks drafting players who couldn't make his team. I said, 'Those picks are worth money. If you don't think the guy's got a chance, trade the pick for a pick the following year.' That's what we talked about."

It's no wonder where Belichick derives his draft strategy. Trading forward for picks in a subsequent draft has become a core principle of Belichick's strategy, and it was a huge part of the Cowboys' quick turnaround. Shortly after taking over the Cowboys, Johnson pulled off one of the shrewdest moves NFL history: the Walker trade. The Cowboys and Minnesota Vikings swapped a total of 18 players and draft picks. It became known as the Great Trade Robbery but not because of the players the Cowboys got from the Vikings. As it turned out, the five Vikings players in the trade each had conditional picks attached to their status on the roster. If they were cut by the Cowboys, Dallas would get draft pick compensation. As a result, the Cowboys added a total of three first-round picks, three second-round picks, a third-round pick, and a sixth-round pick from 1990 to 1993.

The Cowboys used some of those picks to add running back Emmitt Smith, wide receiver Alvin Harper, and safety Darren Woodson to the roster. Consider that the Patriots traded out of their first-round pick in 2009 and made a series of moves that netted them four future starters. They missed out on adding a home-run pass-rushing talent in Clay Matthews, but they added Darius Butler, Patrick Chung, Brandon Tate, Julian Edelman, and Rob Gronkowski by trading down to acquire picks.

That strategy is what helped the Cowboys regain their lost glory in the early '90s and it's what helped them maintain that glory even after Johnson left. In his new role as a mentor to other coaches and personnel evaluators, Johnson's fingerprints remain scattered across multiple college and professional football teams.

CHAPTER 12

★ ★ ★

Bill Belichick vs. Chuck Noll

Like Bill Belichick, Chuck Noll was a four-time Super Bowl champion coach who was famously nondescript in his press conferences. "Once, at a Super Bowl, a mimeographed sheet entitled 'Notes From Chuck Noll's Press Conference' was circulated in the media press room," wrote Phil Musick, a Pittsburgh sports columnist. "There was nothing below it."

Like Belichick, Noll was less concerned with manufacturing headlines than wins. "My thing is preparation and teaching, and that's not a good story," Noll said. "I'm not a one-liner guy; I'm not a comedian." Like Belichick, Noll was a quiet winner driven by success who was protective of trade secrets, focused on doing his job as a coach, and with a detailed commitment—bordering on and sometimes crossing into obsession—to do what's best for the team in every way possible.

And like Belichick's Patriots, Noll's Steelers had better results than any other head coach of his era. Some teams won more games, other teams had better stats, but no team in the '70s won Super Bowls like the Steelers. Belichick and Noll share more than their reserved demeanor, their approach to their jobs, and their dedication to winning. They also share eerily similar career numbers.

Noll passed away on June 13, 2014, as the winningest head coach in Super Bowl history. Less than eight months later, Belichick joined Noll at the top of the heap with four Super Bowl victories. The Steelers also enjoyed a run of dominance that lasted more than a decade with nine consecutive winning seasons from 1972 to 1980, eight consecutive playoff appearances from 1972 to 1979, and a total of 14 winning seasons, 12 playoff appearances, and nine AFC Central division titles in Noll's 23-year career, which is just two years longer than Belichick's head coaching career to date at 21 years.

In Noll's first 11 years, he had already won four Super Bowls and had compiled a 100–57–1 record. Belichick was one win shy of the century mark in his first 11 seasons overall at 99–77 with the Cleveland Browns and New England Patriots combined, but his first 11 years with the Patriots brought a 126–50 record. As it stands, their win-loss ratios are only marginally different: Belichick's is .664 in the regular season and .697 in the playoffs, and Noll's is .556 in the regular season and .667 in the postseason.

But even as the wheels began to turn toward parity with the NFL draft order being determined by how the team finished the year before, the league still had not tightened its grip on dynasties and winning organizations in the form of free agency. Sure, teams could still trade players and draft picks, but Noll preferred to build through the draft, and why not? The Steelers were wildly successful at selecting players and not a single player on their Super Bowl XIV roster ever played a down for another team.

Noll drafted nine Hall of Fame players to his team in the late '60s and early '70s: Terry Bradshaw, Joe Greene, Jack Ham, Jack Lambert, Mel Blount, Mike Webster, Lynn Swann, Franco Harris, and John Stallworth. Four players—Swann, Ham, Lambert, and Webster—were all part of one draft class in 1974. Only two of those players ever played in any colors but black and yellow. Harris spent the last year of his career with the Seattle Seahawks, and Webster played his last two years with the Kansas City Chiefs.

Free agency is an instrument of parity designed to hamstring a team's ability to retain all of its best players. At the same time, when used correctly, free agency can also be an instrument for improving a team. It's a tool Belichick has used well, particularly when it comes to finding good bang-for-the-buck value. But free agency was not an option available to Noll when his team was no longer bringing

Tale of the Tape

Coach	Bill Belichick	Chuck Noll
Years as a head coach	21	23
Career W–L	223–113	193–148–1
Ratio	.664	.566
Playoff trips	14	12
Playoff W–L	23–10	16–8
Division championships	13	9
Super Bowl wins	4	4

in haul after haul in the draft. As the well of Hall of Fame players dried up with one retirement after another, the Steelers lost players at a quicker pace than they could feasibly replace them.

Noll will always be synonymous with the greatest defense that ever played: the Steel Curtain. No defense has ever reigned terror on the league like the Steelers of the '70s. In Noll's 23-year career, his defense ranked in the top five in yards on nine different occasions and ranked in the top five in points on eight different occasions. The Steelers had a reputation for their physical play against the run, but it was their brutalization in the passing game that made them the dominant defense of the era.

Before Belichick was concocting a future Hall of Fame game plan in Super Bowl XXV against the Buffalo Bills and before he was recycling elements of that gameplan to help the Patriots defeat the St. Louis Rams in Super Bowl XXXVI, Mel Blount was playing cornerback at such a physical level that he forced rules changes to curb his ability to harass receivers at the line of scrimmage. That's another thing Belichick and Noll have in common.

But their dominance was not about one individual. The 1973 Steelers allowed quarterbacks a combined 33.1 passer rating, the best ever by a defense in the Super Bowl era. That means the Steelers opponents fared worse than if they had intentionally thrown every pass into the ground or the stands, which would have given them a passer rating of 39.6. In that regard, all five Steelers defenses from 1973 to 1977 are among the 20 best pass defenses of the Super Bowl era.

Overall, they ranked in the top 10 in yards every year from 1972 to 1979, and ranked in the top 10 in points from 1972 to 1976 and 1978 to 1979. In 1976, after giving up 14 points or more in their first five games, the Steelers went on a nine-game tear in which they allowed only two total touchdowns to close out the season. Noll's defenses left an indelible mark—on both the league and their opponents—with their physical style.

The Steelers had a few more runs at Super Bowl glory in the '80s, but nothing like their dominance of the previous decade. They made four trips to the postseason—from 1982 to 1984 and 1989—but they only made it to one conference championship game and only won two playoff games in those years. But to take those teams to the playoffs—as the Terry Bradshaws of the world gave way to the Cliff Stoudts and Mark Malones and as the Jack Lamberts gave way to the Robin Coles—was impressive in its own right. Belichick has already done that with so many of his players, but one day, he will have to do the same with Tom Brady. If Belichick's winning ways continue at the pace he's currently set, it would be one of only a few differences in his and Noll's illustrious careers.

CHAPTER 13

★ ★ ★

2005: Apples Falling from the Tree

If Bill Belichick and the Patriots were going to do what no head coach or team had ever done before—win three straight Super Bowls—they would need to do it while enduring two of the biggest departures to date under Belichick's reign. Offensive coordinator Charlie Weis took a head coaching job with his alma mater, Notre Dame, and defensive coordinator Romeo Crennel was scooped up as the next head coach of the Cleveland Browns. Thus began the "Belichick coaching tree."

The scent of a dynasty sent teams into a frenzy, trying to emulate New England's model of winning championships, and the Patriots' success finally caught up to them in the biggest way possible. The circumstances were as difficult as (or more difficult than) anything the Patriots had faced up to that point. Little-known defensive backs coach Eric Mangini was promoted to defensive coordinator, but Belichick did not fill the vacancy at offensive coordinator in 2005. In that area, one prominent name began to move up the rankings. A year earlier, Josh McDaniels, formerly a defensive assistant, was named the quarterbacks coach.

The Patriots had a slew of free agents, including David Givens, Jarvis Green, and Troy Brown. They also signed Mike Vrabel and Tom Brady to long-term contract extensions. Obviously, they couldn't make all these moves without making some room. Apart from the departures in the coaching staff, the Patriots also hemorrhaged veteran defensive talent in the 2005 offseason, releasing cornerback Ty Law, linebacker Roman Phifer, and nose tackle Keith Traylor in salary cap moves while also losing linebacker Ted Johnson to retirement just days before the season began.

The 2005 season would be the truest test yet of Belichick as a head coach. And although the Patriots were losing important building blocks of their dynasty, they weren't acquiring talent at their usual pace. Yes, left guard Logan Mankins was their best offensive lineman for a long time, and Nick Kaczur was a starting right tackle for six years. Ellis Hobbs was an effective cornerback and explosive kick returner in four years with the Patriots, safety James Sanders developed into a starter after beginning his career as a rotational player on defense while contributing on special teams. But what the 2005 season was missing, however, was the addition of any established talent that could come in and contribute right away.

With so much change in the span of one offseason, the early result to the Patriots' bid at a three-peat should not have been a surprise. The Patriots were off to a slow start, alternating a win and a loss for the first eight games of the season. The main culprit, it seemed, was a defense that paved the way for opposing running backs to race for 234 carries, 995 yards (124.4 yards per game, 4.3 yards per carry) and nine touchdowns from Weeks 1 to 9, during which the Patriots yielded 220 points (27.5 points per game), the fourth most by any defense through the first eight games of 2005. At no point in Belichick's previous five years as head coach of the Patriots had his defense allowed so many points in an eight-game stretch.

The offense had its own troubles as well. They were a very middle-of-the-road group, scoring 180 points (22.5 points per game). McDaniels' work with Brady was paying off, as the quarterback ranked among the top 10 passers in most major categories through eight games (passing yards, yards per pass attempt, passing touchdowns, passer rating), but their rush attack averaged just 77.6 yards per game and 3.5 yards per attempt in the first eight games of the season, ranking in the bottom 10 in both categories.

It was 2003 all over again except the Patriots had already brought in the back who was supposed to fix it. Unfortunately, Corey Dillon wasn't quite the same back that he had been in 2004, and that was even before an injury took him out of action for four weeks in the middle of the season.

Patriots 2005 Draft Picks

Round	Pick	Player	Position	Games played w/ Patriots
1	32	Logan Mankins	OG	130
3	84	Ellis Hobbs	CB	63
3	100	Nick Kaczur	OT	68
4	133	James Sanders	S	84
5	170	Ryan Claridge	LB	0
7	230	Matt Cassel	QB	30
7	255	Andy Stokes	TE	0

As a team, the theme was not hard to find: the Patriots couldn't consistently beat the other good teams. A home-opening 30–20 win against a lowly Oakland Raiders team was followed by a 27–17 road loss to the Carolina Panthers in a Super Bowl rematch of two years prior. In the rematch the Patriots turned the ball over three times and watched their comeback attempt slip through Ben Watson's hands, as the tight end fumbled near midfield, allowing the Panthers to run out the clock.

The Patriots did rebound with a 23–20 win against the Pittsburgh Steelers in an AFC Championship rematch of just eight months prior. Belichick established a 4–1 record against Bill Cowher with this win, which would also mark the last meeting between the two coaches. That win was followed by a 41–17 beatdown at Gillette Stadium at the hands of the San Diego Chargers. Drew Brees and LaDainian Tomlinson had their way with New England's defense. Each scored two touchdowns.

Two of their first four losses were at the hands of the two teams that would ultimately finish with the No. 1 and 2 seeds in the conference: the Denver Broncos and Indianapolis Colts.

Jake Plummer had been known as a game manager, so when the Broncos quarterback heaved 72- and 55-yard strikes against the Patriots secondary, people took notice. "We knew we were going to get a couple of shots," Plummer said after the game. "They panned out like that."

To hear those words spoken about a Belichick defense was startling and alarming. Opponents previously couldn't have been confident trying to air it out against the Patriots defense. The downturn of that group in 2005 was evidence that the times were changing in New England.

Law's presence was sorely missed, but he wouldn't have stopped running back Tatum Bell and the Broncos' rush attack from rattling off 34 carries for 178 yards and two scores against the Patriots front seven. The Patriots were down 28–3 in the third quarter before mounting a furious comeback with 17 points in about eight minutes. The Patriots appeared poised for another signature Brady moment with five minutes left and two timeouts, but they started the drive at the 8-yard line. Three complete passes moved the Patriots 30 yards, but three straight incomplete passes forced a punt, and the Broncos ran out the clock. As bad as that loss was, it was about to get worse.

When it came to the Patriots and Indianapolis Colts, a common trope was, "it's not a rivalry unless both teams win once in a while." Well, in that case, the rivalry really began on *Monday Night Football* on November 7, 2005, with a 40–21 blowout victory for the Colts. It took Peyton Manning and Tony Dungy two years together, but the combo finally got the upper hand on Brady and Belichick—and at Gillette Stadium no less. Manning finally looked like Manning against a Belichick defense, throwing three touchdowns and just one interception—only the fourth time in nine games against Belichick in which he had more scores than picks. Together with a running game that piled up 132 yards and two touchdowns, the Colts caught the Patriots defense with its pants down. They had been weak all season, and the Colts were the ones that exploited them.

On the other side, it was the Colts' defense that held the Patriots offense in check. Brady had a good day with 265 passing yards and three scores, but after a 69-yard touchdown drive on their first possession, the Patriots' next four possessions ended like this: punt, fumble, end of half, punt. In that time the Colts' drives ended in a touchdown, an interception, a touchdown, and another touchdown. To that point, the world knew that the Patriots had Manning's number. On that night, Manning proved that he could do the same things to the Patriots that he was doing to every other team.

With a 4–4 record at the midway point, the 2005 season was looking a lot like the 2002 season, and the race for the AFC East title was still a dead heat. The

Bill Belichick stands next to Josh McDaniels, who began to take on more offensive responsibilities in 2005. (USA TODAY Sports Images)

Miami Dolphins and Buffalo Bills both sat at 3–5—just one game behind the Patriots, but New England still had five division games ahead, and one division win already in the bank over the Bills. For all the Patriots' success throughout the years, this was the first time they had truly benefited from a weak division. The Patriots won six out of their final eight games and four out of five against their division rivals.

To Belichick and Mangini's credit, the defense was corrected in the second half of the season. The Patriots allowed the fourth most points on defense in the first half of the season but the fourth fewest points in the second half. The transition on offense without Weis went a bit more smoothly than it did on defense. The Patriots improved from a middling 14th in points scored in the first half of the season to eighth in the second half and finished 10th in scoring.

Once again, Belichick's team didn't start out the season as it would have liked but finished out the season playing its best football of the year. But this year was different than the 2003 season, when the Patriots overcame the 2–2 start. With two wins against the 4–12 Jets, two wins against the 5–11 Bills, and only three wins against teams with winning records, the Patriots looked more like the beneficiaries of a good schedule than the dominant team of the new millennium.

The Patriots were in the playoffs and had a home game as division champions, but for the first time under Belichick, they played on wild-card Sunday. A dominant, 28–3 win against the Jacksonville Jaguars had the Patriots looking like championship material again. But looks can be deceiving.

The Patriots made the trip to the Mile High City, where they had already been handed a loss earlier in the season. This time, though, it was the Patriots shooting themselves in the foot more than anything the Broncos did. With five turnovers to Denver's one, eight penalties to Denver's four, and 420 yards of offense to Denver's 286, New England might have won if they had just played smarter and been more careful with the football.

For the first half, the Patriots defense brought the same intensity it had shown over the previous eight games and held the Broncos with no points in the first 28 minutes of the game before a questionable pass interference penalty gave the Broncos an easy touchdown. Ellis Hobbs fumbled the ensuing kickoff, and the Broncos had another easy score on a 50-yard field goal.

It was still a close game late in the third quarter. The Patriots were trailing 10–6 and were facing third and goal at the Broncos' 5-yard line, when Brady threw off his back foot while evading pressure and launched a pass right into the waiting arms of Broncos cornerback Champ Bailey, who returned the pass to the Patriots' 1-yard line before being tackled by Watson. The tight end made a relentless effort and displayed his athleticism by chasing Bailey down across the entire field. It appeared that Bailey fumbled the ball out of the back of the end zone while being hit. Belichick challenged the play, but the ruling was upheld. The Broncos scored on the next play and never looked back on their way to a 27–13 loss. Belichick moved to 2–4 against Broncos head coach Mike Shanahan, and New England suffered its first playoff loss since January 3, 1999.

CHAPTER 14

★ ★ ★

Bill Belichick vs. Bill Walsh

It seems crazy now, but at its inception, the phrase "West Coast Offense" was a derogatory term. Bill Parcells' (and Bill Belichick's) New York Giants had just defeated Bill Walsh's San Francisco 49ers 17–3 in the playoffs in 1985. Smash-mouth Parcells didn't much care for the 49ers' finesse style of play in the passing game and was filled with glee that his defense had suffocated Joe Montana and company in the NFC Championship Game. "What do you think of that West Coast Offense now?" Parcells quipped.

Well, judging by the surge of offenses that borrow extensively from the philosophies and concepts of the West Coast Offense, it's safe to say that people's opinions haven't completely soured.

In the 1970s the passing game was chunky and clunky. Teams predominantly focused on a vertical passing game that complemented a hard-nosed running game. But even as the wide receivers coach and quarterback coach of Paul Brown's Cincinnati Bengals from 1968 to 1975, Walsh was beginning to form the basis of his offensive blueprint.

In that sense the term "West Coast Offense" is a misnomer. Walsh's system was born in the Midwest but had its proverbial coming of age when Walsh took his teaching to the Bay Area.

With so many West Coast variations in the NFL, its root strategies and philosophies continue to show up in the game we watch today—perhaps increasingly so given some of the rules changes that have made the concepts of the system more difficult to defend and the strategies of the system even more effective.

But at first, Walsh's innovation spawned from desperation. In its infancy, the West Coast Offense was an answer to the Bengals' sudden crisis at quarterback. Greg Cook, the Bengals' starting signal-caller, suffered a torn rotator cuff in 1969. The big-armed quarterback had been the central figure of Walsh's offense, but after the injury Walsh was forced to go back to the drawing board to design an offense tailored to Virgil Carter, who did not have the downfield throwing ability of Cook.

Instead of speed Walsh focused on timing. Instead of vertical deep routes, Walsh emphasized horizontal short routes. Instead of watching a particular receiver and waiting for him to come open, a quarterback needed to look at all the receivers until he found the open one or anticipated a receiver coming open.

When you hear about a quarterback and receiver being "on the same page," it's usually in reference to elements of the West Coast Offense, which asks its receivers to be in a specific location on the field at a specific time while the quarterback would be dropping back to throw, reading the defense, setting his feet, etc. The impact of Walsh and the 49ers' offense created a ripple effect in the NFL waters that has spread and continues to be felt as we approach a half-century since its inception.

Walsh is a legend as a coach, but he does not get nearly the credit he deserves as a team-builder. Tom Brady is arguably the greatest NFL draft steal of all time. I say "arguably," because if Brady is No. 1 on the list of all-time draft steals, Joe Montana is 1A. The 49ers made Montana a third-round pick in 1979, and the rest of the NFL spent the next decade kicking themselves for letting him fall that far as he led the 49ers to four Super Bowl wins.

Walsh's teams also played some of the best defense in the NFL, too. They regularly ranked among the top five scoring defenses in the '80s with the likes of safety Ronnie Lott, defensive ends Charles Haley and Jeff Stover, defensive tackle Michael Carter, and other players added by Walsh during that time. In fact his teams were so good on both sides of the ball, you would hardly believe that they drafted Jerry Rice in 1985—after the team had already won two Super Bowls and four years before they would win a third.

Walsh took over a 2–14 team in 1979, and by the end of the 1981 season, the 49ers were hoisting him onto their shoulders for their first Super Bowl victory in their first trip to the playoffs since 1972. He only had three losing seasons in his head coaching career, and two of them were at the onset as he rebuilt the team in his vision. Even during that arduous process, the teams showed signs of progress. Six of the team's 10 losses in 1980 were by seven points or fewer.

When a player or coach retires after winning a Super Bowl, there will always be some lingering wonder as to whether he could have added to his accolades with just a few more years in the NFL. Walsh was a perfectionist. Like his system, he wanted everything to be precise. Of course, nothing ever goes off without a hitch in the NFL, and the resulting stress wore on Walsh as his team struggled to get back to the Super Bowl and win it all. Years after he did it, he was filled with regret. "I wasn't really thinking clearly when I did it," he told *USA TODAY*. "I left the best team in the history of the NFL. I can't remember any coach doing that."

Look at their careers now, and Belichick's accomplishments surpass Walsh's across the board. But, like Jimmy Johnson, Walsh's truncated tenure in the NFL is unfortunate given what he may have left on the table. There's almost no doubt that he would have won a fourth Super Bowl to match both Belichick and Chuck

Tale of the Tape

Coach	Bill Belichick	Bill Walsh
Years as a head coach	21	10
Career W–L	223–113	92–59
Ratio	.664	.609
Playoff trips	14	7
Playoff W–L	23–10	10–4
Division championships	13	6
Super Bowl wins	4	3

Noll. The 49ers won it all in 1989, the year after Walsh retired, under new head coach George Seifert, and they won it again in 1994.

With a 10–4 playoff record, Walsh's .714 win ratio in the postseason is the best for any head coach with more than 11 games of playoff experience. At that rate Walsh would have an even better playoff record than Belichick.

Even with Walsh's short career, though, he continues to have a huge impact on the game today. There are so many coaches off the branches of Walsh's tree in the football today, it's hard to keep track of them all. Lovie Smith, Mike Tomlin, Jack Del Rio, Gary Kubiak, John Fox, Mike McCarthy, John Harbaugh, and Andy Reid are just some of the head coaches. Mike Holmgren, Mike Shanahan, Tony Dungy, Brian Billick, and Jon Gruden are among the notable alumni from other branches of the Walsh coaching tree. But while that may be one tangible way to quantify Walsh's impact, the best way to visualize Walsh's legacy is to simply turn on the television and watch as nearly every NFL offense hearkens back to his philosophies.

CHAPTER 15

★ ★ ★

Bill Belichick vs. Tom Landry

Today the 4-3 defense is commonplace. But when Tom Landry rolled out the defensive package as the defensive coordinator of the New York Giants in the 1950s, it was revolutionary. The league had swung from primarily six to nine-man fronts before the advent of the forward pass to the four to six-man fronts during the '40s.

Like any new strategy, the 4-3 (four defensive linemen, three linebackers) was a response to the dawn of the passing age in the NFL, where speed and spread formations were paramount on offense. The 4-3 addressed the new rising threat without hurting the defense against the run. Initially, two of the three linebackers were flex players who dropped into coverage at the snap. Once the element of surprise wore off, the flex players became full-time linebackers.

The 4-3 had (and still has) its weaknesses, but Landry tweaked certain elements by moving linemen into different spots—horizontally across the line and even flexing them off the line—to nullify an offensive lineman's advantage. These adjustments only added to the success of the scheme. The league took notice, and Landry sparked a revolution that remains a prominent part of the game today.

Another element that is seen every Sunday that often gets taken for granted is pre-snap motion, and that is yet another novel concept introduced by Landry. By moving a receiver around, Landry could create a match-up, expose a weakness in a defense, and/or glean information on what the opponent might do.

Landry's concepts were innovative, and his players were supremely talented. He had seven future Hall of Famers on his roster: quarterback Roger Staubach, offensive tackle Rayfield Wright, defensive back Mel Renfro, defensive tackle Randy White, running back Tony Dorsett, defensive tackle Bob Lilly, and wide receiver Bob Hayes. But it was Landry's coaching and ingenuity that helped maximize the potential of those players.

As a former Olympian, "Bullet" Bob Hayes earned a reputation and a nickname as "The World's Fastest Human," and Landry knew how to use his game-breaking speed for big-play production. Hayes finished his career with 71 receiving touchdowns and 20 yards per reception, the sixth highest average all time. Hayes' speed forced teams to rethink their approach, as defenses tried to account for his speed. Thus, the zone defense was born. In a roundabout way, Landry was innovating the game both directly and indirectly.

As the first coach of the expansion Cowboys, Landry had a big job ahead of him from the very beginning. Fortunately, that wasn't *his* beginning. He had already been seasoned from his time as the Giants defensive coordinator, where he coached alongside soon-to-be Green Bay Packers head coach Vince Lombardi, the Giants offensive coordinator at the time.

Alongside Lombardi and head coach Jim Lee Howell, the Giants went 8–3–1 in 1956, finishing in the top five in scoring on both offense and defense with units that excelled particularly in the running game (No. 3 on offense, No. 1 on defense). It's no surprise that Landry's Cowboys were eventually the league's No. 2 run defense back-to-back years in 1964–65 before they were the No. 1 defense against the run for four years straight from 1966 to 1969.

Part of the credit goes to a talented group of players assembled by Landry, which came to be known as the "Doomsday Defense," but part of the credit must also go to a 4-3 defensive scheme that plugged the gaps in the line with big, heavy linemen.

Despite those dominant defenses of the '60s, Landry's best teams were in the '70s, when they won 105 of a possible 144 regular-season games and 119 of a possible 165 games when you include the playoffs. In that decade they appeared in five Super Bowls and won two in dominant fashion: 24–3 against Don Shula's Miami Dolphins in 1971 (the year before the Dolphins' undefeated season) and 27–10 against the Denver Broncos in 1977.

The Cowboys didn't stop competing after the '70s. Landry went to the playoffs five times in his final nine years as Cowboys head coach, but his team fell below .500 for three straight seasons from 1986 to 1988. Jerry Jones purchased the team and dismissed Landry as the head coach.

While Belichick was the defensive coordinator in New York, the Giants met Landry's Cowboys eight times with the Giants winning three of the eight games. The Cowboys scored an average of 22.9 points in those games and posted 28 points or more in half of them. For the sake of comparison, the Giants only allowed 28 points or more on 10 occasions from 1985 to 1988.

Comparing their accomplishments, it might be easier to just say both coaches are in the top five and in some cases Nos. 1 and 2 in nearly every record imaginable. In fact, Belichick became the winningest head coach in playoff history during the 2014–15 playoffs, surpassing Landry's 20 postseason victories and currently standing alone at the top with 23 playoff wins.

But if you think Belichick's Patriots have been a model of consistency, Landry's Cowboys posted a winning record in 20 straight seasons, an NFL record that still stands. Belichick's Patriots are currently on a 15-season streak with winning records, which is tied for the fourth longest streak in history. Two teams are tied

Tale of the Tape

Coach	Bill Belichick	Tom Landry
Years as a head coach	21	29
Career W–L	223–113	250–162–6
Ratio	.664	.607
Playoff trips	14	18
Playoff W–L	23–10	20–16
Division championships	13	13
Super Bowl wins	4	2

for second with 16 straight winning seasons, and one more winning season would give Belichick's Patriots a tie for the second longest such streak of all time.

One of Landry's most impressive feats was his appearance in 10 NFC Championship Games from 1970 to 1982, a span of 13 years. Belichick has led the Patriots to nine AFC Championship Games in 13 years from 2003 to 2015 with seven appearances in the past 10 years. Belichick could match Landry's 10-in-13 mark with three straight trips to the AFC Championship Game in the next three years.

Landry's 18 trips to the playoffs are second most all time behind Don Shula's 19. Belichick ranks fourth with 14 behind Paul Brown with 15. Landry's 250 career wins are the third most all time, and Belichick's 223 are fifth most. Belichick's six conference championships are tied with Shula for the most all time, and Landry's five conference championship wins are third most.

CHAPTER 16

★ ★ ★

2006: A Missed Opportunity

The attrition that began in 2005 continued in 2006, and the Patriots were losing talented players at a quicker rate than they could add them. Eric Mangini, who had earned a quick promotion to defensive coordinator, earned an equally quick offer for his first head coaching job with the New York Jets, marking the second straight year in which a Patriots defensive coordinator had been hired to be a head coach elsewhere. Two years after earning his first NFL coaching job, linebackers coach Dean Pees was promoted to replace Mangini as defensive coordinator.

Pees' connection with Nick Saban likely helped. Saban worked with Belichick with the Cleveland Browns, and Pees and Saban coached together at University of Toledo in the early '90s when Pees was defensive coordinator and Saban was head coach. The Saban connection had to have something to do with it because it was rare at the time—and remains rare to this day—for Belichick to hire assistants from outside the organization. He preferred and still prefers to promote from within.

The transition on offense was smoother. Quarterbacks coach Josh McDaniels was promoted to coordinator of the offensive side in a move that would eventually define the Patriots' offense. The bigger problems were in personnel, where the Patriots lost a handful of high-profile players who helped build the championship success of the organization. Willie McGinest, Adam Vinatieri, David Givens, Tyrone Poole, and Deion Branch each had started and played a key role in a Super Bowl run for the Patriots at some point in the previous four seasons. McGinest, Vinatieri, and Branch's significance to the team went beyond that. All three were leaders and they were loved in the locker room and the region. McGinest was released, but Vinatieri (free agent) and Branch (holdout) were absent for monetary reasons.

Belichick cares far more about making the best decision for the team than about appeasing the fanbase or locker room by keeping their favorite players on the team. The Patriots made wise decisions mostly. None made significant contributions after leaving the team. McGinest, Givens, and Poole were all out of the league by the end of the 2008 season. Branch achieved moderate success with the Seattle Seahawks but could never stay healthy—before ultimately returning to New England for another run in 2010.

Each departure left a unique hole. The Patriots filled very few—if any—of them. By losing both Givens and Branch, the Patriots lost two receivers with experience in the offense and rapport with Tom Brady. By losing McGinest, the Patriots lost one of their most experienced defenders and one of their best pass

Patriots 2006 Draft Picks

Round	Pick	Player	Position	Games played w/ Patriots
1	21	Laurence Maroney	RB	45
2	36	Chad Jackson	WR	14
3	86	David Thomas	TE	32
4	106	Garrett Mills	FB	0
4	118	Stephen Gostkowski	K	152*
5	136	Ryan O'Callaghan	OT	26
6	191	Jeremy Mincey	DE	0
6	205	Dan Stevenson	OG	0
6	206	Le Kevin Smith	DT	31
7	229	Willie Andrews	CB	30

*=still with Patriots

rushers. By losing Vinatieri, the Patriots lost their clutch foot. Coupled with the losses of Ty Law, Ted Johnson, Roman Phifer, and Keith Traylor the year before, the Patriots were losing veterans, leaders, and talented players everywhere you looked.

The draft haul also was uninspiring. There were some solid picks in the 2006 class. David Thomas made contributions, Stephen Gostkowski went on to become one of the best kickers in the league, and Jeremy Mincey was a solid player despite never playing for the Patriots. But the Laurence Maroney and Chad Jackson picks blew up in New England's face—an interesting result, considering the contentious in-house debates that took place between Belichick and his scouting staff over those two specific players.

Maroney flashed the potential to be a great running back, especially as a rookie with 175 carries for 745 yards and six touchdowns in his first season. But in the long run, he never hit that game-breaking potential that should be expected of a first-round running back. Jackson never flashed more than his glaring lack of work ethic. He nabbed just 13 receptions as a rookie and was unable to crack the top eight pass catchers on a team that featured aging veterans and cast-offs at receiver.

Free agency didn't do the Patriots many wonders either. They signed wide receiver Reche Caldwell, who would have been a third receiver on most teams but led the team in receptions in 2006. The Patriots also signed linebacker Junior Seau, who had retired four days earlier, and the 37-year-old Seau started 11 games at inside linebacker.

Specifically, the lack of talent at wide receiver came to define the 2006 season. The Patriots geared their offense toward a very controlled, low-volume passing attack coupled with feeding a smashmouth tandem in the backfield.

With no explosive threat in the passing game, the Patriots' best bet was obvious: rely on a veteran defense to set up the offense with good field position for easy scores. The Patriots were holding things together with duct tape in some areas and they were integrating new parts into the equation in other areas; the 2006 season was shaping up to be a tough ask for Bill Belichick before it even began.

Headed into the 2006 season, Belichick was on the doorstep of a milestone: his 100th victory as head coach. Thirty other coaches already held this claim, and as long as the Patriots didn't finish 0–16, Belichick was going to become No. 31

sooner than later. He didn't have to wait long. The Patriots picked up their first win of the season in their first game of the season against the Buffalo Bills. The win itself, however, did not come easy.

The Patriots almost immediately began to feel the pinch of their lack of weaponry in the passing game. Brady was sacked on the opening play of the game when he couldn't find an open receiver, and after his fumble, Bills linebacker London Fletcher recovered and ran it back five yards for the score. Brady finished a pedestrian 11-of-23 passing for 163 yards, two touchdowns, one interception, a fumble, and was sacked three times. The leading receiver that day was tight end Ben Watson with three catches for 50 yards. Behind huge performances from the Patriots' running backs—41 carries for 183 yards as a team—the Patriots offense stayed on schedule long enough to keep the team in the game, and the Patriots scored the final 12 points of the game (touchdown, field goal, safety) to pull off the 19–17 win.

The Patriots had another close encounter with the same problems the very next week. The Patriots passing game never got off the ground, as Brady completed 15 of his 29 attempts for 220 yards, one touchdown, one interception, and was sacked once. The leading receiver was Troy Brown with four catches for 51 yards. But the combination of Maroney, Corey Dillon, and Kevin Faulk was working wonders for the Patriots offense. The running game was once again the driving force of the offense with 39 carries for 147 yards and two scores against the New York Jets.

It appeared we had seen Belichick's response to a lack of offensive firepower: run the ball a lot. In the first two games of the season, the Patriots had 80 rush attempts against 56 pass plays. That strategy was about to be tested by the same team that gave the Patriots a nightmare finish to the 2005 season: the Denver Broncos. This time, though, the Patriots would be playing from the comfort of their own home. But it didn't help them pull off the win.

Unable to mount a consistent rush attack (21 carries for 50 yards), they were forced to put the ball into Brady's hands (31-of-55, 320 yards, one touchdown)— far from the Patriots' recipe the previous two weeks. A mess of third and long situations forced the Patriots to punt on six of their first nine drives. One ended on downs, the other on a blocked field goal, the other at the end of the first half. The Patriots didn't get on the board until the fourth quarter of the 17–7 loss. With three straight losses to the Broncos from 2005 to 2006, Belichick was now 2–5 with the Patriots against Mike Shanahan.

The loss didn't linger long, however, and the Patriots got right back to their recipe in a 38–13 win against the Cincinnati Bengals. As a team, the Patriots had 236 rushing yards on 41 carries in that game, and Maroney had his breakout performance with 15 carries for 125 yards and two touchdowns. Brady attempted 26 passes and completed 15. The Patriots' leading receiver was Doug Gabriel with four receptions for 57 yards. But, hey, the Patriots scored 38 points, so all seemed to be well in Foxborough.

Next week's win wasn't nearly as pretty. The Patriots capitalized on good field position and three Miami Dolphins turnovers en route to a 20–10 win at Gillette Stadium, but the offense once again looked out of sorts. Brady was efficient once again, going 16-of-29 for 140 yards and two touchdowns, but the running game was held to just 34 carries for 79 yards.

The Patriots were 4–1 headed into the bye and went 2–0 coming out of it. The defense ruled the day in the Patriots' 28–6 win against the Bills, but Brady earned his second 300-yard game of the season in a 31–7 win against the Minnesota Vikings. Brady was 29-of-43 for 372 yards, four touchdowns, and one interception. Caldwell and Watson tied for a team-high seven receptions, the most by a Patriots pass catcher in a single game that year to that point.

The Patriots were playing some of their best football of the season headed into Week 9, and yet it was somehow a surprise that they were favored by 2.5 points over the Indianapolis Colts. Even with the game taking place at Gillette Stadium, the undefeated Colts were everyone's pick to represent the AFC in the Super Bowl. It appeared the Patriots would use the same strategy they had used against Peyton Manning in the past: run the ball to keep him off the field. It's hard to do that, though, when your quarterback throws four interceptions and the offense has five turnovers total.

With back-to-back wins over Belichick, Tony Dungy inched closer to .500 with a 3–2 record against the Patriots head coach. Manning's third straight 300-yard game helped improve that record and so did a strong defensive performance from a unit that hadn't given them many that season. Dungy always had the coaching acumen to hang with Belichick. In much the same way Belichick had done his first handful of years in the league competing with the Bill Cowhers and Shanahans of the league, Dungy was finally showing the world that he could compete with the best in the league.

Even coming off their loss, the Patriots didn't have much to complain about. They were 6–2, comfortably perched atop the AFC East once again. They were losing ground in the battle for a first-round bye but were still in the hunt with the Colts and two other two-loss teams: the Baltimore Ravens and San Diego Chargers. Little did anyone know that the Patriots' third loss would be the one that would ultimately take them out of the hunt for the No. 1 seed and that this loss would take place the week after the Patriots' loss to the Colts at the hands of Eric Mangini and the Jets.

Maybe, in his time preparing for the Patriots offense in practice, Mangini picked up a thing or two on what might work against Brady. A mix of blitzes and unique coverages gave Brady problems, and the Patriots offense was held out of sync in a 17–14 loss. The Patriots hadn't lost consecutive games since Weeks 15 and 16 of the 2002 season. Fifty-seven straight games went by without the Patriots losing back-to-back games, and that was just three games short of the league record.

A 35–0 blowout of the Green Bay Packers at Lambeau Stadium was just the kind of game this team needed to get back on track. The Packers finished with 120 yards of total offense to the Patriots' 357, five first downs to the Patriots' 22, and just above 20 minutes time of possession to the Patriots' 40. The offense took advantage of good field position with four out of five touchdown drives traveling fewer than 70 yards, including one that traveled 23. These were the layups the Patriots' coaching staff had to have been hoping for.

But the Patriots dropped the ball on a lot of those layups the next week against the Chicago Bears. Lovie Smith's Bears defense was one of the best the league had seen in years. They rolled into New England with a streak of forcing multiple turnovers in all nine games that year. But it was still surprising to see the Patriots, normally very careful with the football, waste away on offense with five turnovers.

The Patriots went into the locker room with a 10–3 lead, and the way the two offenses were playing, that seven-point lead felt like it might as well have been 70 points. But another mistake by the Patriots offense—this time a Brady interception—gave the Bears a short field, which they turned into a tying touchdown after a long pass-interference penalty. The Patriots clawed their way back into the game on the strength of three third-down conversions on the following drive. On one Brady found Watson for 40 yards. On the next Brady scrambled for a gain of 11 yards and juked Bears linebacker Brian Urlacher clean to the ground. Brady ran for three yards on the next third down as well, and two plays later, the Patriots capped off the touchdown drive and eventually closed out a 17–13 win.

The following week's 28–21 win against the Detroit Lions was another in which the Patriots did not put forth a sterling offensive effort, but thanks to a stingy defense and a late two-touchdown rally, they were still able to sneak out with the win. But there was no sneaking anything in Miami, when the 9–4 Patriots visited the 5–7 Dolphins in what ended up looking like a sick rerun. Brady was smacked from pillar to post, sacked four times on the day, and held to just 78 passing yards. The offense couldn't get anything going, and eventually the defense stopped bending and started breaking. After forcing five punts and two field goals on the Dolphins' first seven drives, the Patriots defense yielded two touchdowns on the final three drives, leaving the Patriots with a shutout loss.

The Patriots still had another chance to claim the AFC East title with a 10th win of the season in Week 15 and they delivered a 40–7 beatdown of the 4–9 Houston Texans. In many ways, it was exactly the kind of beatdown the Patriots had suffered just the week before. Their defense swarmed quarterback David Carr, causing four sacks and four interceptions, and their offense kept things safe and efficient (no turnovers) with a high volume running game (38 carries for 105 yards by the Patriots) and a high efficiency passing game (19-of-27, 129 yards, two touchdowns for Brady).

The Patriots got their formula working again just in time for the stretch run and the playoffs. In total the Patriots forced eight turnovers in the final three games, did not turn the ball over once, ran for 393 yards (10th highest mark in that stretch), and completed 68.1 percent of their passes (third highest). Whoever faced the Patriots in the playoffs would be facing them at their best.

★ ★ ★

For the second straight year, the Patriots played on wild-card Sunday, albeit at home. With the Jets coming to town once again, the storyline machines were in full force headed into Mangini's third meeting with Belichick, but none of it mattered. The Patriots scored quickly on their first drive with Brady taking them down the field and setting up an 11-yard Dillon touchdown run. The Jets seized an opening to take a 10–7 lead, but the Patriots offense went on to score on their next five possessions (two touchdowns, three field goals), and the defense contributed a sixth when Asante Samuel returned an interception for a touchdown.

Brady was kept cleaner from the Jets' pressure packages this time around. He was sacked just once and completed 22 of his 34 passes. Wide receiver Jabar Gaffney ripped through the Jets secondary with eight receptions for 104 yards. Those numbers nearly matched his production from the entire regular season (11 receptions, 142 yards, one touchdown), but he wasn't done yet. The Patriots weren't either.

The 14–2 San Diego Chargers, the Patriots' next opponent, were the NFL's dominant team in 2006. The Patriots had been bludgeoned by the Chargers in '05, but in '06 San Diego was simply the best team in the league that year. Led by legend-in-the-making LaDainian Tomlinson at running back with an NFL-record 31 total touchdowns, the Chargers had the league's highest-scoring offense. Led by outside linebacker Shawne Merriman with a league-high 17 sacks, the Chargers defense tallied a league-leading 61 sacks in 2006.

But despite arguably having the better talent and despite having home-field advantage, the Chargers still couldn't pull off the win—and it was largely because of the imbalance on the sideline. Chargers head coach Marty Schottenheimer has a tricky legacy with great regular-season success (200–126, .613) but terrible luck in the postseason (5–13, .278). He made a number of blunders against the Patriots, which might have been benign on their own but combined to a confluence of circumstances that resulted in a Chargers loss.

The Chargers might have otherwise overcome their failure to convert an early fourth and 11 at the Patriots' 30-yard line instead of kicking a field goal. They might have even overcome their decision to go into a shell with a seven-point lead in the fourth quarter had Marlon McCree not fumbled his interception of Brady. They might have overcome all of that had Schottenheimer not foolishly challenged the play, failing to believe what his eyes had told him, and lost a timeout in the process.

It was Brady's third interception of the day, but it was the Patriots who would overcome their own circumstances. They overcame it all in a crazy seven-minute frenzy that included the interception that wasn't, a touchdown, a two-point conversion, a three-and-out defensive series, a ridiculous catch-and-run down the sideline by Caldwell, a 31-yard field goal by Gostkowski, and a missed field goal by Chargers kicker Nate Kaeding (after a spike because they had no timeouts). It was a crazy finish to a crazy game, but by comparison, things were about to go to the looney bin as the stakes were raised, and the Patriots' dominance over an old foe would be tested.

At this point in the Patriots-Colts rivalry, there were so many storylines and match-ups, it's hard to keep track of them all. In the Brady-Manning rivalry, this would be the ninth chapter (advantage Brady, 6–2); in the Belichick-Manning rivalry, this would be the 11th chapter (advantage Belichick, 7–3); and in the Belichick-Dungy rivalry, this would the seventh meeting (advantage Belichick, 4–2).

No matter which lens you were looking through, the story was the same: the Patriots had owned this rivalry in the beginning, but the Colts were gaining ground. A Colts win would propel them to the Super Bowl and would go a long way to exorcising some of those old playoff demons, while a Patriots win would validate Belichick and Brady as the power couple of the NFL playoffs with a fourth trip to the Super Bowl in six years.

Once again, the winner of the regular-season meeting found itself to be hosting the playoff rematch. Unfortunately for the Patriots, it wasn't them this time. The Colts run defense was the worst in the league that season, but they had played better in the two previous playoff games (44 and 83 yards allowed, respectively) with the return of star safety Bob Sanders. The Patriots showed their intent to test that group early on. The Patriots were off to the races on their second drive, running through the Colts defense like a battering ram through drywall with seven carries for 53 yards including a 35-yard scamper by Dillon.

The scoring play was an attempted quarterback sneak by Brady, where the quarterback fumbled and left guard Logan Mankins recovered in the end zone. Not exactly how Belichick drew it up, but the drive that got them there was exactly what they wanted. And that success continued on the next drive with six carries for 23 yards and a seven-yard touchdown run by Dillon to put the Patriots up 14–3.

Two plays later, some Patriots fans would begin booking planes and searching for tickets to the Super Bowl. Manning was a split-second late firing a pass to Marvin Harrison, Samuel got a good read on the pass, stepped in front of Harrison, made the interception, and ran it back 39 yards for a touchdown and a 21–3 lead.

Headed into the AFC Championship Game, the Colts weren't your typical Colts. Manning was a dreadful 45-of-68 for 438 yards, one touchdown, and five interceptions in their first two playoff games. The defense, meanwhile, allowed a combined 14 points through two rounds. For once, Manning wasn't carrying the team. But it was his turn to take over.

A field goal at the end of the first half cut the halftime deficit to 21–6, and the Colts would receive the second-half kickoff. Fourteen plays, 76 yards, 6:47 later, it was touchdown Colts to make the score 21–13. Manning was a crisp 5-of-6 for 44 yards on the drive, and the Colts ran the ball eight times for 32 yards and the score.

Four plays and 1:23 later, the Colts had the ball, and the Patriots defense was back on the field again. Six plays, 76 yards, 2:50 later, the Colts were in the end zone again on a clever touchdown pass to offensive lineman Dan Klecko, but the Colts didn't get there without 23 yards worth of penalties, including a neutral zone infraction on a third and 5 defensive pass interference in the end zone. A two-point conversion made it 21–21. The Colts had found rhythm, and the Patriots defense, exhausted from being on the field so much, was playing with poor discipline.

When the Patriots finally got the ball back, an 80-yard return by Ellis Hobbs set the Patriots up with good field position. That was good news for the offense, but not so good news for a defense that was already gassed. The Patriots managed to take 2:35 off the clock on that touchdown drive, but the Colts blew the doors off the Patriots defense again with another flawless drive, moving 67 yards in seven plays and just 3:01 and scoring in similar fashion to the Patriots' first touchdown when Dominic Rhodes fumbled into the end zone and Jeff Saturday recovered.

At the time, it was just peculiar that three offensive linemen scored in the same game. In hindsight, the symmetry of those touchdowns was almost like a before and after shot of the game and really the Patriots-Colts rivalry to that point.

The scoring flurry breathed at 28–28, and the two teams traded late field goals as the Patriots edged out to a 34–31 lead. But it was at this particular moment in time that one glaring weakness of the Patriots all season had come to the forefront;

Caldwell dropped two key passes on what could have been a touchdown drive for the Patriots, including one where the receiver was uncovered on the right sideline and another in the end zone.

And thus, the stage was set. With 2:17 left Manning got the ball at the 20-yard line, needing a field goal to tie the game and send it to overtime. It turned out the Colts barely needed half that to secure the win. Manning hit three passes for 57 yards, and Joseph Addai ran three times for 11 yards and the game-winning touchdown.

The season ended when Brady threw an interception on a pass intended for Watson. The Colts were going to the Super Bowl after dethroning the Patriots. The 2006 season felt like a missed opportunity. Even with the shortage of talent at wide receiver, even with all the turnover on defense, the Patriots were still one game—and just a few plays—away from an unprecedented fourth Super Bowl in six years. But although the 2006 season ended painfully, it would play an important role in shaping the future of the Patriots.

CHAPTER 17

★ ★ ★

2007: Chasing Perfection

The heartbreak of 2006 gave way to an all-in approach the likes of which we had never seen before. Bill Belichick put all his resources into building the best team possible and in doing so built what looked like the best team *ever*. Before the Patriots could build, there were some losses that needed to be addressed. Running back Corey Dillon had asked for his release, and the 2006 season ended up being his last in the NFL. Safety Tebucky Jones, tight end Daniel Graham, and outside linebacker Tully Banta-Cain also left the team.

But the Patriots gave a record-setting contract to outside linebacker Adalius Thomas to the tune of five years and $35 million. Before joining the Patriots, Thomas had proven to be one of the most versatile defenders in the NFL. He had lined up at defensive tackle, defensive end, outside linebacker, inside linebacker, and even cornerback the year before with the Baltimore Ravens. With Thomas in the fold, the Patriots now had a four-man linebacker group of Tedy Bruschi and Mike Vrabel on the inside, and Rosevelt Colvin and Thomas on the outside. But with versatile linebackers like Thomas, Colvin, and Vrabel in the fold, it was never as simple as plugging guys into their spots and leaving them there. The Patriots could continue to shapeshift on defense in order to best suit their opponent.

Cornerback Asante Samuel, who had emerged as a viable starting cornerback, was set to become a free agent before the Patriots hit him with the franchise tag that year of $7.79 million guaranteed. The franchise tag at the time guaranteed the player the average of the top five salaries at their position but only for one year. Free-agent running back Sammy Morris gave the Patriots a nice relief option behind Laurence Maroney, but—aside from first-round pick Brandon Meriweather, who was brought in for Jones' old role—virtually none of their draft choices made any kind of impact.

The biggest offseason addition was made during the draft, but it wasn't a prospect chosen out of college—it was a veteran added via trade. The Patriots had already sent a second and seventh-round pick to the Miami Dolphins for Wes Welker in late March, but during the draft, they sent a fourth-round pick to the Oakland Raiders for Randy Moss. The two moves completely changed the complexion of the Patriots offense in ways that are still being felt nearly a full decade later. Along with the addition of wide receivers Donte Stallworth and Kelley Washington, the Patriots had taken their weakest position and turned it into a strength.

This began a new approach to the offseason. I've called it the "volume approach," which focuses on the principle of playing the odds. By adding a handful of players at a position of need, Belichick was taking a very calculated gamble that at least one or more of those players would make solid contributions to the team. Of course, this was about as beneficial as the volume approach has ever been.

Moss gave the Patriots a dynamic downfield threat the likes of which they'd never had. Welker gave the team a shifty slot presence that could capitalize on all the extra space that would be created by Moss' deep ability. Stallworth was seen as the boundary complement opposite Moss, and everything else was icing on the cake.

The Moss trade had the potential to create a divide in the team the way Andre Rison had done to the Cleveland Browns more than a decade earlier in 1995, but there was one major difference. Belichick had already built a team-first, winning culture in New England that permeated the organization from top to bottom. A player like Moss had two choices: fall in line or fall to the wayside. Moss chose the former.

The 2007 Patriots offense rewrote the record books, but perhaps the most impressive element was the complete 180-degree shift in philosophy. The Patriots had gone from a smashmouth, run-first offense to a high-flying, aerial assault.

Patriots 2007 Draft Picks

Round	Pick	Player	Position	Games played w/ Patriots
1	24	Brandon Meriweather	S	64
4	127	Kareem Brown	DT	0
5	171	Clint Oldenburg	OT	0
6	180	Justin Rogers	LB	0
6	202	Mike Richardson	CB	10
6	208	Justise Hairston	RB	0
6	209	Corey Hilliard	OG	0
7	211	Oscar Lua	LB	0
7	247	Mike Elgin	C	0

The Patriots went from starting games with three tight ends to virtually never taking the field with fewer than three wide receivers. Having a quarterback like Tom Brady covers a lot of blemishes and allows an offense to be much more versatile, but Belichick and Josh McDaniels showed their own versatility by willingly changing their approach to fit the players on their roster.

★ ★ ★

It was clear right away that the Patriots were on a warpath. Week 1 brought us the fourth chapter in the Bill Belichick-Eric Mangini rivalry, which was a decisive victory for Belichick. An early defensive stop was followed by a 12-play, 91-yard touchdown drive, in which Brady hit four of his five passes for 48 yards and a touchdown, while the Patriots' two-back tandem combined for seven carries and 43 yards. The two teams traded four combined empty possessions before the New York Jets got on the board with their first touchdown, but the Patriots responded with another long touchdown drive of nine plays and 73 yards, and that was capped off by Brady's second touchdown pass to Ben Watson.

Ellis Hobbs took the second-half kickoff for a then-NFL record 108-yard touchdown, the Jets punted on the ensuing possession, and the Patriots were off to the races. Moss proved what kind of game-changing player he can be when he streaked through the Jets secondary right past rookie cornerback Darrelle Revis and two other defensive backs for a 51-yard touchdown en route to a 38–14 victory.

That kind of bomb to Moss would come to define the Patriots season. The victory, however, would come with some controversy. During the game video assistant Matt Estrella had been found on the Jets' sideline videotaping the team's signals. The scandal would come to be known as "Spygate," a play on words of the political scandal "Watergate." NFL rules state that "no video recording devices of any kind are permitted to be in use in the coaches' booth, on the field, or in the locker room during the game," and also that any videographer shooting video for team coaching purposes "must be enclosed on all sides with a roof overhead.

"Any use by any club at any time, from the start to the finish of any game in which such club is a participant, of any communications or information-gathering equipment, other than Polaroid-type cameras or field telephones, shall be prohibited, including without limitation videotape machines, telephone tapping, or bugging devices, or any other form of electronic devices that might aid a team during the playing of a game."

In 2006 NFL executive vice president of football operations Ray Anderson had sent a memo re-emphasizing that "videotaping of any type, including but not limited to taping of an opponent's offensive or defensive signals, is prohibited on the sidelines, in the coaches' booth, in the locker room, or at any other locations accessible to club staff members during the game."

Belichick issued a statement "to apologize to everyone who has been affected," and claimed that his "interpretation of a rule in the Constitution and Bylaws was incorrect." Since Spygate there have been several explanations offered about the events that transpired. In an interview with Armen Keteyian, Belichick said his misinterpretation stemmed from the phrases "during the game" and "during the playing of a game." Belichick thought that, since he was not using those materials during the game, he was in the clear, though he acknowledged his failure in clarifying the legality of his methods after the Anderson memo.

But none of it mattered. The Patriots had been found guilty of cheating. In the eyes of the rest of the NFL, their success was now tainted. So, the Patriots did the one thing they could do to prove everyone wrong.

Providing the deep threat in 2007 that Tom Brady sorely needed, Randy Moss catches a 65-yard touchdown pass, which was Brady's 50th touchdown pass of the year, a single-season record, and Moss's 23rd touchdown reception, also a single-season record.
(AP Images)

Tom Brady, First Eight Games, 2006–07

Year	Comp	Att	Comp %	Yds	YPA	TD	INT	Rate
2006	155	267	58.1	1799	6.7	14	8	83.5
2007	198	267	74.2	2431	9.1	30	2	136.2

In a rematch of the playoff game the year before, the San Diego Chargers traveled to Gillette Stadium for the Patriots' home opener. Initially, it looked like the Chargers didn't even get off the bus. The Patriots drove 69 yards in 2:46 for their first touchdown—Brady's fourth scoring throw of the season. Chargers quarterback Philip Rivers' first pass was intercepted, but the ensuing drive stalled, and Stephen Gostkowski missed the 41-yard field goal. Three plays later, the Chargers had to punt, and 10 plays, 75 yards, and 5:58 later, the Patriots had a two-touchdown lead following a 23-yard touchdown pass to Moss.

With the score 17–0 midway through the second quarter, Rivers committed his third turnover of the game when Thomas intercepted him and ran it back 65 yards for a touchdown. Brady hit his third touchdown pass of the game, and his sixth of the season, on a 24-yard pass to Moss. The Brady-to-Moss connection was on fire. Moss had 17 receptions for 288 yards and three touchdowns in two games. His 288 yards to start the season was the most by any Patriots receiver in the first two games of a season.

The war on the record books, and on the NFL, continued. The Patriots scored 34 points or more in their first eight straight games. It was only the second team to ever accomplish that feat.

They rolled through those first eight games almost without a hitch, even bludgeoning the 5–0 Dallas Cowboys (the eventual No. 1 seed in the NFC) 48–27 in the first game in which the Patriots faced a second-half deficit. That was the first time Welker's impact was felt in a big way. He had five or more receptions in three of the first five games, but he finished with 11 receptions for 124 yards and two touchdowns against the Cowboys, including four third-down conversions. His presence underneath and in the slot was the perfect complement to "deep to Moss" on the outside.

Some of these wins drew the ire of some around the NFL, who felt the Patriots were running up the score to help pad Brady's stats and to send a message to the rest of the league.

But perhaps the most important unit—at that point and throughout the season—was the offensive line. Through eight games Brady was sacked just eight times. On the season he was sacked just 21 times. That group kept Brady upright, giving him the time to go deep to Moss or anywhere else on the field.

It was well before the midway point of the season that the talk of a "path to perfection" began to circle the team, challenging Belichick's one-game-at-a-time, ignore-the-noise approach to the fullest extent. But the noise got much louder with a looming showdown of two undefeated teams in a rematch of the 2006 AFC Championship Game.

★ ★ ★

It was billed as Super Bowl 41.5. Easily the biggest regular-season game of the Belichick era to that point, the 8–0 Patriots rolled into Indianapolis to take on the 7–0 Colts in what marked the latest ever meeting between two undefeated teams. It was Brady-Manning X, Belichick-Manning XII, and Belichick-Dungy VIII. With the win the Patriots maintained the head-to-head lead in the first two and regained the head-to-head lead in the last category of those match-ups. (Brady moved to 7–3 against Manning, and Belichick moved to 8–4 against Manning and 5–3 against Dungy.)

But the victory did not come easy. The Patriots had to fight back from a 13–7 deficit at halftime after Colts running back Joseph Addai scored a 73-yard touchdown on late-first half dump-off. The Colts even built a 20–10 fourth-quarter lead, but Brady commandeered back-to-back touchdown drives, going 7-of-11 for 134 yards (including a 55-yard pass to Moss) and two touchdowns without a single run play called.

So, the Patriots closed out the victory while overcoming their biggest challenge to date. After having beaten their first eight opponents by an average of 25 points per game (still the biggest point differential ever through eight games), it was the first time the Patriots had trailed in the fourth quarter. "This is the first time we were in a ballgame late," Brady said after the game. "There wasn't any loss of confidence or determination."

The Patriots' path to perfection was never as clear after this point. They hung a 50-burger on the Buffalo Bills in a 56–10 win in Buffalo, in which Brady picked up 373 passing yards and five touchdowns, and Moss racked up 10 receptions for 128 yards and four touchdowns. The Patriots were rolling, but that roll would be threatened by two backup quarterbacks playing for average to below-average teams.

The wheels started to come off a little against the Philadelphia Eagles in Week 12, a game in which the Patriots were 22-point favorites—and no one saw anything wrong with that line. The Patriots were 10–0, and with A.J. Feeley and the 5–5 Eagles coming to town, no one expected this game to be any different than any of the Patriots' early-season blowouts.

But "deep to Moss" didn't explode quite the way it had throughout the season; he finished with just five receptions for 55 yards. For another thing, Eagles defensive coordinator Jim Johnson went back to some of the blitz schemes and pressure packages that worked against Brady in Super Bowl XXXVIII. It was also the first game that season in which Brady failed to throw three touchdown passes. In fact, the only reason the Patriots won was because of their defense, as Samuel started the game with a Pick-6 and had an interception late in the game to thwart an Eagles scoring drive.

If there wasn't much fear of the Patriots' perfect season coming to an end after that game, the fear kicked into high gear the following week, when the Kyle Boller-led Baltimore Ravens went blow-for-blow with the Patriots. Ravens defensive coordinator Rex Ryan threw the kitchen sink at Brady, blitzing him nearly every snap, and holding Brady to fewer than three touchdown passes for a second straight week while also holding him to just a 47.4 percent completion rate.

Were it not for a late string of bad calls by the referees, the Patriots might have been handed their first loss right then and there. But while the path to perfection was still clear, these two games were akin to Rocky landing a right hook in the second round against Drago, cutting the seemingly unbeatable Russian. The Patriots were still undefeated, but now the rest of the world knew they could bleed.

The Patriots, though, would receive some extra motivation from Pittsburgh Steelers safety Anthony Smith before their next game. "People keep asking me if we're ready for the Patriots," Smith said. "They should be asking if they're ready for us." He wasn't done talking. "We're going to win," Smith said. "Yeah, I can guarantee a win, as long as we come out and do what we got to do. Both sides of the ball are rolling, and if our special teams come through for us, we've got a good chance to win."

In much the same way the Eagles' preemptive parade plans gave the Patriots extra fuel to the fire before Super Bowl XXXIX, Smith's jawing had the same effect. It was almost as if the previous two weeks were just a bump in an otherwise perfect ride. Brady went back to hurling long touchdown passes, including one to Moss for 63 yards. On a razzle-dazzle triple-pass, Brady threw a backward lateral to Moss on the right sideline. Moss dropped it but picked it back up with Steelers defenders bearing down on him and got it back to Brady in time. Brady found Jabar Gaffney for a 56-yard touchdown pass—against Anthony Smith. Beating him with that play made the 34–13 home victory even sweeter, and Brady wasted little time letting Smith know after the play, getting right in his face to delivery the message.

Following the win, the Patriots were 13–0 and on the precipice of history. Brady was five touchdown passes away from the single-season NFL record, and Moss was four touchdown receptions shy of the single-season NFL record.

The Patriots spent one game mud wrestling with the Jets in a 20–10 win that fell short of the "Spygate revenge game" hype and they spent the next game airing it out from Brady to Moss 11 times trying to break the records. Brady had 48 touchdown passes; Moss had 21 touchdown catches. One more by each would tie the respective records, and two more by each would break them.

On December 29, 2007, the New York Giants were the only team that stood between the Patriots and a perfect regular season. It was obvious almost immediately that the Giants would not roll over for the Patriots. Eli Manning marched the team downfield 74 yards in four minutes for a touchdown. The Patriots responded with a field goal drive, and the next drive tied the touchdown record for Brady. Still, the Patriots went into the locker room trailing for only the second time all year.

A Giants touchdown handed the Patriots a 28–16 deficit, but Brady marched the team quickly downfield for a score, and after trading a few punts, the Patriots landed a haymaker on the Giants and on the NFL record books with a 65-yard connection from Brady for touchdown pass No. 50. For Moss it was touchdown catch No. 23.

The Giants gave the Patriots a tough game because they were able to keep up with New England on the scoreboard. The Patriots came away with a 38–35 win, and the march to a perfect regular season was complete. But the path to perfection was still on, and the stakes were higher than ever before.

Two weeks later, Brady had one of the most efficient performances by a quarterback in NFL history when he completed 26 of his 28 passes against the Jacksonville Jaguars in the playoffs. The Jaguars rarely blitzed, playing it safe instead, and Brady burned them. His 92.9 percent completion rate was the highest completion percentage in a playoff game ever by a quarterback with 10 attempts or more. The two teams traded blows into the third quarter on the way to a 31–20 Patriots victory.

The next week brought a rematch with the Chargers in the AFC Championship Game. This time the roles were reversed. The Chargers were the underdog that had knocked off a heavyweight team, taking down Manning and the Colts the week before. Though short-handed with LaDainian Tomlinson hurt and Rivers having come back from a torn ACL suffered weeks earlier, the Chargers put up a fight. Their defense picked Brady off three times in the playoffs for the second straight year.

An efficient running game kept the Patriots offense moving, but it was the defense that carried New England to victory with two interceptions, holding the Chargers to just three third-down conversions on 12 tries and keeping them out of the end zone. That being said, it was an underwhelming entry to the Super Bowl for a team that had dominated the NFL by breaking records left and right.

★ ★ ★

There might not have been a worse opponent for the Patriots to face in Super Bowl XLII than the Giants. That was a team tailor-made to beat the Patriots. In Week 17 the Giants kept pace with the Patriots on the scoreboard in a three-point loss. They had the firepower on offense to stay efficient in the passing game and to move the chains in the running game. They also had the pass rush up front to take over a game on defense and to keep an aerial assault such as the Patriots' in check. The coaching matchup between Belichick and Tom Coughlin saw two main branches from the Bill Parcells coaching tree going head to head.

But on the field, the Patriots looked like they were in trouble from the very beginning. The Giants dictated the tempo right away with a 16-play, 63-yard field goal drive that took 9:59 off the clock. The Patriots' very first play from scrimmage was a double-reverse-fake screen pass to the running back, but the Giants' pressure was so quick to Brady that the play never had a chance before he spiked the pass into the ground in front of Maroney. The drive ended in a touchdown, thanks in large part to a defensive pass interference penalty in the end zone on third and 10, but the message had been sent: the Giants could play their style on both sides of the ball and rough up the Patriots doing so.

Brady faced immense pressure nearly every time he dropped back to throw, but the Giants were getting that pressure almost entirely with a four-man rush. There were no tricks or exotic blitzes—just defensive linemen beating offensive linemen. It wasn't the first time that season in which the Patriots offensive line had been dominated. It was just the most thorough domination they had suffered. They allowed five sacks, their highest of the season, in that game. The Giants' defensive domination extended to the running game, where the Patriots mustered just 16 carries for 46 yards and a touchdown.

Of course, all of that was washed away by key plays for the Giants and missed opportunities by the Patriots in the final minutes. A great escape by Eli Manning, coupled with a hand on both the football and his helmet by David Tyree, who had struggled during Super Bowl week practices, was followed by a corner end zone touchdown catch by Plaxico Burress. The Burress score gave the Giants a 17–14 lead with 39 seconds left. Yet, with three timeouts, the Patriots still had enough time to tie the game. Instead of trying to drive down the field methodically, though, they just went deep to Moss two more times to end the game.

The Patriots' pursuit of perfection ended with an 18–1 record. Had Belichick been outcoached? Or had the Patriots been outplayed? The answer is probably somewhere in between. A better performance from the offensive line might have yielded better results for the offense, but the same could be said for adjustments by the coaching staff when they realized their gameplan wasn't working. One thing is almost universally agreed upon: the Patriots faced mounting pressure each week. One of the mantras on the door at Gillette Stadium is "ignore the noise." The pursuit of perfection, coupled with Spygate, created noise at a decibel level that blew those doors off their hinges.

CHAPTER 18

★ ★ ★

Bill Belichick vs. Don Shula

Don Shula was once the youngest head coach in NFL history. He was not only the first—and presently, the only—head coach in NFL history to lead an undefeated season, when his 1972 Miami Dolphins went 17–0 and won the Super Bowl, he is also the all-time winningest coach in NFL history. Shula's legacy is so much more than just one Super Bowl team and one perfect season.

Some coaches benefited from a dominant roster, some employed a system that was tough to stop, some coaches were master motivators. Shula was a bit of all three with the Baltimore Colts from 1963 to 1969. He had Hall of Fame talent in quarterback Johnny Unitas, tight end John Mackey, tackle Jim Parker, running back Lenny Moore, and wide receiver Raymond Berry on offense alone. Offensively, they were in the top 10 in both points and yards every year under Shula and they only fell outside the top 10 defensively in points and yards in Shula's final year. Those teams were regularly among the best in the NFL, but they never won a Super Bowl and posted a postseason record of 2–3.

But everything would come together in Miami. He had good players on offense in the form of future Hall of Famers like quarterback Bob Griese, running back Larry Csonka, offensive linemen Larry Little and Jim Langer, and wide receiver

Paul Warfield. That offense ranked in the top five in rushing every year from 1970 to 1975 and in the top five in scoring in 1971 from 1974.

He coached teamwork and hard work, along with an aggressive scheme, in maximizing a "No-Name Defense," as it was called. There were some good players on those defenses, such as defensive tackle Manny Fernandez and Hall of Fame linebacker Nick Buoniconti. However, they weren't the only ones contributing to a Dolphins defense that ranked in the top five in scoring every year from 1971 to 1975 except in 1974, when they ranked sixth.

Shula's success with the Dolphins was instantaneous. For the first four years of their existence, the Dolphins were a combined 15–39–2. And then Shula came aboard. In their next four years, they were 46–9–1 in the regular season alone and another 8–2 in the playoffs, including three trips to the Super Bowl.

As time wore on, his roster began falling apart due to massive, unmatchable offers from the newly formed and now defunct World Football League for his key players such as Csonka, Warfield, and running back Jim Kiick. The Dolphins missed the playoffs three straight years after that, despite winning 10 games in two of those three years.

The decade turned, and the Dolphins kept winning, even appearing in a Super Bowl in 1982. Once again, their success was predicated on the running game and a stingy defense. The current crop of Dolphins quarterbacks wasn't cutting it, so Shula added Dan Marino in the first round of the 1983 draft after several teams passed on him, including the Patriots who drafted Tony Eason.

From there, the Dolphins rode the passing game to another Super Bowl appearance in 1984 and to much of their success for the remainder of Shula's tenure. The team bounced back and forth between mediocre and playoff-caliber for his final decade in the league, though, with only six winning seasons, three seasons of 10 or more wins, and a playoff record of 3–4.

In New England, he's remembered more for the salvos he has lobbed at Bill Belichick over the years. Shula has been so vocal in his distaste for Belichick, it might call for a whole extra chapter to recap everything the legend of yesteryear has said about the legend of the new millennium. Shula, who has repeatedly called the Patriots head coach "Belicheat" (a favorite nickname among the Patriots' worst enemies), is one of only a handful of coaches who stand ahead of Belichick in a number of categories.

Shula's 328 wins are the most in history and 105 more than Belichick. His 172 games above .500 are the most in history and 62 more than Belichick. His 19 postseason trips are the most in history and five more than Belichick. His 36 playoff games are the most in history and three more than Belichick. But his six Super Bowl appearances are tied for the most in history—tied with none other than Belichick.

Shula's legacy stands on its own. He coached 33 straight years from 1963 to 1995. He only had a losing record in two of those seasons and he made the

Then-Cleveland Browns head coach Bill Belichick talks to Don Shula following a 1993 loss to Shula's Miami Dolphins. (USA TODAY Sports Images)

Tale of the Tape

Coach	Bill Belichick	Don Shula
Years as a head coach	21	33
Career W–L	223–113	328–156–6
Ratio	.664	.677
Playoff trips	14	19
Playoff W–L	23–10	19–17
Division championships	13	16
Super Bowl wins	4	2

playoffs more than half the time. The Dolphins failed to win another Super Bowl after 1973, but Shula did not fail to add to his legacy. Shula coached five different quarterbacks in his six trips to the Super Bowl: Johnny Unitas and Earl Morrall with the Colts and Morrall, Bob Griese, David Woodley, and Dan Marino with the Dolphins.

Right now, Belichick has done it with just one quarterback. That's not his fault, of course, but if he hopes to eke out the statistical edge over Shula, the Patriots head coach could benefit from leading his team to another Super Bowl victory after Tom Brady retires. Even without the fulfillment of that set of circumstances, Belichick is still the biggest threat ever to Shula's unprecedented win total. If Belichick coaches 10 more years and continues to win at his career rate of .664, he will surpass Shula's career win total. He will also be 73 years old.

With one more win in the 2007 season, Belichick would hold all the cards in any debate as to the better head coach. Instead, the season is a footnote, and is probably a source of glee for someone who admittedly does not care much for Belichick.

Whether Belichick surpasses Shula in other areas—he's already doubled Shula's Super Bowl wins and has matched Shula's record of six Super Bowl appearances—could determine who has the ultimate edge. But unless Belichick does the unthinkable and coaches a 19–0 team to a Super Bowl win, Shula will always have at least one claim to superiority.

CHAPTER 19

★ ★ ★

2008: A Season Without Brady

How do you retool a team that fell one game short of perfection? For the Patriots, some of that work was done for them. In 2007 the Patriots were aggressive in adding multiple talented players to their roster. In 2008 a long line of in-house free agents mandated that the focus shift toward retaining players already with the team. Tedy Bruschi, Randy Moss, Jabar Gaffney, Kelley Washington, Ray Ventrone, Mike Wright, Wesley Britt, and Pierre Woods were all re-signed, but the Patriots couldn't keep everyone.

The most notable loss was off the field. The Atlanta Falcons hired Thomas Dimitroff, the Patriots' director of college scouting, to be their new general manager. Nick Caserio, the former pro personnel director-turned-wide-receiver-coach, was moved back to the personnel staff as director of player personnel where he would fill both Dimitroff's role and his former role under vice president of player personnel Scott Pioli.

Rosevelt Colvin, once an integral component of the Patriots defense, was released before the beginning of free agency. Wide receiver Donté Stallworth did not have his option picked up, so he became a free agent. Asante Samuel, who had taken Ty Law's place atop the depth chart at cornerback, was not re-signed after his 2007 franchise tag expired. Starting defensive backs Randall Gay and Eugene

Wilson also left the team, and between the three defensive backs, the Patriots lost 122 combined games of starting experience.

That led to a season-long search to find the right pieces in the secondary. No sooner had the Patriots begun retooling their defense than they started to lose more pieces. With so many losses at defensive back, the Patriots used the volume approach once again. Between rookie cornerbacks Terrence Wheatley and Jonathan Wilhite and veteran cornerbacks Jason Webster and Deltha O'Neal and safety Tank Williams, the Patriots were hopeful to find a combination of defensive backs that could help the team make the transition on defense from the dynasty to a new era.

With one first-round pick, though, the Patriots made a move that would help more than all of the others combined. They had been docked their own first-round pick by the league due to Spygate, but thanks to a draft-day trade the year before, the Patriots still had an early first-round pick. After trading down a few spots, the Patriots selected linebacker Jerod Mayo: the eventual 2008 Defensive Rookie of the Year, an immediate starter, and an important versatile piece for their defense for years to come. It's a good thing they got Mayo from that crop, though, because they didn't yield much else in the draft.

Overall, the 2008 offseason had a different feel to it. There wasn't much of an effort by the Patriots to evolve; instead, they were—understandably—trying their

Patriots 2008 Draft Picks

Round	Pick	Player	Position	Games played w/ Patriots
1	10	Jerod Mayo	LB	103
2	62	Terrence Wheatley	CB	11
3	78	Shawn Crable	LB	6
3	94	Kevin O'Connell	QB	2
4	129	Jonathan Wilhite	CB	39
5	153	Matthew Slater	S	119*
6	197	Bo Ruud	LB	0

*=still with Patriots

best to maintain the status quo. There were some minor strategical tweaks, but mostly, the Patriots sought to continue using a formula that had worked to near-perfection the year before.

If that formula had a list of ingredients, the main one would be Tom Brady. The Patriots were soon going to have to concoct a winning formula without their main ingredient. Brady's season was over just minutes after it began. While Brady was stepping into a deep throw to Randy Moss, Kansas City Chiefs safety Bernard Pollard hit the Patriots quarterback at the knee, tearing the ACL and MCL on his left leg.

Out went Brady, taking his string of 128 consecutive starts with him, and in came Matt Cassel, a former seventh-round pick with zero regular-season starts since high school. The feeling might not have been so gloomy if Cassel had shown any signs of life in the preseason, but the backup was a paltry 19-of-34 for 185 yards and an interception in those four games.

Much like the Patriots had done when Brady took over for Bledsoe, the focus shifted to a heavy dose of the running game (28 carries, 126 yards, one touchdown) and a stout performance by the defense (284 total net yards). Cassel steered the ship to a 17–10 victory against the Chiefs in Week 1, but it felt like the Patriots had lost.

With one quarterback down and a new high-profile veteran quarterback in the AFC East, the Patriots were about to have their dominance tested. Brett Favre's retirement saga with the Green Bay Packers came to an ugly end and resulted in the NFL's all-time touchdown leader playing for the New York Jets instead. The Patriots defense pulled through for a second straight week, though, holding Gang Green to just 10 points and 256 yards of offense. Just two weeks into the season, it appeared that the best-laid plans of Belichick and Pioli had gone awry, but thanks to great coaching, they kept winning.

What happened next was one of the most memorable beatdowns of a Belichick team. It was one of the rare occasions where the Patriots head coach had been caught completely and egregiously off guard. The 38–13 loss is known as the "Wildcat Game" for the Miami Dolphins' utilization of a unique formation where the running back lines up as a quarterback in the shotgun with the quarterback flanked out wide as a receiver. The defense didn't know where to match up their assignments, and the confusion resulted in supreme domination.

Dolphins head coach Tony Sparano's surprise scheme gashed the Patriots with 216 rushing yards and four rushing touchdowns, along with a whopping 461 total net yards on the day. Chad Pennington was an efficient 17-of-20 for 226 yards against the Patriots pass defense, and running back Ronnie Brown even threw a 19-yard touchdown pass. The Dolphins had so much success with the Wildcat that it spurred a mini-revolution with teams searching for Wildcat weapons. To think that this success was at the expense of a Belichick defense, typically among the most disciplined in the NFL, was stunning.

The Patriots had their bye in Week 4, and while that would typically be considered early, the whirlwind of the first three weeks made the early bye feel like it was right on time. It allowed the Patriots to regroup and find more ways to transition to a Brady-less offense. Cassel had played efficient football, completing two-thirds of his throws with two touchdowns, one interception, and an 87 passer rating, but the offense just wasn't dynamic enough. Through three games, the Patriots had scored 49 points, tied for fifth-fewest points in the league. Even with one of the best deep threats ever in Randy Moss at his disposal, Cassel attempted just three passes that traveled farther than 20 yards through three games.

At least they were efficient in the passing game. Their bigger concern was in the running game, where their 80 rush attempts had yielded just 308 yards (3.9 yards per carry) and two touchdowns. Without Brady behind center, they needed more from the running game and they got it. Over the next four games, the Patriots ran the ball a collective 136 times for 605 yards (4.4 yards per carry) and six touchdowns. Cassel attempted five passes that traveled farther than 20 yards, and the Patriots scored 104 points, eighth most in the league.

The dominant running game hit its apex with a stunning 257 yards against the Denver Broncos in a 41–7 shellacking that moved Belichick to 3–5 against Mike Shanahan. They revamped their offense with a smashmouth approach and they did it without their best young running back in Maroney. Sammy Morris, Kevin Faulk, and LaMont Jordan were the team's top three rushers in carries and yards, and all three were 30 years or older in 2008. Yet, Belichick was able to look at this group and find ways to patch together a productive offense.

Faulk and Morris ranked third and fourth, respectively, in yards from scrimmage on the team. The Patriots, as a team, ranked in the top 10 in nearly every major rushing statistic and also in both scoring and total yards. But even during that stretch, the offense was inconsistent—scoring 30 points one week and 10 the next, then 41 points against Denver, and a respectable but modest 23 against the St. Louis Rams. And the Patriots were just about to hit the toughest part of their schedule, which would determine their playoff fate.

★ ★ ★

Since Brady and Peyton Manning were both NFL starters beginning in 2001, there have only been three games played between their teams in which one of them did not make the start. This was the first. We still were treated to the ninth meeting between Belichick and Indianapolis Colts head coach Tony Dungy and Belichick's 13th encounter with Manning. But these were not your typical Colts, bringing a 3–4 record headed into the Week 9 showdown. It just so happens, a Brady-less Patriots teams was the cure for their uncommon start to a season.

Manning gave an efficient performance, not a dynamic one, but he accounted for 254 of the Colts' 301 yards of offense and completed 21-of-29 throws with two touchdowns and a 121.9 passer rating. What hurt the Patriots the most in that game was their inability to finish drives in the red zone. They kicked three field goals on drives that stalled inside the Colts' 20-yard line. A touchdown on any of those drives could have been the difference in what ended up an 18–15 Colts victory.

The running game remained the focus in the Patriots' next game, a 20–10 win against the Buffalo Bills in which they ran the ball 43 times and threw it 34 times. But they wouldn't continue to have that luxury in a rematch against the Jets, facing an offense that could put points on the board. The Jets jumped out to a 24–6 lead on the strength of two Favre touchdown passes and a Leon Washington kickoff return before Cassel finally did something he hadn't done all season: took over the game. Cassel threw touchdowns to Jabar Gaffney at the end of the first half and Ben Watson at the end of the third quarter and also led a field-goal drive in the fourth quarter.

But the Patriots were facing a seven-point deficit with a minute to go. Eight plays later, Cassel completed five passes for 67 yards and hit Moss in the corner of the end zone for a tying touchdown. But it was all for naught, as the Jets drove 64 yards in 14 plays for the game-winning field goal in overtime. The loss was another indication that the 2008 Patriots couldn't beat the conference's elite teams.

The Patriots put a dent in that notion the next week with a resounding 48–28 win against the Dolphins, which featured a second straight 400-yard, three-touchdown performance by Cassel. The defense exacted some revenge on the Dolphins as well by holding them to 66 rushing yards as a team (150 yards fewer than the previous meeting).

New England's final loss of the season came the very next week, though, as the Pittsburgh Steelers rolled into Gillette Stadium with one of the AFC's best records at 8–3. Cassel's two weeks of dominance were brought to a swift end as the Steelers held him below a completion percentage of 50 and sacked him five times. The Patriots turned the ball over five times, four coming from Cassel (two interceptions, two fumbles), and the Steelers rolled to a 33–10 victory.

At 7–5 with four games left, the Patriots needed a winning streak and a little help to make the playoffs. They took care of their own business with four straight wins, but thanks to a late-season surge by the Dolphins, the Patriots were held out of the playoffs for the first time since 2002.

On one hand, the Patriots' 11–5 record was a sign that Belichick could coach a winning team with or without Brady. On the other hand, they fell short of the playoffs, which is the objective for every team. Is Brady-Belichick a zero-sum game? The question remains. But despite missing the playoffs, Belichick proved that he could coach a winning team even without one of the greatest quarterbacks of all time.

CHAPTER 20

★ ★ ★

2009: Defensive Overhaul

Matt Cassel's performance in 2008 left the Patriots with some interesting discussions headed into '09. There, of course, was never any serious debate as to whether Tom Brady should be the team's starter when he returned from a torn ACL. The crux of the debate was whether Cassel's value was greater as a trade option or as a backup to one of the best quarterbacks ever.

The Patriots concluded the former, sending Cassel and veteran linebacker Mike Vrabel to the Kansas City Chiefs for a second-round pick—an underwhelming haul given what the Patriots gave up. Nonetheless, the move showed clear confidence that Brady would be back at full health in time for the season. Brady's return was hailed as the return of a king and the return to the Patriots' dominant ways. The Patriots fell short of the playoffs in 2008 for the first time in more than half a decade.

As it turned out, Brady's return was more necessary than anyone thought it would be.

One thing that sets Bill Belichick apart from other head coaches is his successful transition from winning by defense to racking up victories by lighting up the scoreboard. This is a transition that took place gradually from 2005 to 2009. And by the time Brady came back in '09, the transition was nearly complete.

Patriots 2004 Starting Defense
(at least 8 games started)

Player	Position	Super Bowl wins w/ team	Year departed
Ty Warren	DE	2	2011
Keith Traylor	NT	1	2005
Richard Seymour	DE	3	2009
Willie McGinest	OLB	3	2006
Ted Johnson	ILB	3	2005
Tedy Bruschi	ILB	3	2009
Mike Vrabel	OLB	3	2009
Randall Gay	CB	1	2008
Asante Samuel	CB	2	2008
Rodney Harrison	SS	2	2009
Eugene Wilson	FS	2	2008

The '05 season was the first sign of symptoms of the end of the Patriots dynasty; the '09 season was (arguably) the final nail in the coffin. This is not to say that the Patriots' run of dominance was over. On the contrary, it is remarkable that the Patriots remained as competitive as they were even while completely overhauling a defense, which had been the lifeline for three Super Bowl championships in four years.

In the four-year stretch since their last Lombardi Trophy, the Patriots lost nearly every defensive starter who had contributed to the team's success. Yet, despite all those setbacks, the Patriots finished in the top 10 in both scoring defense and total defense from 2006 to 2008.

The 2009 offseason marked the departure of four greats. Linebacker Tedy Bruschi and safety Rodney Harrison both retired. Vrabel was part of the trade package with Cassel, and defensive end Richard Seymour was traded to the Oakland Raiders in a shocking move just a few days before the beginning of the season. They lost more than one-third of what was a championship-caliber defense in one offseason and yet they still ranked fifth in scoring and 11th in total defense in 2009.

As all those pieces fell off, Belichick's system was tested. New players were plugged in when they could approximate the value and fill the role of former starters. That's how you end up with Jarvis Green replacing Seymour, Gary Guyton replacing Bruschi, Jonathan Wilhite replacing Ellis Hobbs, who was replacing Samuel, who was replacing Ty Law.

Even aside from all the long-term turnover, the Patriots had also turned over the cornerback position between 2008 and 2009. Neither Hobbs nor Deltha O'Neal returned to the team in '09, and the tried-and-true volume approach continued with the addition of two veteran free agents in Shawn Springs and Leigh Bodden, as well as a draft pick in Darius Butler. Adding to a depth chart that already included second-year cornerbacks Wilhite and Terrence Wheatley, Belichick was clearly hoping that a trio of young stars would emerge from the group of cover men he had assembled.

This all might help explain Belichick's decision to trade down in the draft. The Patriots had more needs than picks. One Clay Matthews might have had a tremendous impact on the defense, but if Belichick could find three or four helpful players for the price of one Matthews, that was a trade he was willing to make. And the 2009 draft marked the first of many occasions where Belichick would willingly make that exchange.

This strategy was made more necessary by the fact that similar changes were happening on offense but at a much quicker rate. Over the previous two years, the Patriots had shifted to a spread offense that used several receivers or more on the field at a time. They started in 2007 with a handful of new receivers. In 2009, though, the Patriots entered the season with only two reliable receivers at their disposal: Randy Moss and Wes Welker. They would need Laurence Maroney, free-agent signee Fred Taylor, and the running game to step up.

And amid all these personnel changes on both sides of the ball, Belichick lost more important people within the organization. Offensive coordinator Josh McDaniels took a head coaching job with the Denver Broncos after the firing of Mike Shanahan, and vice president of player personnel Scott Pioli took a gig with the Kansas City Chiefs as general manager.

Caserio, who had been Pioli's assistant, was promoted to his superior's vacant position—an example of Belichick staying in-house with organizational moves. Belichick opted to stay within the organization in naming an offensive

Patriots 2009 Draft Picks

Round	Pick	Player	Position	Games played w/ Patriots
2	34	Patrick Chung	DB	81+*
2	40	Ron Brace	DT	39
2	41	Darius Butler	CB	29
2	58	Sebastian Vollmer	OT	88*
3	83	Brandon Tate	WR	18
3	97	Tyrone McKenzie	LB	0
4	123	Rich Ohrnberger	OG	5
5	170	George Bussey	OT	0
6	198	Jake Ingram	LS	24
6	207	Myron Pryor	DT	24
7	232	Julian Edelman	WR	87*
7	234	Darryl Richard	DT	0

+ = two separate stints with Patriots, *=still with Patriots

coordinator. But in doing so, he made an unorthodox move: Belichick made himself McDaniels' replacement. He was already beginning the process of grooming a new offensive coordinator, though, by moving wide receivers coach Bill O'Brien to McDaniels' vacant post as quarterbacks coach. The ingredients combined to form a concoction of excitement and concern for what was ahead.

★ ★ ★

The last time we saw the bend-don't-break defense might have been the third quarter of Super Bowl XLII. Since that point the Patriots had made more of a habit of breaking than bending. But initially, the Patriots held fast by holding the Buffalo Bills to just 17 points on offense—seven came via a Pick-6—in a 25–24 win and the New York Jets to just 16 points in a 16–9 loss.

The offense was stagnant in both games with 43 rush attempts for just 156 yards (3.6 yards per carry) and one touchdown. Brady threw the ball a whopping 100 times in two games with 62 completions for 594 yards, two touchdowns, and two interceptions. The focus was clearly on Moss and Welker. In Week 1 each had

12 receptions. Welker was injured in Week 2, and Julian Edelman stepped in with eight receptions for 93 yards, but the Jets focused on taking away Moss and held him to just four receptions for 24 yards.

It was Belichick's first head-to-head matchup with the Jets' new head coach, Rex Ryan, and it was a loss in exactly the manner the Jets had scripted it, employing stifling defense and efficient offense. Brady completed less than 50 percent of his passes for the first time since Week 13 of the 2007 season. Ryan's aggressive defensive scheme used overload blitzes to cause confusion on the offensive line, allowing unblocked defenders to rush the quarterback, and the free rushers got Brady off rhythm.

The Patriots bounced back with back-to-back wins in Weeks 3 (26–10 against the Atlanta Falcons) and 4 (27–21 against the Baltimore Ravens) with Brady finding rhythm against the Ravens secondary, but the Ravens, thanks to big plays on defense (three sacks, one fumble recovery for a touchdown) and offense (116 rushing yards on 17 carries), kept it close. In a dose of foreshadowing, running back Ray Rice rattled off a 50-yard gain in the third quarter to set up the Ravens' third touchdown of the day.

But the next week brought one of the biggest Belichick storylines, when he faced his former protege McDaniels and the Broncos in Colorado. The Patriots held a 17–7 lead in the first half, but after narrowing the gap to seven, Kyle Orton led a 98-yard touchdown drive to tie the game with just above five minutes remaining. The Patriots had the ball at mid-field with less than two minutes to go, but Brady was sacked on back-to-back plays and fumbled the ball both times. The Broncos recovered the second of those fumbles. Overtime began, and 11 plays and 58 yards later, the Broncos kicked the game-winning field goal.

McDaniels had left the Patriots before their offseason preparation, but he knew what everyone else knew and what Belichick said privately after the game. "Offensively, all they really—and we've seen this now twice, really—if you just take Moss away in the deep part of the field and get down on Welker, we're done," Belichick said in a coach's meeting documented on NFL Films. "We're done. We can't run the ball. We can't throw it to anybody else. We're done."

Welker finished that game with a respectable eight catches for 86 yards and a touchdown, but Moss had just one reception for 36 yards on the day. Edelman and running back Kevin Faulk each had three receptions, and running back Sammy

Morris and tight end Ben Watson each had two. The Patriots simply didn't have enough options in the passing game. Meanwhile, Patriots running backs picked up just 97 yards on 26 carries in that game.

Belichick felt that it wasn't just a personnel problem; it was a mentality and a work ethic problem. "It started on Wednesday. That Wednesday practice was over, and where did the receivers go? Straight in," he said. "Do we stay out there on Wednesday after practice with the receivers and Brady? No, because we're all set. We got it down. We're all set. We don't need any extra work. That sums it up right there."

To create the spark that would turn the offense around, Belichick needed better effort from everyone. If effort is determined by points, the Patriots put forth more of an effort against the Tennessee Titans than they did in the previous two games combined. It was a snow-swept 59–0 slaughter that included touchdowns of 45, 40, 28, 38, and 30 yards. This came just days after he chided the team for its lack of big plays, as they had been the only team in the NFL without a 20-yard run or a 40-yard pass. Against the Titans they had two such rushes and two such passes.

The big plays came and went, but the big wins continued as the Patriots tacked three consecutive victories onto their record to get to 6–2 ahead of the annual midseason showdown between the Patriots and the Colts.

Belichick had spoken to the media after his team's 26–10 win against the Atlanta Falcons in Week 3 and was asked about his decision to run the ball on fourth and 1 at the Patriots' 25-yard line. "Short-yardage in our own end, I felt like we could get a yard," he said. "I'm sure there would have been plenty of criticism if we didn't."

He couldn't have possibly known the degree to which he was foreshadowing future events. This was the 14th chapter of Belichick's rivalry with Peyton Manning, the 10th chapter of the Brady-Manning saga, and the first meeting between Belichick and new Colts head coach Jim Caldwell, following the retirement of Tony Dungy. This game remains one of the most debated and analyzed chapters in those long storied rivalries. And it all boils down to one play on fourth and 2.

Before that one play, the Patriots were cruising to a dominant win. The offense scored on four of its first five drives on the strength of two long passes by Brady to Moss. The defense forced punts on four of its first five drives, including three

three-and-out series. A fourth-quarter touchdown to Moss gave the Patriots a 31–14 lead.

But the script flipped quicker than an M. Night Shyamalan thriller. Manning led two 79-yard touchdown drives, carving up the Patriots secondary along the way, while the Patriots offense sputtered to a stall. Suddenly, the Patriots went from rolling to victory to staring down the barrel of an unbelievable comeback defeat. They took the ball at the 20-yard line with 2:23 left and a 34–28 lead. After gaining eight yards on second down, the third-down pass fell incomplete, bringing up fourth and 2 and a ton of confusion. Belichick had decided earlier in the week that if this situation arose he was going to try to pick up the first down, as he had (successfully) done against the Falcons. This wasn't communicated perfectly on special teams, and the punt unit began to take the field before being waved off by the coaching staff.

Brady's pass was complete to Kevin Faulk at the first-down marker, but the official ruled that he had been stopped short. With no timeouts the Patriots couldn't challenge. The Colts took the ball and scored four plays later, walking away with a 35–34 win.

The decision was widely panned, but even when statisticians got involved to defend the decision, it boiled down to this: get two yards and win the game; don't get two yards and you still have a chance to get a stop on defense. Some people said he lacked confidence in his team, but that couldn't have been further from the truth. "If you guys don't think I have confidence in you, I don't know what you guys are doing every day," he told the team in a meeting.

He put a lot of pressure on the defense, but he also put a lot of trust in them in the process. He knew there was a possibility the offense wouldn't get it, but he had faith the defense could get a stop, as they had done for most of the game prior to the previous 13 minutes. It, though, was the wrong decision when the Patriots lost.

The Patriots bounced back from that emotional loss with a 31–14 shellacking of the New York Jets at Gillette Stadium. In the process the Patriots also exacted revenge on a team that beat them earlier in the year and pulled out a two-game lead in the division. It was a completely different game this time around. Brady had Welker as an outlet to on short passes when blitzed, and that's exactly what he did to the tune of 15 catches for 192 yards. The defense pounced on Mark Sanchez with four interceptions. The offense had plenty of layups with three scoring drives that traveled fewer than 60 yards. But that success wasn't sustainable against teams that weren't turning the ball over five times in one game.

The Patriots found that out the hard way the very next week in one of the most thorough losses in Belichick's history with the buzzsaw of the New Orleans Saints offense rolling through the Patriots to a 38–17 victory. Saints quarterback Drew Brees picked apart the Patriots cornerbacks with 371 passing yards, five touchdowns, and a perfect 158.3 passer rating.

The offense had three turnovers, but the Saints didn't need the help. They had 480 net yards of offense, and four of their five touchdown drives traveled farther than 70 yards. "I just can't get this team to play the way we need to play," Belichick told Brady on the sideline after the loss. "I just can't do it."

Brady reminded him that they can do it in spurts, just not for four quarters. Belichick got another reminder of that the very next week in another one-point loss on the road. While visiting the Dolphins, the Patriots fell short when their offense couldn't score any points in the final 27 minutes of the game after establishing a 21–10 lead. Their final six drives amounted to four punts and two interceptions. Once again, the Welker-Moss show wasn't enough. Welker had 10 catches for 167 yards, and Moss had just two catches for 66 yards and a touchdown. The lack of other options in the passing game and the inability to run the ball consistently hurt the Patriots once again.

December usually means it's time for the Patriots to play their best football. At this point in his career, Belichick's Patriots had amassed a 29–7 record in the final four games of his previous nine seasons. The defense found some swing, holding the final three December opponents to a combined 27 points en route to three straight victories: 20–10 against the Carolina Panthers, 17–10 against the Bills, and 35–7 against the Jacksonville Jaguars. At this point in the season, Moss' production had dipped dramatically. From Weeks 13 to 15, Moss had six receptions for 149 yards, a touchdown. That was capped off by a bad day against the Panthers in which he had just one catch, which he fumbled. Belichick fielded questions from a reporter about Moss' recent dip in production, which opened the door for one of Belichick's finest soundbites. "Really, stats are for losers," he said. "Final scores are for winners, and that's really what it's about."

Moss proceeded to bounce back by tallying 14 receptions for 190 yards and four touchdowns in the final three games. Welker, on the other hand, had been a machine all season with more than five receptions in 12 of his first 13 games of the year. He also tied an NFL single-season record with 10 or more receptions in seven games.

With wins in Weeks 14 to 16, the Patriots locked up the division, making the season finale a meaningless exercise for the Patriots. Their status as the No. 3 seed for the playoffs was set in stone. That meaninglessness made it all the more painful when Welker went down with a torn ACL on a non-contact injury after trying to plant and cut on what Belichick has described as "terrible" turf at Reliant Stadium.

The Patriots lost six games during the regular season, and all of them were on the road. They won just two road games all of 2009, and one of them wasn't even a true road game because the Tampa Bay Buccaneers were calling Wembley Stadium home in Week 7. None of those losses hurt them as much as losing Welker the week before the playoffs.

Brady was about to find out just how much that injury hurt when the Ravens came into town for a rematch of their Week 4 matchup. The game was over before Baltimore quarterback Joe Flacco even broke a sweat. Rice ran 83 yards for a touchdown on the Ravens' first play from scrimmage, and Brady was sacked for a fumble three plays later. The Ravens recovered and scored a touchdown on a five-play, 17-yard drive. Just under five minutes into the game, the Ravens had a 14-point lead, and Flacco hadn't even attempted a pass yet.

That lead became a 24–0 lead before the first quarter was over. Pressure was in Brady's face throughout, generating three sacks and three interceptions on the day. Edelman (six receptions, 44 yards, two touchdowns) was the backbone of the offense on a day where it had lost its heart without Welker. The Patriots were unceremoniously bounced from the playoffs in a 33–14 loss. The dynasty had technically died years ago, when the Patriots won their last Super Bowl, but this felt like the closest thing to a funeral for that dynasty.

CHAPTER 21

★ ★ ★

Bill Belichick
vs. Joe Gibbs

Joe Gibbs' Washington football team was respected across the league for his fierce, massive, athletic offensive line known as "The Hogs," but Gibbs' coaching career shouldn't be reduced to a nickname for five offensive linemen. Just look at the names of the quarterbacks with whom he won Super Bowls: Joe Theismann (1982), Jay Schroeder and Doug Williams (1987), and Mark Rypien (1991). Gibbs coached some Hall of Fame talent like guard Russ Grimm, cornerback Darrell Green, running back John Riggins, and wide receiver Art Monk.

He was even the calming presence that soothed the tensions between Riggins and the franchise, following Riggins' nasty holdout of 1980. Not only was Gibbs a great motivator, but he was also innovative in ways that are still having an effect on the game today.

No wonder Washington owner Dan Snyder called upon Gibbs when his crestfallen team had just one winning season in a six-year stretch from 1998 to 2003. Gibbs had been out of football for more than a decade at that point, and the magic had worn off, but his legacy had been etched in stone long before his career came to a close. Gibbs was on the cutting edge of offensive innovation in the 1980s and he won multiple Super Bowls.

Gibbs' roots were as the offensive line coach for Don Coryell's San Diego State team from 1964 to 1966 and as the offensive coordinator for Coryell's San Diego Chargers from 1979 to 1980. The "Air Coryell" offense, which features a heavy emphasis on vertical routes, was a big part of Washington's system. It draws the defense up close with a punishing ground attack and then hits them with a big play through the air.

Gibbs' ability to blend a physical running game with an explosive passing game helped Washington put together one of the most feared offenses of the 1980s despite lacking a dominant quarterback. In fact, Washington's offense ranked among the 10 highest scoring offenses in eight of Gibbs' 12 years in his first run as their head coach.

New England linebacker Tedy Bruschi brings down Washington Redskins running back Clinton Portis during a 2007 contest when Bill Belichick's Patriots annihilated Joe Gibbs' Redskins 52–7. (USA TODAY Sports Images)

Tale of the Tape

Coach	Bill Belichick	Joe Gibbs
Years as a head coach	21	16
Career W–L	223–113	154–94
Ratio	.664	.621
Playoff trips	14	10
Playoff W–L	23–10	17–7
Division championships	13	5
Super Bowl wins	4	3

Sometimes, their quarterback threw it all over the field (No. 2 and No. 1 in passing in '88 and '89, respectively). Sometimes, their running backs throttled their way through the defense. (Washington was top five in rushing from 1983 to 1985.)

Turn on the television to any game on Sunday during football season and at some point you'll see the one-back set made famous by Gibbs. When Gibbs first started using one-back sets as the basis of his offense, though, it looked a little out of place. Traditional offenses featured two receivers, a tight end, and two backs (one fullback, one running back). Instead of a fullback, who traditionally did nothing but block or carry the ball, Gibbs swapped in a third wide receiver to take a defender away from the middle of the field, which had a dual benefit for the offense. In the passing game, the quarterback had a more spread-out field of vision. And in the running game, there were more open lanes and one less defender to block. The third receiver could also be a second tight end, who would present the dual threat of either blocking or catching the ball.

Washington was much like the Patriots in that it sought to create favorable match-ups and run similar plays out of different formations to keep the defense guessing. With pre-snap motion and bunch formations (wide receivers crammed together on one side of the field), Washington's offense sought to create confusion in the defense's assignments. But even with all that Washington was doing to keep its opponents guessing, they had their bread-and-butter: the "Counter Trey." The running back would take the handoff with three linemen holding their ground at the line of scrimmage in front of him and two more linemen from the other side sprinting out in the direction the play was headed.

The Counter Trey was one of the main reasons Washington ranked in the top 10 in rushing in seven of Gibbs' first 12 years with the team regardless of whether it was John Riggins, George Rogers, or Earnest Byner. But between his efficient running game, dynamic passing game, and changing formations on offense, Joe Gibbs built a multi-faceted, mind-bending, physical offense. There were two strike-shortened seasons in the 1980s and only one Super Bowl champion coach during the two: Joe Gibbs.

Like the three quarterbacks Gibbs coached to Super Bowl victories, the Washington coach was able to get the most out of his players no matter where they fell in the pantheon of all-time greats. That's because Gibbs coached discipline into his teams at an elite level. Washington was frequently among the best teams in the league when it came to turnovers. In his 16 years, the Redskins ranked in the top 10 fewest giveaways on offense eight times and six times ranked in the top 10 most takeaways on defense.

His teams were disciplined year round, but they also played some of their best football in the most important games. Washington went to three Super Bowls in Gibbs' first seven years and won two of them. His 17–7 (.708) playoff win-loss ratio is the best such ratio for any head coach with more than 15 playoff games in his career. Belichick's ratio of .697 is close, but he would need to pick up the pace a bit to match Gibbs' lofty record.

If there's one thing working against Gibbs, however, it's that his success was tethered to the 1980s and early '90s. He had been out of coaching for more than a decade when he returned to the game, and the situation in Washington was not as stable and nurturing in the mid-2000s as it had been some 20 years prior.

The only thing that's left for Belichick is to win a Super Bowl with not one but two more quarterbacks—though if Tom Brady somehow stumbled on a fountain of youth, Belichick probably wouldn't do much complaining. Likewise, it's fair to wonder whether Gibbs could have been even more successful with a Hall of Fame quarterback running the show. Given the legacy Gibbs left behind, it's clear he didn't need one.

CHAPTER 22

★ ★ ★

2010: Moss Moves On, Gronk Moves In

Bill Belichick juggled two jobs in 2009—serving as the team's head coach and offensive coordinator that year. But if you thought his plate was heavy then, things only got more difficult in 2010.

Dean Pees parted ways with the organization after four years as the defensive coordinator, leaving Belichick to handle both coordinator jobs and his own job as head coach. Granted, he had a staff of strong position coaches in place. In particular, quarterback coach Bill O'Brien is believed to have been a de facto offensive coordinator in 2010, but the job was massive nonetheless.

But before he could play any of those three roles, he first had to play general manager, where his cabinet remained largely unchanged. And after what transpired the previous year, everyone knew exactly what needed to be done in order for the Patriots to build themselves into one of the dominant powers in the conference. The team's lackluster play on pass defense and its lack of receiving targets on offense were two of the key themes in '09 that prevented the team from realizing its full potential. They took two very different approaches to these issues.

On defense, Belichick looked at the NFL and saw an increasing focus on spread formations, special personnel packages, and a general focus on offensive speed. In turn, the inclination was to build a defense that mastered the art of specialization. In 2010 Belichick would often make wholesale personnel changes on defense depending on situations that called for more of a focus on the run or the pass. This strategy was in stark contrast to what the Patriots had done on defense throughout the years. Belichick knew how to use players to their strengths, but that often involved the same subset of players working within the scheme in different roles.

At linebacker, rookie Brandon Spikes played almost exclusively against the run because he lacks the speed against the pass but was a thumper against the run while Gary Guyton was the guy in coverage for his speed and athleticism. On the edges, Tully Banta-Cain and Eric Moore were options as pass rushers for their relative explosiveness, while Rob Ninkovich and rookie Jermaine Cunningham played more balanced roles for their combination of speed and power. Mike Wright and Myron Pryor were pass rushers in the defensive interior, while Vince Wilfork and Gerard Warren were closer to a 50-50 split.

On offense, however, the changes were much less subtle but much fewer in numbers. The real meat of the offseason was the selection of two tight ends in the

Patriots 2010 Draft Picks

Round	Pick	Player	Position	Games played w/ Patriots
1	27	Devin McCourty	DB	91*
2	42	Rob Gronkowski	TE	80*
2	53	Jermaine Cunningham	DE	36
2	62	Brandon Spikes	LB	51
3	90	Taylor Price	WR	4
4	113	Aaron Hernandez	TE	38
5	150	Zoltan Mesko	P	48
6	205	Ted Larsen	C	0
7	208	Thomas Welch	OT	3
7	247	Brandon Deaderick	DT	34
7	248	Kade Weston	DT	0
7	250	Zac Robinson	QB	0

*=still with Patriots

draft: Rob Gronkowski in the second round and Aaron Hernandez in the fourth round. This gave the Patriots not only two more receiving threats to complement their two wide receivers Wes Welker and Randy Moss, but it also helped them establish an identity, one that was completely different from any identity they had ever taken before and different from anything else in the NFL at the time. Welcome to the return of the two-tight end offense. Instead of employing three wide receivers in spread sets, The Patriots acknowledged that they no longer had the firepower at wide receiver to run that kind of formation. So, they shifted to a two-tight end offense. Gronkowski was a traditional tight end for his ability to both block and catch, and Hernandez bucked the positional prototype as a smaller, athletic matchup nightmare in the passing game, rarely if ever contributing as a blocker, especially early in his career.

Of course, hindsight being 20/20, the Patriots would definitely take a mulligan on the latter of those two picks. But in the brief time the Patriots enjoyed Hernandez's talent, he rewrote the playbook of what a player with his skillset could mean to a team.

This also continued Belichick's penchant for picking up players within his college pipeline. Hernandez, Spikes, and Cunningham were all Florida products under Urban Meyer; defensive tackle Brandon Deaderick was fresh out of Nick Saban's program at Alabama; and, as we would learn about over time, first-round pick Devin McCourty was a product of a Patriots breeding ground, Rutgers, and their head coach Greg Schiano.

Overall, the offseason was a resounding success. The Patriots found building blocks for the future and they re-fortified their nucleus with extensions for Wilfork and Tom Brady. There were some losses along the way, including tight end Benjamin Watson and outside linebacker Adalius Thomas (though, given Thomas' publicly contentious relationship with Patriots coaches, it wasn't a huge surprise). But the biggest loss of them all was yet to come.

★ ★ ★

The storylines about the Patriots' offseason moves didn't come to an end when the regular season got under way, even following a resounding 38–24 win in the home opener against the Cincinnati Bengals. Randy Moss had five catches for 59 yards that day and afterward took to the podium to vent his frustrations that the

2010 season might be his last with the team with whom he had helped set records just three years before.

Publicly, he talked about not feeling appreciated while lamenting the fact that this might be his last year with the Patriots. Privately, he reportedly requested a trade and seemingly hoped to be out soon. The next week saw the return of Moss' rivalry with New York Jets cornerback Darrelle Revis—a match-up that saw Moss humbled by Revis, though he did make a spectacular one-handed over-the-shoulder touchdown catch in stride against him before halftime. That loss was particularly painful because Jets head coach Rex Ryan had spent much of the previous six months searching for mountaintops upon which he could shout his proclamation that the Jets wanted to "kick Belichick's ass." Brady looked to Moss time after time with 10 targets on the day. Moss had two catches for 38 yards and a touchdown, and one of Brady's passes for Moss was intercepted (though it was the last interception he would throw for a long time). But the Patriots had another problem in the loss of running back Kevin Faulk. One of Brady's security blankets, Faulk, was vital in blitz protection and as a receiver out of the backfield.

The Patriots lost 28–14 but bounced back with wins against the Buffalo Bills (38–30) and Miami Dolphins (41–14). Danny Woodhead, a free-agent pickup who had been released by the Jets, found his stride and had 11 carries, 78 yards and one catch for 11 yards and two total touchdowns. It was clear from the onset that Woodhead would be plugged right into Faulk's role.

While Moss again put the Patriots on the board with two catches for 42 yards and two scores against the Bills, he was held without a catch for the first time in his Patriots career against the Dolphins. Moss' diminished role in the offense wasn't necessarily a referendum on lost ability as much as indication of the direction of the Patriots offense as a whole. The two-tight end offense was the future, giving the Patriots the flexibility to have either a run or pass on any given play while giving them the ability to run the same concepts out of multiple formations—a major tenet of the Erhardt-Perkins offense.

The previous year, Belichick saw an obvious problem with his offense on the field and he began to feel an underlying problem with the work ethic of that group. It did not take Belichick long to make all the key determinations about his approach. The Moss revolution was over, and a new revolution had arrived. Time and time again, Belichickian foresight has helped the Patriots stay mostly ahead of the curve on personnel moves. That being said, given Moss' seemingly vital role to the offense—his unbridled ability to take the top off the defense with long speed and leaping ability—it would appear unwise to trade the one player on the team who fit the bill and one of the all-time best in those areas. Yet, without batting an eyelash, the Patriots traded Moss to the Minnesota Vikings for a third-round pick.

And away the national media went. Of course, Moss was a divisive enough figure before he arrived in New England that there were quickly reports of dissension between Moss and the coaching staff. There was also the much easier explanation that Moss was an aging player in a role defined by athleticism and a role that was decreasingly vital to the Patriots' approach. And when the Patriots traded for wide receiver Deion Branch, it fed the narrative on both levels. Not only had the Patriots specifically targeted a player who already has familiarity in the offense and rapport with Brady and the coaching staff, but also one who—despite his age—still had the quickness to fit the Patriots' new, heavy focus on the short passing game.

This was not the 2007 offense. Brady now had two rookie tight ends, two experienced but undersized receivers who both lacked big-play ability, and a solid but unproven running game. Instead of an offense that spread everything out, this was an offense that still had the ability to field multiple passing threats while also presenting the threat of the run. It sounds great in theory, but initially the theory didn't work out so well.

The Patriots won the first two games after trading away Moss and for Branch (separately) but in less-than-convincing fashion with two 23–20 wins—one in overtime—against the Baltimore Ravens and San Diego Chargers. But the Ravens held the Patriots offense in check in that first game with New England trailing 20–10 before scoring on back-to-back drives to tie the game and then kicking the winning field goal in overtime. Meanwhile, they capitalized on some very short fields to build a 23–6 lead against the Chargers. (They even scored a field goal on a four-play, negative-14 yard drive.)

In those games Brady was a combined 46-of-76 (60.5 percent) for 451 yards (5.9 yards per attempt) with two touchdowns, two interceptions, and a 75.1 passer rating while being sacked seven times. The defense stepped up in those two games, particularly against the run where they allowed just 137 yards on 53 carries and despite giving up 603 yards passing. They used their trademark "amoeba" style defense, changing week to week, series to series, play to play to get

The Patriots drafted Rob Gronkowski, who is known for his emphatic touchdown spikes, in 2010, and he quickly became an integral part of the New England offense. (AP Images)

the best personnel on the field for the situation. They just couldn't find a personnel package to slow down opposing quarterbacks.

They'd have a good opportunity to finally do so by confronting an old friend.

Moss returned to Gillette Stadium as a member of the Minnesota Vikings four weeks after the Patriots traded him. He was held to just one catch for eight yards (before being released shortly afterward), and quarterback Brett Favre hit 22-of-32 passes for 259 yards with no touchdowns and one interception.

But most of his production went to one receiver, Percy Harvin, who had six receptions for 104 yards. This high concentration of production boils down to Belichick's ability to take away an opponent's best weapons and force the opponent to beat them other ways. Moss was persistently double-teamed when he ran deep, which is about all he did that game. That added attention opened up opportunities for Harvin. He capitalized upon those, but none which were of dire consequence to the game. The front seven once again did a great job of buckling down against running back Adrian Peterson, who was held to 25 carries for 92 yards and a touchdown.

But the next week, the Patriots got a dose of their own medicine against the Cleveland Browns, which represented Belichick's eighth showdown with Eric Mangini. Belichick held a 5–2 record against his former protege entering the game, but that was about to be tested when Mangini threw everything he could at the Patriots on both offense and defense.

A wide range of unique strategies—unique formations, trick plays with handoffs to receivers on reverses, and rollouts by quarterback Colt McCoy—bamboozled the Patriots' defense. A battering-ram performance by breakout running back Peyton Hillis left them weary. Meanwhile, the offense scrambled to put anything together. Their first seven possessions resulted in five punts, one fumble, and one touchdown. By then the Browns were up 27–7 in the fourth quarter. The Patriots were outplayed, but they got in their own way with three turnovers, just three third-down conversions on 11 tries, while allowing the Browns to convert seven of 13 third downs. These factors exposed the path to defeating the Patriots, but it would take two months before anyone would put it together.

Despite the Patriots' three-turnover day against the Browns, Brady entered Week 10 with just four interceptions in the first eight games and he had not thrown a single interception since Week 6 against the Ravens. The loss to the

Browns seemed to stoke a fire in the Patriots, as they went on a tear of scoring 31 points or more in the final eight games of the regular season with 100 or more rushing yards in every game, 20 or more first downs in all but one game, and only one turnover in those eight games.

Gronkowski had shown flashes of what he could become in the first half of the season, but he only had 14 receptions for 148 yards and three touchdowns. Then, they went to take on the Pittsburgh Steelers, and everything changed. Suddenly, Brady found Gronkowski not just as a big-bodied red zone target but also as a monster in the middle, running down the seam against linebackers who were too slow and safeties who were too small to cover him. That night, Gronkowski matched his touchdown total (three) from the previous eight games. Meanwhile, Welker (eight receptions, 89 yards) and Branch (seven receptions, 71 yards) were eating up all the extra space Gronkowski's presence was creating. The offensive explosion led to a rolling 39–26 victory for the Patriots.

With another Peyton Manning showdown on the way, the Patriots were back on a winning track and back in the lead for the top spot in the AFC. The defense frustrated Manning early on with disguises in coverage—just as they had done to Manning in the past—and intercepted an errant pass on the Colts' first drive. Meanwhile, the offense pulled away with three straight touchdown drives.

The first half was seamless, as the offense scored on three of their four first-half drives on their way to a 21–7 lead. The Colts stormed back from there, bringing the score to within three mostly on the strength of Manning's arm, but the Patriots closed the deal on a 31–28 win when James Sanders intercepted Manning on the Colts' final offensive play of the game.

And the wins, and the points, just kept coming, including a 45–24 win against the Detroit Lions. Brady's interception-less streak was now up to 199 straight passes—just in time for the big rematch with the big-talking Rex Ryan.

The Patriots prepared to take on the Jets on *Monday Night Football* in a game where the hype nearly matched that of "Super Bowl 41.5" from the 2007 season. Although neither team was undefeated, both were vying for the No. 1 seed in the AFC at the time. A 45–3 win for the Patriots showed the Jets they may not be ready for prime time. The domination was thorough, both on the field and the sideline. Belichick's gambles worked. They turned an early fourth and 3 into a 25-yard touchdown when Branch shook free of Antonio Cromartie.

Conversely, Ryan's decision-making looked jumbled. Mark Sanchez was stopped short on third and 1. Ryan challenged the ruling, but when the play was upheld, he decided to go for it, and Shonn Greene ran the ball for a first down. If his plan all along was to go for it, why waste the challenge? The decision didn't pay off either way because four plays later Nick Folk shanked a 53-yard field goal.

Brady's interception-less streak had reached 228 attempts. The next week against the Chicago Bears, the Patriots won 36–7 in a whiteout snowstorm. Their weakness on third down nearly bit them the next week against the Green Bay Packers, who were able to put up a fight in a 31–27 Patriots victory despite being without Aaron Rodgers. They held the Patriots to just four conversions on 10 third-down tries while converting 11 out of 19 of their own third downs.

The interception-free streak had now reached 292. But mostly, this game was viewed as a small blip on the radar during another Patriots demolition derby on their way to a No. 1 seed and likely Super Bowl bid. Those beliefs were affirmed by two straight convincing wins thereafter against the Bills (34–3) and Dolphins (38–7).

If you had polled Patriots fans before the divisional round in 2010 as to which team they were most eager to face, anyone would have been foolish not to say the Jets. Thanks to their utterly dominant win just a month and a half prior, the Patriots had a huge psychological edge over a team that was reliant on confidence and swagger.

But all it took was one interception, Brady's first in 340 pass attempts, to take the Patriots' swagger away. The Patriots had two possessions in the first quarter and just a 3–0 lead. That was a good spot to be in for the Jets, who scored on three of their next seven and four of the next nine drives. Meanwhile, the Patriots punted on four of the next six drives. One ended in a turnover-on-downs and the other at the end of the first half. The Jets got a much more controlled performance from quarterback Sanchez, who completed 16-of-25 throws for 194 yards and three touchdowns.

And although Brady completed two-thirds of his throws (29-of-45) for 299 yards, he only threw two touchdowns. Averaging just 6.6 yards per attempt, it was clear: the Patriots missed the presence of a big-play wide receiver, much like the one they had traded earlier in the year.

CHAPTER 23

★ ★ ★

2011: Hello, Old Friend

Unrest set in across the Patriots, as the once-dynastic team found itself staring at a three-year drought since its last playoff win. Although the Patriots were still reshaping parts of the roster, the 2011 offseason finally brought some organizational stability after years of shake-ups to the coaching staff. Quarterback coach Bill O'Brien was officially promoted to the position of offensive coordinator (though he was a de facto offensive coordinator in 2010, too). There were no major changes on the defensive staff and there were no changes in the front office either. Indeed, the 2011 season brought the most continuity at the top of the organization that the Patriots had seen in quite some time.

But the 2011 offseason also brought a unique dynamic: the NFL lockout. The end of the collective bargaining agreement and a dispute between the NFL and the NFLPA—the players' labor union—brought about unique circumstances in which free agency was delayed from March to July. This meant that the draft took place before free agency.

Some teams altered their draft approach by taking players who were seen to fit a position of need. The Patriots didn't fall into this trap, most notably with their selection of left tackle Nate Solder in the first round despite having two starting offensive tackles on the roster. Of course, this proved to be Belichickian foresight at work once again with the Patriots getting out ahead of the curve on the eventual retirement of Matt Light.

Patriots 2011 Draft Picks

Round	Pick	Player	Position	Games played w/ Patriots
1	17	Nate Solder	OT	67*
2	33	Ras-I Dowling	CB	12
2	56	Shane Vereen	RB	42
3	73	Stevan Ridley	RB	52
3	74	Ryan Mallett	QB	4
5	138	Marcus Cannon	OL	65*
5	159	Lee Smith	TE	0
6	194	Markell Carter	OLB	0
7	219	Malcolm Williams	CB	4

*=still with Patriots

The Patriots entered the draft with two first-round picks, but they left with only one after trading one to the New Orleans Saints in exchange for a late-second-round pick the next day along with an additional first-round pick the following year. Once again, Belichick was passing up an opportunity to capitalize on what appeared to be a closing window in favor of playing it forward to give the Patriots the upper hand in the future.

Their next pick was need-based with cornerback Ras-I Dowling filling a void at cornerback. The selection continued the trend of the Patriots picking a defensive back in the first two rounds of every draft from 2007 through 2011 as they frantically tried to piece together a talented secondary. But after that pick, the Patriots went right back to long-term drafting strategies. They added two running backs despite having the talented duo of Danny Woodhead and BenJarvus Green-Ellis at their disposal, they drafted a quarterback despite having Tom Brady under center, and they drafted a tight end despite having just drafted two the previous year.

The Patriots came out of this draft with a big left tackle to pair with a big right tackle in Sebastian Vollmer and pair of running backs to back up Woodhead and Green-Ellis. Coupled with their two tight ends from the year before, the Patriots suddenly had the look of an offense that could run the ball down an opponent's throat.

And when free agency finally kicked off in July, the Patriots methodically went down the list to check off all the unchecked boxes where they still had needs. They added two proven veteran pass-rushers in Mark Anderson and Andre Carter on one-year deals, but those were far from the highest profile additions to the Patriots' roster.

Meet Chad Johnson (Ochocinco) and Albert Haynesworth, two of the most controversial players in the league at the time. Both came to the Patriots within days of each other. Belichick faced a lot of questions about Haynesworth's legal issues (he was facing assault charges at the time) and Ochocinco's bombastic personality. In Belichick's mind, the risk was worth the reward. In the end the reward turned out to be almost zero. Neither player made a huge impact for the Patriots. Ochocinco didn't score a touchdown until Week 15, and Haynesworth didn't even make it to the end of the season.

The lockout also prevented the teams from working out, practicing, and going through the usual offseason motions. This change forced Belichick to question his allegiance to his complex 3-4 alignment as the base defensive package. Belichick had long ago seen and followed the trend of passing offenses by utilizing a sub-package defense (five or more defensive backs on the field) more often than a base alignment, but the 2011 season marked the first time we began seeing four-man defensive lines as the norm.

But as the Patriots entered the season, there was a lot of reason for optimism: the 2010 draft class was a year older and ready for Year Two. "That's where a lot of players, I'd say almost all players make a big jump," Belichick said. "Whether that is reflective in their status on the field, that's another question. But just from a development as a football player, that second year is a big year. It's a great opportunity for them to take that first-year knowledge that they don't have as a rookie and be able to apply it in their job now."

Between Rob Gronkowski, Aaron Hernandez, Devin McCourty, and Brandon Spikes, the Patriots had plenty of players looking to take that next step. It appeared the Patriots were no longer a team in transition but were instead resting on a foundation that was solidifying by the minute. Across the NFL, the 2011 season brought a statistical boom the likes of which had almost never been seen. In fact, there were more passing yards across the league in 2011 (117,601) than any year before it, and it was also the first year in which not one but two quarterbacks eclipsed the 5,000-yard mark.

One of those quarterbacks was Brady.

The assault on the standard of high-volume passing numbers began immediately, as Brady set a new personal best with 517 passing yards in a 38–24 triumph against the Miami Dolphins in Week 1 and followed it up with a whopping 423 passing yards against the San Diego Chargers in a 35–21 win in Week 2. With 940 passing yards in those two games, Brady set (and still retains) the record for most passing yards in the first two games of a season.

You'd think the higher passing numbers would have something to do with the addition of Ochocinco, but he caught just three passes for 59 yards in those two games. Rather, it was the quartet of Wes Welker, Deion Branch, Hernandez, and Gronkowski that made the Patriots' offense so dangerous. But the most dynamic threats were Hernandez and Gronkowski, who combined for 24 receptions, 337 yards, and five touchdown in the first two games of the season.

Hernandez suffered a knee sprain in the second game of the year, though, which put the Patriots offense in a bind. No longer able to employ their two-tight end formula, the Patriots had to change on the fly. The initial result was just a heavier focus on Welker. He surpassed the numbers from the first two games in the Patriots' next game, which came against the Buffalo Bills. Brady and Welker's chemistry was always very good, but their red hot start to the 2011 season was a threat to the record books. Welker's value in the slot never appeared to be higher. His 31 receptions through three games were a tie for the NFL record.

But stats are for losers, which is what the Patriots ended up being in Week 3. After building a 21-point first-half lead against the Bills, Brady threw four interceptions en route to a 34–31 loss. It was the first time the Patriots lost to the Bills since their 31–0 blowout defeat in Week 1 of the 2003 season. But that wasn't the larger story. Instead, the focus was on a pass defense that looked like Swiss cheese. The Patriots allowed no fewer than 369 passing yards in their first three games.

One of the big reasons was a decline in performance from McCourty, the team's top cornerback who was burned repeatedly that season. Opponents began targeting him almost immediately, and he allowed at least 100 receiving yards in each of the first three games—though admittedly, he had some tough assignments in Dolphins receiver Brandon Marshall, Chargers receiver Vincent Jackson, and Bills receiver Steve Johnson. The most startling thing about it, though, was that McCourty hadn't given up more than 100 receiving yards at all in the previous season. Only after the Patriots allowed 344 passing yards to journeyman Jason Campbell in a 31–19 win against the Oakland Raiders did anyone begin asking the question: can the Patriots win with a pass-defense so porous?

At 3–1 the Patriots headed into a Week 5 showdown with the New York Jets, hoping to exact revenge on Rex Ryan and the Jets for eliminating New England from the playoffs the year before. For the week leading up to the game, Ryan touted his winning 3–2 record against the Patriots, but the Patriots were the ones to come away with the 30–21 win.

For once, Brady wasn't carrying the team. The week before, in their win over the Raiders, the Patriots put up 30 carries for 183 yards and two touchdowns. Against the Jets it was nearly as good with 35 carries for 152 yards and two touchdowns. Brady put up solid numbers, but his best work was in beating the Jets' blitzes with 11 completions on 16 throws when Ryan's defense directed an exotic pressure package at the Patriots quarterback. And where the Patriots' abundance of short-area threats had been seen as a weakness before, it was evident as a strength in this scenario, where Brady had plenty of options to get the ball out quickly.

The offense slowed down the next week against the Dallas Cowboys. Brady was held to below 300 passing yards for just the second time that season. But the Patriots pulled out the 20–16 win, largely because of coaching gaffes by Cowboys head coach Jason Garrett—namely, his decision to run the ball and try to drain the clock on a three-point lead instead of throwing, which had worked against the Patriots all season and on that day.

Despite a 5–1 record, the Patriots had shown some flaws. The Pittsburgh Steelers were ready to expose them. With a spread attack and a controlled passing game, the Steelers took advantage of the Patriots' lack of physical, bump-and-run cornerbacks. Coupled with an unusual defensive strategy by defensive coordinator Dick LeBeau—normally, the Steelers' defensive signal caller would blitz the quarterback time after time, but instead he chose to blitz less and cover more—the Patriots fell into an early 10-point hole and couldn't climb out en route to a 25–17 loss.

Then came time for a familiar matchup with the New York Giants. You know those guys, the ones who thwarted the Patriots' bid for a perfect season in '07. Tom Coughlin, Eli Manning, and crew came to Gillette Stadium threatening to not only hand the Patriots back-to-back losses for the first time since 2009, but also to hand Brady his first home loss in 31 straight regular-season games. (Their last regular-season home loss with Brady was in '06 to the Jets.)

The Giants accomplished both of these things in much the same manner they had thwarted the Patriots' perfect season four years before: a steady four-man pass-rush and some late-game heroics from Eli. Coughlin now boasted a 3–1 record over Belichick. And at 5–3 with two straight losses, the Patriots were not in a panic, but disarray.

★ ★ ★

But for the second straight year, a midseason loss sparked a second-half running of the table. The Patriots scored 31 points or more in seven of their final eight games, Brady's relentless march resumed with 300 or more passing yards in five of those eight games, and the offense had just three turnovers in that stretch. It was during that span where Gronkowski burst onto the scene as a playmaking tight end of historic proportions. He had five touchdowns in the first eight games of the season, but with 12 touchdowns in the final eight games, he set a single-season record for receiving touchdowns by a tight end. Gronkowski's trademark bulldozing style of running after the catch made him a force, as defenders grasped at straws to find ways to stop him. Hit him high and you'll bounce off; hit him low and you might just slide off.

The defense, on the other hand, also continued to allow yards in bunches (274 passing yards on average in the final eight games) but was also generating turnovers at a formidable rate. Blowout wins against the Jets (37–16), Kansas City Chiefs (34–3), and Philadelphia Eagles (38–20) assuaged concerns that the Patriots were descending into mediocrity. A furious comeback by the Peyton Manning-less Indianapolis Colts and quarterback Dan Orlovsky renewed fear about the pass defense, but the winning continued 31–24 against the Colts, 34–27 against the Washington Redskins, and 41–23 against the phenomenon of Tim Tebow and the Denver Broncos.

Tebow is largely remembered as a flash in the pan, but this performance was during that brilliant flash. The Broncos went up 16–7 and scored on each of their first three drives before the Patriots finally got it together, slowing down the rushing onslaught of Tebow and running back Lance Ball, who both capitalized on the Broncos' read-option plays. The Broncos used this scheme to pile up 252 yards and three touchdowns on the ground.

But the Patriots went into a scramble on defense when defensive end Carter was lost for the season. Almost on the spot, the Patriots switched from that four-man front back to Belichick's preferred 3-4. This forced them to get creative with their pass rush, and they stymied the Broncos' onslaught by allowing just one scoring drive out of the Broncos' next eight tries on their way to the victory.

The Patriots fell behind by 17 points to the Dolphins but escaped with a narrow 27–24 win. With 12 wins the Patriots had locked up the No. 1 seed, giving them home-field advantage throughout the playoffs. Their 13th win, a 49–21 blowout against the Bills (after falling behind by 21 points), was the cherry on top to put the Patriots into the playoffs on a high note.

Belichick had devised a good plan to slow down Tebow a month before, and in the divisional round, the Patriots coach would have to do it again. Even with the resounding victory in Week 15, there was breathlessness surrounding the Patriots' struggles in the postseason over the past two years. Those fears were abated by a curb-stomping, 45–10 win at home. Before that game, though, the Patriots had made an important addition to the staff. Josh McDaniels, who had joined the St. Louis Rams as offensive coordinator prior to the 2011 season, had been fired.

The Patriots signed him on as a consultant, and the wrinkles came out almost immediately. Hernandez, who had proven to be a dynamic receiver, was suddenly taking handoffs out of the backfield. His first went for 43 yards and set up a touchdown on the very next play. But the Patriots might have blown out the Broncos with or without the wrinkles. Brady became the first quarterback in playoff history to throw five touchdown passes in one half. The defense, meanwhile, kept the Broncos read-option in check once again and sacked Tebow five times while holding Denver to just 252 yards of offense.

For the first time since the 2007 season, the Patriots had not only won a playoff game, but they were back in the AFC Championship Game. But they couldn't advance to the Super Bowl without first making it past an old rival, the

Baltimore Ravens. The two teams traded blows, which is more than could be said of the last time they met in the playoffs when the Ravens simply landed one hay-maker after another. But the Patriots' old concerns in pass defense came back as Ravens quarterback Joe Flacco suddenly looked more like Joe Montana, complet-ing 22 of 36 passes for 306 yards, two touchdowns, and one interception. Clearly, though, that was preferable to allowing Ray Rice to run wild all over the Patriots defense, as he had done in the '09 divisional round.

The Patriots' offense didn't do them any favors with three turnovers, includ-ing an interception by Brady on a throw to special teams ace-turned-temporary-wide-receiver Matthew Slater in triple coverage. The hard-fought battle appeared headed to overtime, when Belichick's postseason kicker luck continued as Ravens kicker Billy Cundiff missed a chip-shot 32-yard field goal with seconds left on the clock.

The Patriots were back in the Super Bowl but not without anxiety both during and after the game. Gronkowski's historic season appeared to be in jeopardy, as the prolific tight end left the Ravens game with an injury, leaving his status for the Super Bowl in doubt.

Leading up to the Super Bowl, there was a very interesting narrative develop-ing: Belichick and the Patriots had a chance to right all the wrongs of their seven seasons since winning a Super Bowl. The Broncos, who eliminated the Patriots in 2005, were eliminated by the Patriots; the Colts, who had beaten the Patriots in 2006, failed to make the playoffs due to Peyton Manning's neck surgery causing him to miss the season; they had knocked out the Ravens, their usurpers in 2009; and the Jets missed the playoffs after a three-game losing streak to end the season.

First, they would need to exact revenge for their ultimate wrongdoing: Super Bowl XLII, 18–1, and a thwarted shot at a perfect season against the Giants. Yes, the same Giants who beat the Patriots in thrilling fashion just a couple months prior were once again back to put a thorn in their side. A win in the Super Bowl might have given Patriots fans the vindication they wanted for those losses, but it also would have given Belichick his fourth Super Bowl ring as a head coach and would have moved his Super Bowl record to 4–1.

Instead, another one-possession loss sent the Patriots home with a pit in their stomach at a missed opportunity. The Patriots had a chance to put the game out of reach in the fourth quarter, but a dropped pass by the usually sure-handed

Welker forced the Patriots to punt. Another improbable catch—this time by Mario Manningham for 38 yards down the left sideline—gave the Giants a good probability to score. When they made it inside the 10-yard line, Belichick even instructed his defense to let the Giants score that go-ahead touchdown so that the Patriots could get the ball back on offense with enough time to score.

It wasn't the fierce pass-rush that did the Patriots in this time—though that certainly had something to do with it, as Justin Tuck was once again a nightmare with two sacks. Truth be told, Gronkowski's injury was as big a story as Patriots fans feared it might be; the tight end was nowhere near the game-changing player he had been all season, and if he were 100 percent, who knows what the outcome would have been.

The Patriots were also dogged by a running game that simply couldn't take enough advantage of its opportunities, finishing with just 83 yards on 19 carries. The running game had been formidable for the Patriots all season, but when they needed to run in obvious running situations, they couldn't get the yards they needed. Meanwhile, Eli Manning spent most of the game dissecting the Patriots secondary, completing 30-of-40 passes for 296 yards and a touchdown. It was clear now as it had been the previous year: the Patriots still needed to improve their pass defense, and their running game still needed to prove it could be as consistent and reliable as the passing attack.

CHAPTER 24

★ ★ ★

Bill Belichick vs. Tom Coughlin

Year after year—particularly near the end of his tenure in New York—the hot seat under Tom Coughlin just kept getting warmer and warmer. That's because his team had a losing record in each of his final three seasons in New York. He won 10 or more games in only seven of 20 seasons as a head coach, but he also delivered the Giants as many Super Bowl wins as legendary coach Bill Parcells did. Moreover, he's likely to be inducted into the Hall of Fame.

Any time Coughlin was approaching disaster, along came Belichick and the Patriots for the Giants to earn another Super Bowl win. And in that respect, Coughlin's legacy is viewed far more favorably because of those two Lombardi Trophies and because he defeated one of the greatest head coaches of all time—two times, as well as thwarted the Patriots' perfect season.

In 2007 the Giants became one of only four teams to win the Super Bowl after beginning a season 0–2. They faced some tricky circumstances, too, in 2011. At 7–7 the Giants needed two more wins and also needed the 8–6 Dallas Cowboys to lose their next two games, including one head-to-head. The Giants took that four steps further with six straight wins.

Coughlin batted 1.000 in Super Bowls but .531 in the regular season. (Interestingly, his win-loss ratio was the exact same in 12 years with the Giants as

Bill Belichick vs. Tom Coughlin, Head to Head

Year	Teams	Score	Winner	Belichick's Record
1995	Browns vs. Jaguars	24–21	Coughlin	0–1
2007	Patriots vs. Giants	38–35	Belichick	1–1
2007*	Patriots vs. Giants	17–14	Coughlin	1–2
2011	Patriots vs. Giants	24–20	Coughlin	1–3
2011*	Patriots vs. Giants	21–17	Coughlin	1–4
2015	Patriots vs. Giants	27–26	Belichick	2–4

*= denotes playoff game

it was in his eight years with the Jacksonville Jaguars.) His record in the playoffs was 19–12 (.632). The Giants fared better when expectations were low and worse when they were high. Coughlin's Giants squandered two division titles—an 11–5 finish in 2005 and a 12–4 finish in 2008—with first-round exits.

Bill Belichick and Tom Coughlin are cut from the same cloth, having coached together with Bill Parcells and the Giants from 1988–90. "I have a lot of respect for Tom and his family, the way he approaches his job and the way he coaches," Belichick said. "We had a great relationship at the Giants when we were on the same staff and have had good relationships throughout our respective careers. A lot for him to be proud of and unfortunately a couple of his biggest wins came at our expense. He deserves a lot of credit for all that he's accomplished in his career."

But their coaching styles are very different. Sure, Coughlin knows how to motivate his players. He is strict (demanding his players arrive to team meetings early, not just on time) and he is smart. There aren't as many wrinkles in his coaching style. When they have one, though, it's usually very effective. Take, for example, Coughlin's implementation of a four-man defensive line featuring all defensive ends from left to right. The speedy pass-rush personnel grouping, known as a "NASCAR" package, helped the Giants generate fierce pressure on the quarterback while also making use of their deep depth chart of defensive ends like Osi Umenyiora, Mathias Kiwanuka, Justin Tuck, and Jason Pierre-Paul.

In fact, that was part of what gave the Patriots such a hard time in the Super Bowls. Tuck was matched up on Patriots guard Logan Mankins and beat him soundly in both games. Tuck's quickness was simply too much for Mankins to handle. Tuck had two sacks in each of the two Super Bowls between the two teams. The Giants also rolled out a big nickel package, which gave the Patriots some problems. The defensive grouping features six players up front (some combination of linebackers and defensive linemen) and five defensive backs (two cornerbacks and three safeties). By using a third safety, the Giants were sacrificing speed for size. The Patriots had some success passing against this package in Super Bowl XLVI, as Aaron Hernandez caught eight passes for 67 yards and a touchdown, but the Giants held the Patriots running game to just 19 carries for 83 yards.

So, how does Coughlin stack up to Bill Belichick? His overall record is much worse, but he leads the head-to-head match-up 4–2, and that includes victories

Two Bill Parcells proteges, Bill Belichick and Tom Coughlin, embrace following the New York Giants' victory in Super Bowl XLVI. (AP Images)

Tale of the Tape

Coach	Bill Belichick	Tom Coughlin
Years as a head coach	21	20
Career W–L	223–113	170–150
Ratio	.664	.531
Playoff trips	14	9
Playoff W–L	23–10	12–7
Division championships	13	3
Super Bowls	4	2

on the biggest stage. Coughlin has coached just one fewer season than Belichick and has 63 fewer regular-season wins to show for it. Of course, Belichick has had Tom Brady for more than 75 percent of his head coaching career, whereas Coughlin has only had an elite quarterback on a handful of occasions when Eli Manning strung together quality seasons.

In that respect, you could say Coughlin was working with less than Belichick but was still able to achieve greatness with a pair of Super Bowl wins—and oh by the way, Manning wasn't playing lights-out in either '07 or '11 and even led the NFL in interceptions prior to knocking off the undefeated Patriots.

Although Coughlin's unblemished Super Bowl record is impressive, it's not a trump card above Belichick's six trips to the Super Bowl—which are tied with Don Shula for most ever by a coach. Likewise, Belichick has four Super Bowl wins, twice as many as Coughlin. There's also one more obvious blemish on Coughlin's resumé: in his 20-year coaching career, Coughlin has eight losing seasons; Belichick has five losing seasons in 21 years.

Coughlin's legacy is that he had his team playing their best when it mattered the most, and he was able to get that momentum on two separate occasions—and he did so at Belichick's expense. He may not be quite on Belichick's level, but without Coughlin's affect, this wouldn't even be a book worth writing; a 19–0 season, along with six Super Bowl wins, would be unrivaled accomplishments.

CHAPTER 25

★ ★ ★

2012: Hurry Up

The Patriots' trend of winning Super Bowls in the early 2000s created the aura of a dynasty. It stands to reason then that their trend of disappointing playoff exits in the years from 2005 to 2011 created a different kind of aura—one of vulnerability. From 2001 to 2004, the Patriots were 9–0 in the playoffs. In the seven years since then, they had earned an average of just one playoff win per year and had been knocked out of the playoffs six times to compile a record of 7–6.

What was once a team with a defensive wall that could not be penetrated had transformed into a team with an offensive juggernaut that could be slowed—if one could expose its flaws.

So Bill Belichick sought to add a missing dimension to the offense, one that had been absent since the departure of Randy Moss. With the signing of wide receiver Brandon Lloyd, the Patriots once again had a boundary receiver who could force a defense to respect the deep ball. At the time, Lloyd was coming off two seasons in which he posted a combined 147 receptions for 2,414 yards and 16 touchdowns. Most of Lloyd's success had taken place under Josh McDaniels with the Denver Broncos and St. Louis Rams, and now that McDaniels was the Patriots offensive coordinator once again, it seemed like a natural fit.

On defense, the problem wasn't depth; it was top-end talent. They had more than enough players who could fill niche roles, but they needed players who could play almost, if not every single down. Perhaps that helps explain why the Patriots suddenly and dramatically changed their draft philosophy. What was once a systematic approach, which involved a lot of trading down to acquire extra picks, transformed overnight into an aggressive mind-set in which the Patriots traded up to acquire some players of particular interest.

They entered the draft with the 27th and 31st overall picks but moved up six spots with each of their selections to pick defensive end Chandler Jones and linebacker Dont'a Hightower. The renewed focus on the defensive front seven, in addition to their eagerness to add those players, served as proof that the Patriots were committed to improving their front seven.

It was a logical move to make. The Patriots had spent six picks in the first or second round on defensive backs in the previous five years and they made it seven first or second-round picks in six years with the selection of Tavon Wilson. With so many resources used on the secondary, it made a lot of sense to finally start focusing on the front seven.

The selection of Jones and Hightower caused observers to wonder whether the Patriots would be a 4-3 defense, as they had been in 2011, or if they would revert back to the 3-4 now that the lockout was over and they would have a full offseason to install their defense. The picks were not driven by scheme; those decisions would come much later. The selections of Jones and Hightower showed a commitment to finding talented players to build around. In fact, this entire draft was based on improving the defense. The Patriots made seven

Patriots 2012 Draft Picks

Round	Pick	Player	Position	Games played w/ Patriots
1	21	Chandler Jones	DE	55
1	25	Dont'a Hightower	OLB	54*
2	48	Tavon Wilson	S	54
3	90	Jake Bequette	DE	8
6	197	Nate Ebner	DB	57
7	224	Alfonzo Dennard	CB	29
7	235	Jeremy Ebert	WR	0

*=still with Patriots

selections; six of them were on defense. Out of those six players, four started at least four games in their rookie season: Jones, Hightower, Wilson, and Alfonzo Dennard. Every move the Patriots made was the right move in theory, but the real test was about to come.

★ ★ ★

The Patriots' aggressive offseason approach paid off almost immediately. In the second quarter of the first game of the season against the Tennessee Titans, Jones forced a fumble on a sack of quarterback Jake Locker, and Hightower recovered that fumble for a touchdown. Meanwhile, Tom Brady was effective in the passing game, hitting 23 of his 31 passes for 236 yards and two touchdowns, while finding tight ends Aaron Hernandez and Rob Gronkowski for a combined 12 receptions, 119 yards, and two touchdowns. Stevan Ridley steamrolled the Titans defense with 125 yards on 21 carries, and Brandon Lloyd caught five of the eight passes thrown his way for 69 yards. It was an exciting win for all involved—except for Wes Welker, who wasn't very involved (three catches, 14 yards). The team's leading receiver over the past five years, Welker was relegated to the bench behind Julian Edelman and Lloyd in two-receiver sets (a majority, given the presence of the two tight ends).

In fact, had Hernandez not injured his ankle in Week 2 against the Arizona Cardinals, Welker might have been an afterthought all season. Even without one of their most important players on offense, though, the Patriots were clearly the superior team. They outgained the Cardinals by 145 yards, they had 25 first downs to Arizona's 16, one turnover to Arizona's two, and ran 78 plays to Arizona's 61. But the Cardinals snuck away with a 20–18 win at Gillette Stadium because the Patriots punted twice while in enemy territory and also kicked four field goals on promising drives that stalled. Brady's first pass was intercepted, which should have been a bad enough omen on its own. Also, one of the Patriots' punts was blocked, and the Cardinals recovered to begin their next possession at the 2-yard line. The Cardinals defense held the Patriots in check, but the Patriots nearly overcame it all to win. A 5-yard touchdown pass to Gronkowski was followed by a defensive stand with a forced fumble by Brandon Spikes, which was recovered by the Patriots. A go-ahead touchdown was waved off for a holding penalty, and Stephen

Gostkowski's 42-yard field goal attempt was wide right, giving the Cardinals the win and the Patriots a rare home loss.

If the Patriots wanted to get back in the win column, they would have to do so against the team they narrowly defeated in the 2011 AFC Championship Game: the Baltimore Ravens.

Despite opening up a 13–0 first-quarter lead, the Patriots found themselves in a dog fight.

Their biggest problem was long passes. Time and time again, Ravens quarterback Joe Flacco hit his receivers deep with nine passes that gained 20 yards or more. As the season wore on, this proved to be more of a trend than a fluke.

But long passes weren't the Patriots' only problem. Questionable officiating from replacement refs (while the NFL Referees Association negotiated their new collective bargaining agreement) drew the ire of Bill Belichick and John Harbaugh, as 24 penalty flags were thrown. Some of those flags helped stymie the Patriots momentum, while giving the Ravens opportunities to get back in the game. That's exactly what they did, and before the first half was over, we had a back-and-forth game on our hands. There were five lead changes in the final 32 minutes of the game, including one with no time left as a field goal went over the upright. The officials ruled that it went through the uprights, but replay was less conclusive.

It made sense, then, when roughly a year and a half later, Belichick proposed a rule that would extend the field goal posts by five feet. Obviously, it was too late to prevent the Patriots from falling to 1–2, but it could help prevent over-the-bar inconclusive field goals from happening again.

For a minute, it looked like the Patriots would fall to 1–3 at the hands of the Buffalo Bills. Trailing 21–7 in the third quarter, the Patriots had just given up a 68-yard catch-and-run touchdown pass to wide receiver Donald Jones. There were seven more pass plays that gained 20 yards or more that week. But after falling behind by 14 in the second half, the Patriots scored 35 unanswered points on their way to a 52–28 win. Rob Gronkowski had an off day against the Ravens, but he came roaring back with five catches for 104 yards and a touchdown against the Bills.

But as it turned out, we hadn't even seen the beginning of the Patriots' offensive prowess. The next week, with Peyton Manning's Denver Broncos rolling into town, the Patriots unveiled their newest weapon: the no-huddle offense. More specifically, the one-word offense. With many receivers and linemen who had been entrenched in the system for years, the Patriots began operating at warp speed by using one-word play calls to get everyone's assignments from formation, to blocking scheme, to directions for run plays, to routes for receivers on pass plays, and everything in between.

It was a perfect use of his personnel but also a testament to Belichick's willingness to change with the times and to borrow influence from other coaches. Right around this time, Chip Kelly was making the same kind of impact with the same kind of college offense, running plays at a breakneck speed to catch the defense off guard and prevent them from catching their breath between plays.

Time after time, the Patriots hurried to the line and would snap the ball before the Broncos defense was ready. This was especially effective in the running game, where the Patriots piled up 54 carries for a whopping 251 yards and three touchdowns. With the Broncos front seven out of their stance, the Patriots line could fire off the ball and easily knock the defense backward, paving the way for easy rushing yards. It was also an effective strategy in the passing game, where Welker caught one quick pass after another for 13 receptions for 104 yards and a touchdown.

That week the Patriots ran 89 offensive plays, tied for the eighth most plays run by any offense in a non-overtime game since 2000 and the third most by the Patriots in any non-overtime game in their history. With a 31–21 win against the Broncos, the Patriots moved to 3–2 on the season, but they weren't out of the woods yet.

The warp-speed offense continued the next week, as the Patriots ran 85 plays against the Seattle Seahawks, but their dominance in the running game did not continue. With just 85 yards on 26 carries, one of the most successful areas of the Patriots offense the previous week was almost a non-factor. The lack of running game was not an issue for much of the first three quarters, though, as the Patriots built a 20–10 lead behind Brady, who finished the game with 36 completions on 58 pass attempts for 395 yards and two touchdowns. But two second-half interceptions cut into the Patriots' momentum and gave the Seahawks new life to mount a comeback.

The Patriots even doomed themselves a little, as they suddenly began trying to run the ball in the fourth quarter right into the teeth of the Seahawks defense that had slowed them down for much of the day. Then, with less than two minutes left, Seahawks rookie quarterback Russell Wilson, as he had done for much of the game to that point, threw another successful long pass over safety Tavon Wilson's head for the go-ahead touchdown. That day, Russell Wilson hit a total of six passes that gained 20 yards or more, and through Week 6, the Patriots allowed 33 such pass plays, the most in the NFL.

Belichick fell to 0–1 against Pete Carroll as a head coach, and a new cross-conference rivalry was born as the Seahawks took to social media to stake their claim over the Patriots. After the game Seahawks cornerback Richard Sherman taunted Brady, generally an Internet meme. More importantly, New England was now 3–3 and locked in a four-way tie for the division lead.

The Patriots snuck by the New York Jets with a 29–26 overtime win in Week 7 and earned the outright division lead for the first time all season. They extended that division lead with a 45–7 blowout win against the St. Louis Rams at Wembley Stadium. The offense was humming right along, as their two-tight end sets were creating matchup nightmares for opponents. Gronkowski was on a tear with 14 catches for 224 yards and four touchdowns in those two wins.

But all the while, their defensive woes continued. Jets quarterback Mark Sanchez connected on six passes that gained 20 yards or more, and Rams quarterbacks Sam Bradford and Kellen Clemons combined for three more. Despite every effort to improve their pass defense, long pass plays were still flying over their heads. Countless defensive backs and pass rushers had been tried, but something just wasn't working.

Desperate times called for drastic measures. With the trade deadline approaching, the Patriots gave up a fourth-round pick to the Tampa Bay Buccaneers in exchange for talented but troubled cornerback Aqib Talib. The move completely shook up the defensive backfield. Talib's presence allowed several unsettled pieces to find their best fit. Cornerback-turned-safety-turned-cornerback Devin McCourty returned to safety full time, cornerback Kyle Arrington moved from the outside (where his size had been exposed) to the slot (where his quickness would be a better fit), and rookie Alfonzo Dennard staked his claim to the top cornerback spot opposite Talib.

The trade took place on Wednesday of their bye week, which gave them a little extra time to sort everything out. Overnight, the complexion of the defense changed. The Patriots were suddenly a more physical group on the back end and they went from more zone coverage to man coverage in the secondary as a result. And once Talib returned from a drug-related suspension in Week 10, the Patriots defense immediately felt different. Yes, the Patriots still gave up 27 pass plays of 20 yards or more in the final seven games of the season. That was tied for second most in the league, but it felt more like 2001 than 2011.

No one could pass on the Patriots. The Indianapolis Colts' new golden boy quarterback, Andrew Luck, found out the hard way in his first experience against the Patriots, when he had a similarly nightmarish performance to many of Manning's worst defeats in a Colts uniform. Luck barely completed 50 percent of his throws and threw two touchdowns with three interceptions, two of which were returned for Patriots scores, one by none other than Talib.

But while the complexion was changing for the better on defense, the Patriots were met with adversity on offense, and they were reminded—once again—that the only thing that can stop Gronkowski is an injury. The All-Pro tight end was campaigning for similar numbers to the historic totals he posted in 2011, when a broken forearm put him on the shelf. Before Gronkowsi's injury, the Patriots scored 30 points or more in seven out of 10 games. After his injury they scored 30 or more in four of the final eight games of the season (including the playoffs).

Before and After the Trade

Patriots defense	Without Aqib Talib	With Aqib Talib
Games	9	7
Completions	220	150
Attempts	333	262
Completion %	66.1	57.3
Yards	2,690	1,867
Yards/attempt	8.1	7.1
Touchdowns	19	8
Interceptions	10	10
Passer rating	97.3	73.8
20+ yard passes	47	27

The Patriots won four straight with Talib in the fold and six overall. In Talib's first four games in a Patriots uniform, their opponents averaged 18.3 points per game and 253.5 passing yards per game. In fact, the Patriots lost just one game in the second half of the regular season and it also happened to be the one game in which they gave up more than 30 points to an opponent.

The upstart San Francisco 49ers came into Gillette Stadium at 9–3–1 looking to validate some of their success under their new quarterback, Colin Kaepernick. With an athlete behind center and several talented running backs beside him and behind him, the 49ers gave the Patriots fits with their running game in multiple formations and they piled up 180 yards on 39 carries. Kaepernick was also effective in picking the Patriots apart from the pocket with 14 completions on 25 pass attempts for 221 yards and four touchdowns.

This was a Murphy's Law kind of game for the Patriots; everything that could go wrong, did. The 49ers fumbled six times, but the Patriots only recovered one, and Frank Gore scooped up one of his own fumbles and ran it in for a touchdown. Meanwhile, the Patriots turned the ball over four times in the first half with two interceptions and two fumbles of their own. It all led to a 31–3 third-quarter deficit for the Patriots. And despite all that went against them up to that point, the Patriots mounted a thrilling comeback to tie the game at 31. The breakneck offense went to work with touchdown drives of 13 plays, 73 yards; nine plays, 86 yards; six plays, 66 yards; and seven plays, 92 yards. The 49ers returned the ensuing kickoff to the Patriots' 38-yard line and scored on the very next play (a 38-yard pass to Michael Crabtree). It all proved that the Patriots could still compete with a good team, even when playing at their worst. That being said, it also proved that the Patriots needed to clean up their mistakes if they wanted their Super Bowl dreams to stay alive.

During the divisional playoff game, the Patriots unveiled a unique wrinkle with running back Shane Vereen split out wide, matched up with a linebacker, and running stop-and-go routes that left Houston Texans defenders in his dust. Vereen caught five passes for 83 yards and two touchdowns. And Brady was on fire with 25 completions on 40 attempts for 344 yards and three touchdowns. The Patriots beat the Texans 41–28, but they were dealt a crushing blow. Gronkowski returned to the lineup just in time to re-injure his forearm in the Patriots' first playoff game. And for a second straight year, the sting of a Gronkowski injury had a negative impact on the Patriots' chances of a fourth Super Bowl victory.

In a rematch with the Ravens, the Patriots suffered the same turnover imbalance that spelled their demise against the 49ers. The Ravens recovered their one and only fumble; the Patriots lost theirs, along with two Brady interceptions, to give the Patriots a turnover margin of minus-three.

If Gronkowski's injury wasn't enough, the defense suffered its own significant departure when Aqib Talib went down with an injury in the first quarter. The injury caused some major shakeups in the secondary. Instead of Talib on Anquan Boldin, it was young cornerback Marquice Cole. That was a matchup that Flacco targeted time and time again.

This time, it wasn't long passes or bad officiating that did the Patriots in. It was a pair of major injuries, efficiency by the Ravens, and the Patriots' offensive struggles. The Patriots' 13 points was their lowest total of the season. Despite running 82 offensive plays, the offense did not have the same speed it had shown before; 54 of those plays were pass plays, and 25 of them were incomplete. The Patriots' 28 run plays gained only 108 yards (3.9 yards per carry).

For a fourth straight year, the Patriots postseason had ended with defeat. This was now their seventh postseason loss since their last Super Bowl win. For a team that had already proven so much, it began to feel like there was still so much left to prove. And it began to feel like their opportunity to prove it was diminishing right before their eyes.

CHAPTER 26

★ ★ ★

2013: The Fall of Gronk

No offseason in Bill Belichick's Patriots career had as much drama as the 2013 offseason. Chronologically, the first thing on the docket was free agency. There were two crown jewels of the Patriots' free-agent class: cornerback Aqib Talib and wide receiver Wes Welker.

In Welker's six years with the Patriots from 2007 to 2012, he was at times the only thing keeping the offense moving. Even when he fought back from a 2009 ACL injury in six months despite a nine-month timetable, the slot machine hardly missed a beat. With the exception of that 2010 season, Welker was good for no fewer than 110 catches each season. In just half a season, Talib had been the piece that brought the defense together and settled everyone else into more comfortable positions. In half a season, Talib had proven he could be what the Patriots had been needing for years: a legitimate No. 1 cover cornerback.

Belichick wasn't choosing between the two; it wasn't a one-or-the-other decision. In fact, had Welker accepted the Patriots' initial offer—a two-year, $10 million contract with incentives that could have pushed it to $16 million—he would have stayed with the team in 2013 and beyond. But Welker knew he had interest elsewhere, and the Broncos offered him a two-year, $12 million contract to join Peyton Manning in Denver. Welker gave the Patriots a chance to match, but they had already signed a new slot receiver, Danny Amendola.

On one hand, you had Welker, an aging but reliable veteran who had demonstrated durability, a deep understanding of the offense, and a great rapport with Tom Brady. On the other hand, you had Amendola, a younger, more athletic but less-proven, and more injury-prone player.

Thus, 118 receptions worth of production taken away from the 2012 team. In a salary cap move, the Patriots also released wide receiver Brandon Lloyd, cutting his three-year deal short at one year. Lloyd took his 74 receptions with him. Danny Woodhead signed with the San Diego Chargers and with him went 40 receptions, the most by a Patriots running back in 2012.

In total, the Patriots lost eight players who caught at least one pass for them in 2012 and a total of 305 receptions out of 402 (75.9 percent)—and they weren't done losing receivers. But first they at least tried to add some. In addition to Amendola, the Patriots re-signed Julian Edelman to a one-year deal roughly a month after he became a free agent. Edelman didn't draw much interest on the open market, and the Patriots wouldn't realize until later just how lucky they were to have had him back at the veteran minimum.

The volume approach was back, and the Patriots were looking to add multiple wide receivers to find the best combinations and create a new-look offense. The Patriots drafted their big-bodied, lanky downfield receiver in Aaron Dobson and a smaller, shiftier receiver in Josh Boyce.

That wasn't all they got during the draft, though. With Stevan Ridley's contract expiring soon and because of his recurring fumble problems, the Patriots decided to trade for Tampa Bay Buccaneers running back LeGarrette Blount. Whether he was to be the bell-cow or simply a relief option for Ridley, the immediate plan wasn't clear. But the Patriots were clearly cognizant of the possibility that they might have to rely more heavily on the running game in 2013 because of all the changes in the passing game.

Then, in the short period of time between the team's mandatory mini-camp in mid-June and the start of training camp in late July, tragedy struck when a young man named Odin Lloyd was allegedly murdered by Aaron Hernandez, and the tight end was taken to jail where he awaited trial. Once Hernandez was arrested, the Patriots wasted no time in releasing him. He was ultimately found guilty of

Patriots 2013 Draft Picks

Round	Pick	Player	Position	Games played w/ Patriots
2	52	Jamie Collins	LB	43*
2	59	Aaron Dobson	WR	24*
3	83	Logan Ryan	CB	48*
3	91	Duron Harmon	S	47*
4	102	Josh Boyce	WR	10
7	226	Michael Buchanan	DE	18
7	235	Steve Beauharnais	LB	2

*=still with Patriots

murder, but in the meantime, Belichick was juggling two massive undertakings: figuring out how to rework the offense without Hernandez and keeping his team focused despite all the outside distractions.

Belichick's strategy in dealing with this horrific turn of events could not have been more clear: address it head-on and turn the page as quickly as possible. Belichick, Brady, and several other team captains spoke with the media in the two days before training camp officially began, and the Patriots were immediately onto the 2013 season.

With so many major changes taking place on offense and with tight end Rob Gronkowski still recovering from offseason forearm surgery, it was no surprise to see the Patriots stumble out of the gates with just 36 combined points in their first two games. Amendola caught 10 of the 14 passes thrown his way for 104 yards and converted several key third downs as part of a comeback 23–21 victory against the Buffalo Bills in Week 1. In that effort, though, he tore ligaments in his groin and was forced out of the lineup for three weeks.

Just in time to help compensate for Amendola's injury, rookie wide receiver Dobson made his debut, and along with the emerging undrafted rookie Kenbrell Thompkins, the Patriots appeared to have a young, athletic duo of wide receivers. But that all came into question after a dreadful performance in a 13–10 win against the New York Jets. Dobson dropped three passes that week, Thompkins dropped one, and the two receivers were out of position for countless other passes. Brady completed just 19 of his 39 throws that night, and 13 of those completions and 18 of those targets went to one man: Edelman. With seven receptions for 79 yards and two touchdowns the week before, Edelman was off to a red hot start to the season as the team's top slot receiver.

Everyone had expected Amendola to be Welker's replacement; it ended up being Edelman. After four years of work, the former college quarterback had developed into a quality NFL receiver. Edelman pulled in seven passes in Weeks 3 and 4 as the Patriots offense slowly found its footing. Thompkins took off as one of the better weapons in the passing game and hauled in three catches for 41 yards and two touchdowns in Week 3, followed by six catches for 127 yards and a touchdown in Week 4.

Meanwhile, the Patriots continued to apply an even heavier emphasis on the running game. Brady attempted 36 passes against the Tampa Bay Buccaneers in Week 3, and the Patriots ran the ball 33 times as a team. The next week, Brady attempted 31 passes against the Atlanta Falcons, and the Patriots ran the ball 31 times as a team.

While the offense had been finding its footing, the defense had been keeping the Patriots afloat. The Patriots yielded 57 points in those four games, the fifth best for any team in the league to start the 2013 season. But in that fourth game of the season, defensive tackle Vince Wilfork was lost for the year to a torn Achilles' tendon. That injury proved to be just the first crack in the foundation of the Patriots defense. Now it was a question of whether they could make it to the end of the season before it all came crumbling down.

At 4–0 the Patriots were undefeated but far from perfect—as their next game, and first loss, would reveal. The Cincinnati Bengals handed the Patriots a 13–6 loss in a game that had proven just how far the Patriots had to come on offense. The Patriots dropped six passes, Edelman was a non-factor (two catches, 35 yards), and Brady's completion percentage dipped below 50 for the second time in the season. Meanwhile, the injuries kept piling up. Defensive tackle Tommy Kelly joined Wilfork on injured reserve, which left a gaping hole in the middle of the Patriots defense. Right tackle Sebastian Vollmer was also injured against the Bengals.

The injuries continued the next week against the New Orleans Saints, as line-backer Jerod Mayo suffered a season-ending torn pectoral muscle. The Patriots were trailing 27–23, when Brady threw an interception that sent the Saints side-line into celebration and sent the Gillette Stadium faithful to the exits. Those fans quickly regretted their decision, as the Patriots forced the Saints to go three-and-out. Trailing by four points with 1:13 left and no timeouts, the Patriots needed a great plan with perfect execution. With minimal time left, common sense dictates that the offense should go for the sideline to get the ball out of bounds and stop the clock. As such, the defense is on high alert for the boundary and wants to keep the offense in-bounds to keep the clock running. The Patriots knew this and capitalized on it by attacking down the middle of the field, hurrying to the line and getting the next play off. In three plays, the Patriots had moved 44 yards. Five plays later, Brady found Thompkins in the back corner of the end zone for the go-ahead touchdown with 10 seconds remaining. The Patriots advanced to 5–1. It wasn't pretty, but it was about to get ugly.

Belichick's second meeting of the year with Rex Ryan was another reminder that the Patriots still were not the dominant Patriots of old. Gronkowski finally made his return, and Brady clearly could not have been more thrilled to have a familiar target by his side. He promptly targeted Gronkowski 17 times, and the tight end caught eight receptions for 114 yards.

But Gronkowski wasn't the only receiver with whom Brady had a hard time connecting. In fact, this marked the third time in 2013 that Brady's completion percentage was 50 percent or lower for a single game, matching his career high. In the process, the Jets became the first team to ever do it to Brady twice in a season. Curiously, the balance was all but completely missing from the Patriots offense. Yes, the Jets were one of the league's best run defenses, but the pass attack had been inconsistent all season.

On the flip side, the Jets revealed what would become a common gameplan against the Patriots defense: run the ball and don't stop until the clock strikes zero. The Jets finished with 52 rush attempts (10th most rush attempts against the Patriots all time and most against the Patriots since 1987) for 177 yards and a touchdown. The Bengals began the trend a couple weeks before with 39 rush attempts for 162 yards and a touchdown. The Saints piled on with 26 carries for 131 yards and a touchdown of their own. As the Patriots lost more and more pieces in the middle of their defense, their opponents focused more and more heavily on running the ball right into the teeth (more like soft gums) of that defense.

The Patriots offense was far removed from a full season of ripping through opposing defenses like a hot knife through butter, running plays before a defense could catch its breath, and operating at maximum efficiency in the passing game. This year, they were huddling up at nearly every snap; passes were hitting the ground with a harmless, comical thud; and Brady's patience was tested as his new receivers dropped passes, while his old receivers were elsewhere. The defense was a fresh-paved road of young, inexperienced players in the middle. Joe Vellano and Chris Jones, two unheralded rookies, filled the defensive tackle vacancies of Wilfork and Kelly, while second-year linebacker Dont'a Hightower played slightly out of position filling in for Mayo.

A second-half surge put the Patriots past the Miami Dolphins 27–17 but not before the Patriots fell behind 17–3 in the first half. The Dolphins pounded the rock into the Patriots' midsection 31 times for 156 yards. On the other side, it finally seemed the offense had hit its stride. Everyone had a turn to make big plays in a 55–31 Week 9 win against the Pittsburgh Steelers. Dobson broke out with five receptions for 130 yards and two touchdowns; Amendola had his biggest performance to that point with four catches, 122 yards, and his first touchdown of the season; Gronkowski got back to his old self with nine catches for 143 yards and a touchdown. It looked like the Patriots were getting into midseason form right on cue.

Belichick's teams had always done well coming out of a bye week in previous years, but after losing to the Steelers following their bye in 2011 and barely getting past the Bills after their bye in 2012, it wasn't all too surprising to see the Patriots stumble against the Carolina Panthers. Brady found rhythm with his receivers, hitting 29 of his 40 pass attempts, and running back Shane Vereen made his return to the lineup after half a season away. The defense clamped down against the run, despite yielding 103 yards on 23 carries, though 24 of those yards were on one carry by Cam Newton. An exciting game was ultimately decided on a questionable officiating call, where a referee picked up a flag on what appeared to be pass interference by the Panthers in the end zone against Gronkowksi, resulting in a 24–20 loss for the Patriots.

At 7–3 the Patriots were still among the AFC's elite but not *the* elite. In 2013 that distinction belonged to the Denver Broncos. Peyton Manning's Broncos offense was threatening the record-setting 2007 Patriots for many of the marks they set just six years prior. This was the same offense that snatched Welker away from the Patriots. And how did the Patriots respond to this offense? By inviting them to run and loading up against the pass. The linebackers and defensive tackles spread away from the middle of the field, opening up lanes for the Broncos to get some easy yards in the running game.

On a chilly night in Foxborough with winds of 22 miles per hour and gusts that were even stronger, Manning was all too eager to take advantage of the giant holes the Patriots left in run defense. Whether he audibled out of pass plays into run plays or whether the Broncos simply ran the plays as called from the sideline, the strategy worked. Manning threw for just 150 yards, his lowest passing yardage total in any game that year. At first, though, he didn't need the yards. The Patriots offense was coughing up the football left and right with fumbles by Ridley and Blount that were recovered by the Broncos and turned into touchdowns. The Patriots entered the locker room with a 24–0 halftime deficit, but within seven minutes of the second half, they had cut the deficit to 24–7 and had forced a turnover by the Broncos. In fact, the Patriots scored on their first five possessions of the second half with four touchdowns and a field goal to put New England up 31–24 before the Broncos could respond to tie the score and send the game

★ ★ ★ ★ ★ ★ ★

"Coach Belichick is the best coach that I've ever competed against, and I think it's safe to say he'll go down as the greatest NFL coach of all time. The teams that he has coached that I've competed against have always been well coached, always been prepared, always played hard for 60 minutes. I think that's a couple things that stood out about the teams he's coached. I played against him when he was the defensive coordinator with the Jets and then the head coach in New England. Those things jump out every single week, and to me that speaks to his coaching."

—Peyton Manning, four days before the 2013 AFC Championship Game

Quarterback Tom Brady stands next to Bill Belichick in 2013 during the Patriots' 34–20 win against the Buffalo Bills in quagmire-like conditions. (USA TODAY Sports Images)

to overtime. That's when Belichick made one of the most questionable in-game decisions of his coaching career.

The Patriots won the overtime coin toss. Up against a record-setting offense, they elected to choose which direction they wanted to defend instead of deciding to receive the ball. As a result, the Broncos got to choose whether to receive or kick and thus they ended up with the ball first. Think about that: Belichick willingly put the ball in Manning's hands, giving him an opportunity to seal a win for the Broncos. But when the Broncos failed to do that, the game became sudden death, and Belichick liked his odds better with the wind at his back than in his face. The final sequence might as well have been accompanied by Belichick waving an "I told you so" banner over his head when Patriots punter Ryan Allen sent the ball high into the air, where the wind caught it. Welker could not judge where it would land. He waved off the punt, but it was too late, as specialist Tony Carter ran into the ball, allowing the Patriots to recover inside the Broncos' five-yard line. The Patriots sealed the shocking comeback with a field goal and a 34–31 win. This has to be considered one of Belichick's finest singular performances as a coach.

That win was not without its losses, though. Dobson suffered a foot injury that took him out for a month, just as it looked like he was beginning to heat up. Even without Dobson, the offense was hitting stride because it once again had its best playmaker, Gronkowski. But that wouldn't last long. After narrowly escaping the Houston Texans 34–31, the Patriots were in a nail-biter with the Cleveland Browns in Week 14 when safety T.J. Ward hit Gronkowski at the knee, tearing his ACL and putting him on the shelf for the rest of the season. For a third straight year, Gronkowski suffered a major injury that ended his hopes of helping the team in the playoffs. For a third straight year, Belichick would have to work on the fly to adjust the game plan and compensate for the absence of the All-Pro tight end.

That they even escaped the Browns with the 27–26 win was surprising. The Patriots were trailing by 12 points with 2:35 left and one timeout. With a little help from a recovered onside kick, Brady was 10-of-13 for 93 yards and two touchdowns to inch the Patriots past the Browns. Vereen was part of the game plan before Gronkowski's injury, but that role magnified in the wake of the injury. Vereen finished with 12 receptions for 153 yards, but not on checkdowns; he was running a lot of routes from the boundary and the slot as a wide receiver.

At this point, the Patriots' top receiving options, Edelman, Amendola, and Vereen, were the go-to pass-catchers on offense and all less than six feet tall. Without Gronkowski, the Patriots also went to their running game. For three games, it worked. They beat the Baltimore Ravens 41–7, the Bills 34–20, and the Indianapolis Colts 43–22 in the divisional round of the playoffs.

Blount and Ridley were a dominant one-two punch in those three games, and Belichick wasn't afraid to go to that well again and again. The Patriots ran the ball a combined 123 times for 643 yards (5.2 yards per carry) and 10 touchdowns in those three games. Meanwhile, Brady attempted just 75 passes for 492 yards with two touchdowns and one interception.

The Broncos, of course, responded by loading the box with eight or nine defenders every time either Blount or Ridley was on the field when the two teams met in the AFC Championship Game. The Patriots ran the ball 16 times for 64 yards. They punted the ball on their first three drives and they had just three points headed into the fourth quarter.

Brady fared as well as could be expected with an offense that was limping into the biggest game of the year. But Manning was his usual transcendent self with 32 completions on 43 attempts for 400 yards and two touchdowns. He had a little help from an injury to Talib on a play in which Welker ran into the Patriots cornerback head-on while running a route over the middle of the field. As had been the case in 2012, Talib's absence in the AFC Championship Game shifted the matchups in favor of the Broncos. Logan Ryan covered Demaryius Thomas, and Alfonzo Dennard covered Eric Decker. The Patriots' offensive line was beaten in one-on-one matchups by the Broncos defensive line, marking a trend of the Patriots' postseason losses over the past several seasons, to the Giants, Ravens, Jets, Giants (again), Ravens (again), and Broncos (again).

CHAPTER 28

★ ★ ★

2014: Super Again

From 2001 to 2004, the Patriots were 9–0 in the playoffs. From 2005 to 2013, they were 9–8. In Bill Belichick's first five years as head coach of the Patriots, his team won nine playoff games, which is the same number his team won in the next nine years combined. In 2001 the Patriots were the first professional team in a decade and a half to give the New England area a taste of championship success, but in the nine-going-on-10 years since their last Super Bowl victory, each of the three other major Boston sports teams had taken at least one tour of the city while holding championship hardware high above their heads. The question was no longer *when* the Patriots would regain their past glory; now, it was a question of *if* they would ever return to their perch atop the NFL.

Maybe there was a sense of urgency in the Patriots' offseason moves, or maybe the stars (figurative and literal) just fell into place, and the Patriots were simply in the right place to capitalize on those opportunities. Out of nowhere All-Pro cornerback Darrelle Revis became available and signed with the Patriots to (essentially) a one-year contract, and the Patriots had acquired Brandon Browner to put opposite Revis in the secondary.

This was a huge diversion from the Patriots' previous offseason pattern of buying low on free agents and of avoiding top-dollar contracts, but this was a worthy exception. Browner would not be available until Week 7 due to a drug-related suspension, but upon the return of the 6'4", 221-pound cornerback, the Patriots would have one of the biggest and most formidable secondaries in the NFL.

The additions weren't limited to defense either. The Patriots tried their hand with yet another boundary receiver, their third veteran acquisition in the past four years. First, it was Chad Ochocinco in 2011; then, it was Brandon Lloyd in 2012. After a year with Aaron Dobson, the Patriots added an insurance policy at the position with Brandon LaFell. At 6'3" and 210 pounds, LaFell had the size and athleticism to present a dynamic, versatile, unique presence on the outside.

The Patriots were also adding from within. Rookie linebacker Jamie Collins flashed brilliance at the end of the 2013 season; linebacker Dont'a Hightower and defensive end Chandler Jones had both shown signs of growth in their first two years in the league; wide receivers Dobson and Kenbrell Thompkins now had a year of seasoning in the NFL and in the Patriots' system; Rob Gronkowski would be returning from a torn ACL in time for the regular season.

The excitement reached a fever pitch in mid-March, but in the draft a couple months later, it seemed that the Patriots passed up an opportunity to surge forward with their win-now mentality. Their first pick, defensive tackle Dominique Easley, had explosive potential but a reputation of injuries; their second, a quarterback named Jimmy Garoppolo, would not help the team right away. With additions at running back and on the offensive line, the Patriots focused more on building

Patriots 2014 NFL Draft Picks

Round	Pick	Player	Position	Games played w/ Patriots
1	29	Dominique Easley	DT	22
2	62	Jimmy Garoppolo	QB	11*
4	105	Bryan Stork	C	21*
4	130	James White	RB	17*
4	140	Cameron Fleming	OT	19*
6	179	Jon Halapio	OG	0
6	198	Zach Moore	DE	8
6	206	Jemea Thomas	DB	0
7	244	Jeremy Gallon	WR	0

*=still with Patriots

their depth through the draft than adding players who would come in and start immediately. But with their acquisitions earlier in the offseason, there was still a feeling that this team could contend for a Super Bowl.

That was before the Patriots traded left guard Logan Mankins to the Tampa Bay Buccaneers just days before the season. Even with the Patriots' recent history of severing ties with a player with a high salary figure and/or in the last year of his contract, the Mankins trade still came as a shock. First of all, he was viewed by many as their best offensive lineman, and secondly, it opened a huge hole at guard. The Patriots saved $13 million by trading Mankins, who still had two years left on his deal, but they couldn't just pile up $13 million at left guard to keep Tom Brady clean and to open holes in the running game.

The trade resulted in a rough first four weeks of the season. The Patriots entered 2014 with sky high expectations, but after a month, it looked like they were headed for a crash landing. Once again, a trip to Miami resulted in a stunning defeat, as the Patriots coughed up a 20–10 halftime lead to notch a 33–20 Week 1 loss to the Dolphins.

The offensive line became human turnstiles. Brady was sacked four times, including two sack/fumbles and he was under pressure on 25 of his 60 dropbacks. Meanwhile, the running game couldn't get any momentum against the Dolphins' front seven and produced just 20 carries for 89 yards and a touchdown. The run defense struggled like it did at the end of 2013, yielding 38 carries for 191 yards and a touchdown to the Dolphins.

Some of the struggles were pinned on scheme. Jones was playing out of position in the 3-4 scheme, as the 265-pound defensive end was asked to hold steady at the line of scrimmage rather than using his best skill set to rush into the backfield. Some of the struggles were pinned on execution; the Patriots missed nine tackles as a team.

A blowout 30–7 win against the Minnesota Vikings and a narrow 16–9 win against the Oakland Raiders did not assuage concerns. The defense seemed to have corrected some of its issues by allowing 54 rushing yards against the Vikings and 67 rushing yards against the Raiders, but the offense continued to struggle as the offensive line failed to protect Brady, and the receivers struggled to get open.

Then, there was an absolute beatdown. The Patriots have been beaten soundly plenty of times in the Belichick era. So why was it different when the Kansas City Chiefs handed them a 41–14 blowout loss in Week 4? Maybe because it aired in primetime on *Monday Night Football*, maybe because of the mountainous preseason expectations for the team, maybe because the fans in attendance at Arrowhead Stadium set a new Guinness world record for crowd noise level at a stadium, maybe because those fans were extra stoked as their Royals had just clinched a playoff spot for the first time since 1985, maybe because nearly everyone in a Patriots uniform played horribly.

Jamaal Charles and Knile Davis led the Chiefs' charge through the Patriots defense with 199 yards on 34 carries between the two of them. Alex Smith was at peak efficiency and was 20-of-26 for 248 yards and three touchdowns on the night. The Patriots' offense had an equally rough night. Brady was under fire from Chiefs pass rushers Tamba Hali and Justin Houston, who combined for all three sacks on the night, and the Patriots quarterback was a pedestrian 14-of-23 for 159 yards, one touchdown, and two interceptions. The running game didn't do much to help with just 75 yards on 16 carries, but the brunt of the focus was on the offense.

Even in the darkest moment, there was a glimmer of light. LaFell finished with six receptions for 119 yards and a 44-yard catch-and-run touchdown. It was notable as the first 100-yard receiving performance by a Patriots receiver since Julian Edelman and Danny Amendola each had 100 yards against the Dolphins in Week 15 of the 2013 season.

This time, Brady didn't escape criticism. Immediately after the game, Bill Belichick was asked about the future of the quarterback position and whether or not it would be evaluated in the week to come. The Patriots head coach could do nothing but scoff at the question, but that was just the start of the firestorm headed into a Week 5 matchup with the Cincinnati Bengals that felt as close to make-or-break as it could get at the one-quarter mark.

In the six days between the two contests, everyone had different answers as to why the Patriots were .500 after four games. One popular opinion was that the Patriots had not given Brady the supporting cast he needed to succeed. Belichick engaged in a now famous back-and-forth with a reporter, where the reporter peppered Belichick with questions as to whether he had done enough to surround Brady with talent. Belichick's repeated three-word response—"We're on to Cincinnati"—was simply meant to deflect the questions that Belichick deemed irrelevant to the immediate task ahead of defeating the Bengals. Little did he know that it would become a war cry of sorts for the Patriots in 2014.

★ ★ ★

Through four games Gronkowski had 13 receptions for 147 yards and three touchdowns. The Patriots had attempted 105 rushes for 390 yards (3.7 yards per carry) and two touchdowns, ranking 20th or worse in each category. Brady had been sacked 10 times and was a paltry 81-of-137 (59.1 percent) for 791 yards (198 yards per game, 5.8 yards per attempt), four touchdowns, two interceptions, and a 79.1 passer rating. Revis had yielded 11 receptions on 19 targets for 133 yards, one touchdown, and one interception. The defense yielded 117 rushes for 519 yards (4.4 yards per carry) and two touchdowns. With just a six-day turnaround after their blowout loss to the Chiefs, the outlook was bleak up against an undefeated Bengals team that was coming off a bye week.

Revis' slow start was because he didn't begin to feel 100 percent healthy from the ACL surgery he suffered in 2012 until Week 5 of the 2014 season. Gronkowski also said that was when he truly began to feel like "Gronk" again, the dominant, hard-nosed tight end of 2011 and 2012. Two of the central figures of the team, feeling less than 100 percent following knee injuries, helped turn the team around when they were both back to normal.

But one other area that needed correcting—the offensive line—got a much-needed face-lift. The Patriots couldn't settle on their starting guards but eventually landed on a combination of Dan Connolly at left guard, rookie Bryan Stork at center, and Ryan Wendell at right guard. Connolly and Wendell had both been starting centers for the Patriots in the past, so their experience on the inside would be valuable in helping Stork acclimate to the NFL.

Gronkowski racked up six catches for 100 yards and a touchdown against Cincinnati, Revis yielded just three receptions against Bengals wide receiver A.J. Green, but it was more than just those two. The communication on the offensive line improved immediately, and that group kept Brady clean with just one sack. The running game produced 46 carries for 220 yards and a touchdown, and the defense held the Bengals to just 79 yards on 18 carries and forced and recovered three fumbles en route to a 20–3 halftime lead and 43–17 victory.

The Patriots were on to Buffalo, where they scored a convincing 37–22 win against the Bills on the strength of four touchdowns by Brady, including two to LaFell, who continued to showcase his abilities in the offense. As a boundary receiver with size and quickness, the Patriots took advantage of his skillset (as well as the dominant presence of Gronkowski) by getting him the ball on continued play-action passes, where Brady would fake a handoff one direction and throw to LaFell in the other, and there would often be a huge window waiting for him.

Next, the Patriots were on to the New York Jets, where New England snuck away with a 27–25 win despite yielding 218 rushing yards on 43 carries. The Jets' weakness at linebacker was the target, as Shane Vereen caught five passes for 71 yards and two touchdowns while Gronkowski added five catches for 68 yards. Browner finally made his Patriots debut and was not targeted once all day, but he made his presence felt—for better and worse—the very next week against the Bears.

The one-two tandem of Revis and Browner held Bears wide receivers Brandon Marshall and Alshon Jeffery in check. The two combined for just eight catches, 94 yards, and one touchdown. This began a trend that we would see for the remainder of the season: Browner went where his size was most needed, and Revis went where his talent was most needed. Browner's physical style of play made him the target of a lot of penalty flags, though, and he drew two or more in seven out of 12 games he played in 2014. The offense kept on its dominant path. Brady picked apart the Bears defense and had as many incomplete passes (five) as touchdown passes against Chicago. Brady was a perfect 20-of-20 targeting Gronkowski and LaFell.

The Patriots were then on to the Denver Broncos for a rematch of the 2013 AFC Championship Game in what turned into an offensive affair. New England jumped out to a 27–7 halftime lead before finishing off a 43–21 victory. It was Belichick and Peyton Manning's 19th meeting (Belichick was 11–7 headed into this one) and Brady and Manning's 16th (Brady was 10–5). The two teams mustered 870 total yards of offense but only 109 yards on the ground. It was a true quarterback's duel with 110 pass attempts between the two future Hall of Famers.

But this game was important for more than just the passing duel. This was our first extensive look at the ability of cornerback Malcolm Butler. The undrafted free agent had impressed onlookers in training camp, but he was a hidden gem up until Week 9 of the regular season. That week he allowed five completions on nine throws, mostly to Emmanuel Sanders, into his coverage for 77 yards.

The Patriots followed up their Week 9 win against the Broncos with wins in their next two games against the Indianapolis Colts (42–20) and the Detroit Lions (34–9), holding four talented quarterbacks in a row in check: Jay Cutler, Peyton Manning, Andrew Luck, and Matthew Stafford. The next on the schedule—Aaron Rodgers of the Green Bay Packers—would not be as easily disposed. "He has set the standard for an NFL head coach, definitely in my time in the league," said Packers coach Mike McCarthy about Belichick. "It's awesome to go up and compete against his team and no one does it better than what he's done."

Defensively, Belichick has always fared well at taking away options A and B from an opposing offense. The only drawback is when that opponent can make use of options C and D on their way to a victory. That's what Rodgers did against the Patriots. Jordy Nelson was kept relatively quiet, save for a 45-yard touchdown catch on a missed assignment, and Randall Cobb's respectable seven receptions for 85 yards were far from the explosive numbers he'd posted all year to that point, but it was Davante Adams (six catches, 121 yards) and running back Eddie Lacy (21 carries, 98 yards) who did the most damage to the Patriots defense.

So, the Patriots' seven-game win streak came to an end, but three more wins put them at 12–3 and earned them the No. 1 seed in the conference headed into the playoffs. Six of the previous seven times they had the No. 1 seed, they went to the Super Bowl (with 2010 the only exception).

This would prove to be one of the most exciting—and controversial—postseason runs in Belichick's tenure. Controversy No. 1 occurred against the Baltimore Ravens when the Patriots dipped into their bag of tricks to build momentum on offense. The Patriots came onto the field, facing a 14-point third-quarter deficit. Vereen came onto the field, but before the play, he declared himself an ineligible receiver and lined up out wide. Meanwhile, tight end Michael Hoomanawanui lined up at tackle despite being an eligible receiver and ran down the middle of the field. The play call, appropriately known as "Baltimore," was effective. Vereen turned to the quarterback, faking a screen, while Hoomanawanui ran uncovered through the middle of the defense, and the result was a 16-yard gain down the middle.

Two plays later, they ran a similar play, but they altered the formation a little bit and named it "Raven." This time Hoomanawanui was ineligible, and Edelman was the open man on the other side of the field. The result was an 11-yard gain. Two plays later, it was "Baltimore" again. Once again, Vereen was ineligible, and the pass went to Hoomanawanui. This time the result was a 14-yard gain, and an incensed John Harbaugh tacked on five yards for unsportsmanlike conduct as the Ravens coach aired his grief with the referees. "We wanted an opportunity to be able to ID who the eligible players were," Harbaugh said after the game, "because what they were doing was they would announce the ineligible player, and then Tom would take them to the line right away and snap the ball before we had a chance to even figure out who was lined up where. And that was the deception part of it, and it was clearly deception."

But it didn't matter because at that point the Patriots were done with eligible and ineligible receiver trickery. They scored a touchdown two plays later to draw within seven. And after forcing the Ravens to go three-and-out, the Patriots had one more trick up their sleeve: a double-pass. Edelman was a college quarterback, but he hadn't thrown a pass in a meaningful game since graduating Kent State. So, when Brady threw him a backward lateral on the left sideline and when Edelman released a deep pass to a wide-open Danny Amendola, there was some trepidation until it landed in the receiver's hands.

The two teams traded empty possession for the better part of the next 15 minutes with the Ravens kicking a field goal to take a three-point lead with 10:17 left. That's when Brady took over with a 10-play, 74-yard drive capped off by a 23-yard deep touchdown pass to LaFell. The Patriots hung on in the final minutes to clinch a victory but not without kicking up a media storm with their strategies.

Then came the AFC Championship Game, Belichick's fourth meeting with Luck and Colts head coach Chuck Pagano. For a third straight time, the Patriots racked up more than 200 rushing yards against the Colts defense. For a second straight time, the Patriots had held Colts star wide receiver T.Y. Hilton to modest numbers. He had just four catches for 60 yards in the two games. Luck was a combined 35-of-74 (47.3 percent) for 429 yards, two touchdowns, and three interceptions and was now 0–4 for his career against Belichick.

★   ★   ★   ★   ★   ★   ★

"Tennessee had a play [in Week 15 against the Jets] on the last play of the game, where they put four skill players in at guard and tackle. When I saw the play, I thought to myself, *That's something you see on the punt team*. And that's always a problem for us: to identify who's who, who's eligible because you don't want them to sneak somebody out and fake punt, that kind of thing. But it's hard to match up, and a lot of times, the officials don't…they're not going to sit there and say, '54 is eligible, 27 is ineligible, 89 is eligible, 76 is ineligible.' They just kind of…it goes kind of fast. And defensively, you've just kind of got to figure it out…if we split an eligible guy out, and he's a legitimate receiver, like Vereen, defensively, even though that guy is ineligible, it's going to be hard not to cover him—just instinctively. You see Vereen out there, you don't think, *Alright, forget about him*."

—Bill Belichick

But all those stories were pushed to the side. The real story came after the game when Indianapolis sportswriter Bob Kravitz reported that the Patriots had used underinflated footballs during the game and that the NFL had begun investigating the possibility that the Patriots had deflated them. We'll get more into the details of the scandal, known as Deflategate, in a later chapter. But when you strip away the details and get rid of the he-said she-said reporting that ensued, you're left with one simple fact: fair or not, Belichick now had a scandal on his hands two weeks before the Super Bowl.

The national media circus rolled into town as the Patriots geared up for the Super Bowl and they brought with them the full force of questions about who knew what, when they knew it, and how they could expect anyone to believe anything they say given their perceived pattern of controversy. It went on like that all week. Belichick gave a press conference on Saturday, eight days before the Super Bowl, in which he detailed his thoughts on what happened. The end goal of that press conference was to divert attention from the scandal, which was now being called "Deflategate," and back onto the biggest game of the year just days away.

With all those distractions—or rather, one giant circus—you would think the Patriots would be underprepared for the NFC's No. 1 seed, the Seattle Seahawks. But the Patriots never looked underprepared. Despite a distraction that lasted a week, Belichick had his team ready for Super Bowl XLIX and his second ever meeting with Carroll, the man he replaced in New England, as a head coach.

The Seahawks made big plays, as you would expect a team to do when they've made it to the Super Bowl, but the Patriots were right there almost every step of the way. They knew exactly what they had to do. Belichick's strategy of taking away an opponent's best weapon is often applied to the Patriots' defense in response to an opponent's offense; in the Super Bowl, we learned that it can be the other way around. Edelman, Amendola, and Vereen were a huge part of an offensive gameplan that looked to attack the Seahawks underneath rather than trying to force it deep against talented, physical defensive backs like Richard Sherman, Byron Maxwell, Kam Chancellor, and Earl Thomas. The plan worked perfectly. Brady completed 30 of his 35 pass attempts that were within 10 yards of the line of scrimmage. Vereen, Edelman, and Amendola tallied 25 of Brady's 37 completions for 221 of his 328 yards and two of his four touchdowns.

The defensive gameplan appeared to be just as effective at the start. The Seahawks ran 11 plays and gained 22 yards on their first three drives, which all ended in punts. Twenty of those yards were on six carries by Seahawks running back Marshawn Lynch. But he wasn't done wearing down the Patriots' defense. The two teams traded touchdowns early, and the Patriots took a 14–7 lead with 31 seconds remaining in the first half. Then the Seahawks went 80 yards in five plays, and that was capped off by a tying 11-yard touchdown pass by Russell Wilson.

That swing in momentum set the Seahawks on a 17-point scoring streak to take a 24–14 lead headed into the fourth quarter. The Patriots punted, and the Seahawks had a chance to put the game away, but the defense forced the Seahawks to go three-and-out on a predictable set of clock-killing plays. That stop was important because without it the Seahawks could have put the game away right then.

The stage was set. Belichick was in pursuit of his fourth Super Bowl ring as a head coach in the same building where his team's undefeated season was derailed seven years prior. Wisely, he put the game in the hands of his best player, and Brady delivered. He was 5-of-7 for 59 yards and a touchdown on the ensuing drive, and another three-and-out series by the Seahawks gave the Patriots a chance for a game-winning drive with 6:52 left. Brady completed all nine of his passes for 71 yards and the go-ahead touchdown to Edelman.

But what appeared to be a backdrop for glory turned into a house of horrors, as once again an improbable downfield catch seemed to alter the result in favor of the Patriots' Super Bowl opponent. Butler tipped a long pass by Wilson into the air, but Jermaine Kearse caught it on the rebound for a 33-yard gain that put the Seahawks at the 5-yard line. What happened next was the stuff of Super Bowl legend.

To start, Hightower shed an offensive lineman with one arm and tackled Lynch at the 1-yard line with the other arm. Consider that the shoulder on one of Hightower's arms was broken, and the feat becomes even more immeasurable. Then Butler became a Super Bowl legend when he intercepted a pass from Wilson to Ricardo Lockette on a slant. Were it not for Browner's physical coverage on the outside, Butler would never have made it to the play. Right from the snap, Butler began to run toward the spot where the ball was being thrown. That's because the Patriots had practiced against that play all week, and Butler had seen it time after time.

But in between those two plays, something else took place. The Patriots head coach watched the Seahawks sideline where Carroll and his crew seemed to be scrambling with the seconds ticking off. There was a minute left after Lynch's four-yard run, and the Seahawks still had a timeout left. The Patriots had two timeouts of their own, but as Belichick watched the Seahawks trying to figure out their next move, he decided to keep the pressure on them by keeping the clock moving. Belichick put his goal-line defense on the field, and the Seahawks responded with three wide receivers. To respond, the Patriots substituted Butler onto the field, and the rest was history.

The team had taken a roller-coaster ride through the 2014 calendar year from the build-up and the high of an offseason full of big-ticket acquisitions to a four-week start to the season that left some Patriots fans with a pit in their stomachs, and along for the ride they went. But the journey was over, and this was the time to celebrate the destination. Belichick finally had his fourth Super Bowl ring to tie legendary Steelers head coach Chuck Noll for the most by a head coach in NFL history.

CHAPTER 28

★ ★ ★

Bill Belichick vs. Pete Carroll

Pete Carroll wasn't supposed to be a success in the NFL. His undying positivity, enthusiasm, rah-rah sideline antics, and "Big Balls Pete" coaching style were supposed to be limiting factors that would ultimately be Carroll's undoing. That was in January 2010, when Carroll left USC to take the job with the Seattle Seahawks.

A decade earlier Carroll wasn't supposed to be a success in college. He burned out in the NFL with a Patriots team that lost more and more each year on Carroll's watch. He had spent nearly two decades in the pros—away from college football. He didn't have an eye for talent, as evidenced by the Patriots' draft drought from 1997 to 1999.

But Carroll beat expectations at both turns. In college he regularly hauled in recruiting classes that were among the best in the country, and his teams won at rates that were unmatched during the 2000s. In the pros he pumped positivity and talent into a fledgling Seahawks team until it emerged as a Super Bowl champion in 2013.

Prior to his success with the Seahawks, Carroll was one-and-done in his first NFL head coaching gig with the New York Jets. His team got off to a 6–5 start before dropping its final five games of the year after falling victim to the infamous

Dan Marino "fake spike" play in a Monday night loss to the Miami Dolphins. After two years of coaching the San Francisco 49ers' defense to top 10 finishes in both points and yards, Carroll got an opportunity to follow Bill Parcells as the Patriots head coach.

If one accuses Bill Belichick of gaining early success with the Patriots by virtue of acquiring a talented team and piggybacking off of Parcells, one must concede that it's curious why the team regressed each year under Carroll: from 11–5 before

Bill Belichick poses next to Pete Carroll, the man he replaced as Patriots head coach and would also coach against in Super Bowl XLIX. (AP Images)

★　★　★　★　★　★　★

"[There's] not a coach in the NFL I respect more than Pete Carroll. He's a tremendous coach. He and I have kind of come up together in roughly the same era. We've both been defensive coordinators, we've both been head coaches. I have a ton of respect for what Pete does as a coach, how good of a fundamental teacher he is, the way his teams play. I've studied him from afar—we've never worked together...I've learned a lot from what he does and, indirectly, I think he's made me a better coach. I have all the respect in the world for Pete and his staff."

—Bill Belichick on Pete Carroll

his arrival, to 10–6 in his first year, 9–7 in his second, and 8–8 in his third and final year. Carroll's Patriots started 6–2 in 1999 before dropping six of their last eight games to finish at .500.

When it came to the players he brought in, his three drafts produced exactly three players who made a meaningful impact for the Patriots' Super Bowl wins: running back Kevin Faulk, center Damien Woody, and defensive back Tebucky Jones. When it came to the players he took over, his laid-back approach didn't mesh with the blue-collar, hard-working mentality of the Tedy Bruschis, Ty Laws, and Willie McGinests who had been brought in under Parcells. Those were all players who became essential cornerstones to the Patriots' dynasty from 2001 to 2004, but the Patriots were unable to realize that potential until Belichick came along.

That's not to say that Carroll's style is wrong. It didn't work in that situation, as his style wasn't a fit for what the Patriots needed in the head coaching position at the time. That's why when Belichick brought a hard-working, hard-nosed mentality with him to the Patriots, he was welcomed with open arms.

It took a couple of years before the Seahawks became a contender under Carroll, but it didn't take long for them to start making noise. In Carroll's first year, the Seahawks became the first team to ever win their division with a losing record and followed up that improbable feat with an even more improbable victory against the reigning Super Bowl champion New Orleans Saints in Seattle.

He achieved all of that while making a whopping 284 roster moves during the course of the season. It was like the Patriots' "volume approach" on speed. No position was spared in Carroll's quest for competition. "We're bigger, we're stronger," Carroll said during the 2011 season. "What we tried to do from the outset is to make the depth chart on this roster more competitive from the bottom up—and it feels like that. We have more choices, we have more opportunities where guys can battle and compete for jobs that are going to make everybody feel pushed. That's a great thing."

In the early stages, the roster churn strategy didn't appear to be working. But over time Carroll was finding the nucleus of his team piece by piece. In his first three years, Carroll added 17 out of 22 players who would start in the Seahawks' Super Bowl XLVIII victory: Richard Sherman, Earl Thomas, Kam Chancellor, Byron Maxwell, Walter Thurmond, K.J. Wright, Bobby Wagner, Cliff Avril, Michael Bennett, Marshawn Lynch, Golden Tate, Doug Baldwin, Zach Miller, J.R. Sweezy, James Carpenter, Russell Okung, and Russell Wilson. That's not even including talented players like Bruce Irvin and Brandon Browner, who didn't make the start in the Seahawks' Super Bowl win but who played big roles on that team.

Five of those players were voted to the Pro Bowl in 2013, and three more were voted another year. But Carroll didn't just succeed in acquiring talented players; he built a team with a clear vision. His secondary earned the nickname "The Legion of Boom" (a play on the professional wrestling tag team known as the

Tale of the Tape

Coach	Bill Belichick	Pete Carroll
Years as a head coach	21	10
Career W–L	223–113	93–67
Ratio	.664	.581
Playoff trips	14	7
Playoff W–L	23–10	9–6
Division championships	13	4
Super Bowl wins	4	1

Bill Belichick vs. Pete Carroll, Head To Head

Year	Teams	Score	Winner	Belichick's Record
1994	Browns vs. Jets	27–7	Belichick	1–0
2012	Patriots vs. Seahawks	24–23	Carroll	1–1
2014*	Patriots vs. Seahawks	24–20	Belichick	2–1

*= denotes playoff game

Legion of Doom) for their size and physicality. Sherman, Thomas, Chancellor, Maxwell, Thurmond, and Browner fit the mold of physical, athletic cornerbacks who could disrupt receivers at the line of scrimmage and had the quickness to read and react to a pass in time to break up the play.

But even as the Seahawks acquired all those pieces, Wilson was the one who brought it all together. At 5'11" Wilson is far from the prototype NFL quarterback, but his speed and athleticism, combined with his intelligence, made him a major threat with the ball in his hands.

Belichick and Carroll have been on-again, off-again NFL head coaches since 1990, but, curiously, they've only been head coaches at the same time for seven years: 1994 and 2010–15. In Week 5 of the '94 season, Belichick's Cleveland Browns handed Carroll's Jets their third straight loss of the year in a 27–7 blowout. The two coaches would not cross paths again on the professional field for nearly two full decades, when Carroll's Seahawks pulled off a 24–23 upset against Belichick's Patriots in Week 6 of the 2012 season.

The rubber match was Super Bowl XLIX. The defining on-field moment in that game, no doubt, was Malcolm Butler's game-winning interception. The off-the-field moments that set up that play—with Belichick closely watching Carroll's every move on the Seahawks sideline, electing not to call a timeout while the clock ran closer to the final whistle—are the defining ones.

Who knows what the narrative would have been if they had run it into the jaws of a goal-line defense and failed to score? That would have been the safe choice because Carroll made the unconventional choice to pass. "Worst play-call in Super Bowl history," wrote Mark Maske of *The Washington Post*. "Worst call in

NFL history," wrote Don Banks of *Sports Illustrated*, taking it one step further. "Not just Super Bowl history. NFL history. Bar none." "Second and Dumb," it was dubbed by Alex Marvez of Fox Sports.

The legacies of these two coaches are separated by that one play. Had the Seahawks been successful, Belichick wouldn't have won his fourth ring as a head coach, and his 2003–04 Patriots would not be the most recent team to have won back-to-back Super Bowls. It just goes to show how small the margin of error can be in the NFL and how different things could be on either side of that margin.

CHAPTER 29

★ ★ ★

Bill Belichick
vs. George Halas

Forty years. George Halas was the Bears' head coach for nearly half a century, setting an NFL record (that might never be broken) for longest head coaching career. It could have been even longer had Halas not taken three brief intermissions from football in 1930–32, 1943–45, and 1956–57. But coaching was not the extent of Halas' NFL career. In fact, Halas had his hands in the Bears organization at every level—as a player, a coach, and as the owner.

How many of today's NFL owners do you think could run a team and call plays on the sidelines? How many of them would be willing to suit up in pads and play both offense *and* defense? Halas' role on the team was so big, his legacy so lasting, that the Bears—to this day—still wear his initials on the sleeve of their jerseys. "It's the Halas Bears, really," longtime Bears coach Mike Ditka told ESPN.

As a split end, defensive end, head coach, and owner, Halas led the Bears (then known as the Chicago Staleys) to the NFL championship in 1921—albeit in controversial fashion. At the time there was no finite finish to the season, and Halas took advantage of this by manipulating the schedule and adding games to help his team match the record of the presumptive NFL champions, the Buffalo All-Americans.

Halas' Staleys defeated the All-Americans in a late-season rematch that Buffalo thought was just an exhibition that wouldn't count in the standings. Instead, the Staleys and All-Americans finished with the same record, and Halas convinced the rest of the owners that the rematch mattered more than the first matchup, therefore awarding the NFL championship to Chicago.

And you thought Spygate and Deflategate were scandalous.

But that wasn't the end of Halas' success. Halas retired as both a player and a coach, following the 1929 season but remained a co-owner before gaining full control of the team in 1932. A year later he was back on the sideline as the head coach in a cost-cutting move during the Great Depression.

And immediately, they were back on top of the NFL as the champions. The Bears went on to dominate the next two decades, winning four NFL championships in a 14-year span from 1933 to 1946. That ended the bulk of Halas' success, but the Bears reached the pinnacle of the NFL once again with another championship in 1963.

★ ★ ★

Obviously, "innovation" in football looked a lot different in the 1930s than it does today. Back then, innovation was Halas' T formation, an offensive set that put the quarterback under center—the quarterback had primarily been a blocker, and the snap instead went straight to the running back—and posed the threat of both the run and the pass.

With multiple potential ballcarriers in the backfield, the T formation opened up the possibility of fakes to either running back. Also, with the quarterback under center, the running back could take the handoff at full speed. In the past we've seen Bill Belichick come up with a crazy strategy (think "Baltimore" and "Raven" in the 2014 playoffs) that left the country buzzing. Halas' Bears created a nationwide ripple effect by using the T formation to utterly dominate the Washington Redskins in the 1940 NFL championship. The Bears won by a 73–0 margin that still has never been matched in league history.

It's fitting, then, that Bears fans pay homage to the T formation every time their team scores a touchdown in a home game by singing their fight song "Bear Down," which includes the lyric, "We'll never forget the way you thrilled the nation with your T formation."

Halas didn't birth the T formation, as its roots trace back to Walter Camp at Yale in the 1880s. In fact, the Bears had used the T formation with mixed results in Halas' first run as head coach. But when the Bears rolled it back out in 1940, its effectiveness caught everyone by surprise (as evidenced by the scoreboard in the NFL championship). That's because Halas had the perfect T formation quarterback in Hall of Famer Sid Luckman, and he had been perfecting the scheme as well. Halas was innovative, but his teams also were just plain good. The Bears ranked in the top five in scoring offense in 29 of Halas' 40 years as head coach and they ranked in the top five in scoring 27 of Halas' 40 years.

When the Patriots finished the 2007 regular season with a 16–0 record, only to fail to win the Super Bowl and cap off the undefeated season, it was touted as an historic moment in league history. Certainly, it was. No team had ever gone 18–0 leading up to a Super Bowl, only to lose the final game of the season. But the Patriots were not the first team to go undefeated in the regular season before losing the championship. In 1934 the Chicago Bears were the defending NFL champions and had just finished ransacking the league to a 13–0 finish. Then the NFL championship rolled around, and who's there to knock them off? The New York Giants. What a bunch of party poopers. The Bears were winning big, too, with a 13–3 third-quarter lead before the Giants scored 27 fourth-quarter points to walk away with a 30–13 victory.

Heck, the Patriots' failed attempt at perfection wasn't even the *second* of its kind; the Bears did it again in 1942 when they ran off 11 straight wins to finish

Tale of the Tape

Coach	Bill Belichick	George Halas
Years as a head coach	21	40
Career W–L	223–113	318–148–31
Ratio	.664	.682
Playoff trips	14	8
Playoff W–L	23–10	6–3
Division championships	13	10
NFL championships/Super Bowl wins	4	6

the regular season without a defeat but lost in the NFL championship against Washington. The defeat broke up a run of two straight NFL championships, ending the possibility of the elusive "three-peat."

Those two missed opportunities at perfection could have furthered Halas' legacy to untouchable levels. He would have finished his career with an NFL-record eight total championships, and the 1972 Miami Dolphins wouldn't be the NFL's only undefeated team ever.

Even without two perfect seasons, Halas' legacy is barely touchable. In 40 years as head coach, he only suffered six losing seasons. His six NFL championships are just one shy of Paul Brown's record of seven. Halas' legacy is proof that no amount of failed attempts at perfection will hold a coach back from being considered one of the greatest of all time. That being said, with one more win at the tail end of those two seasons, Halas could have shed the "one of" from that label.

CHAPTER 30

★ ★ ★

2015: Short-Handed

Bill Belichick was no stranger to the perils of success, even though it had been 10 years between Super Bowl victories. For 2015 the biggest challenge would be replacing so many players from their championship roster. The secondary, which had been a major strength the previous year, was suddenly in major flux. Darrelle Revis, Brandon Browner, Kyle Arrington, and Alfonzo Dennard all departed one way or another, paving the way for Malcolm Butler and Logan Ryan to become starters.

Butler earned the No. 1 spot left vacant by Revis and, though his season got off to a rough start, he proved a formidable cover corner in the long term. But that wasn't the only departure the Patriots had to address. Veteran defensive tackle Vince Wilfork was released as a salary cap casualty; his $8.9 million cap hit was simply too much for a 33-year-old nose tackle. Linebackers Jonathan Casillas and Akeem Ayers and running backs Shane Vereen and Stevan Ridley left the fold to sign with new teams as free agents.

Despite losing so many players, Belichick didn't allow himself or his team to fall behind the curve. Their most important signing was defensive end Jabaal Sheard, who had been a draft target of the Patriots when he entered the NFL four years prior. Now a free agent, Sheard had proven his ability to transition to the pros and to play in both a 3-4 and a 4-3 front. And the Patriots didn't even need him for starter-level production with Chandler Jones and Rob Ninkovich still on the roster.

Patriots 2015 Draft Picks

Round	Pick	Player	Position	Games played w/ Patriots
1	32	Malcom Brown	DT	16*
2	64	Jordan Richards	SS	14*
3	97	Geneo Grissom	DL	15*
4	101	Trey Flowers	DE	1*
4	111	Tre' Jackson	OG	13*
4	131	Shaq Mason	C	14*
5	166	Joe Cardona	LS	16*
6	178	Matthew Wells	LB	0
6	202	A.J. Derby	TE	0*
7	247	Darryl Roberts	CB	0*
7	253	Xzavier Dickson	DE	0

*=still with Patriots

The Patriots took the volume approach at cornerback with free-agent signees Tarell Brown, Robert McClain, and Chimdi Chekwa, along with rookies Jimmy Jean, Darryl Roberts, and Justin Coleman. At the very least, the Patriots were set to have a massive competition at cornerback to determine who would be the starters in hopes that some talented players would emerge from the pack. With all the attention square on the secondary, the Patriots' needs on the offensive line fell out of focus. The Patriots had a need at guard, thanks to the trade of Logan Mankins the year prior, coupled with the retirement of Dan Connolly and an injury for Ryan Wendell that kept the veteran out of offseason practice. Tre' Jackson and Shaq Mason went to the Patriots in the fourth round of the draft, and the two rookies were asked to fill the void of two veterans. One of these positions would be a lingering problem all year long. The other would prove to be a surprising strength.

★ ★ ★

With all the changes in the secondary, at running back, and on the offensive line, it was easy to forget about the one place where the Patriots had consistency: the passing game. The Patriots had come a long way from 2013, when they turned over a vast majority of the receiving corps. In 2015 Rob Gronkowski had the first fully healthy offseason of his career since 2011, and Brandon LaFell, Julian Edelman, and Danny Amendola all stuck around for another year of building rapport with Tom Brady. The positive effects of continuity did not take long to reveal themselves, as the chemistry picked up right where it left off—almost. LaFell missed the first six games of the season with a foot injury, but between Edelman, Amendola, and Gronkowski, Brady had enough firepower at his disposal. Add in the emergence of running back Dion Lewis, and the Patriots offense was humming. Belichick plugged Lewis into that familiar third-down role, the latest clone in a line of similar backs from Kevin Faulk to Danny Woodhead to Vereen, and now to Lewis.

The Patriots had problems on the offensive line right from the start, but they also had a solution: a quick passing attack designed to get the ball out of Brady's hands before a pass rush ever had a chance to get past the offensive line. Fueled by an initial Deflategate suspension, a supremely motivated Brady had an excellent year. He averaged 2.21 seconds in the pocket and 2.13 seconds to attempt a pass in the first 10 weeks of the 2015 regular season. Those were the quickest such times of any quarterback in the NFL through 10 weeks. With slot receivers like Edelman and Amendola to get open quickly and with Lewis leaking out of the backfield, Brady was able to find plenty of options in the short passing game to get the ball out of his hands fast. That rhythm helped Brady rack up 72.5 percent completions, 1,387 yards, 11 touchdowns, and no interceptions in the first four games of the year.

The Patriots rolled through their first four games with wins by scores of 28–21 against the Pittsburgh Steelers, 40–32 against the Buffalo Bills, 51–17 against the Jacksonville Jaguars, and 30–6 against the Dallas Cowboys. The offense scored an average of 37.3 points per game in that time, which had some people flashing back to 2007. But unlike the undefeated season, the Patriots' unrivaled dominance would not last.

In the long run, the Patriots 2015 season was undone by injuries. Looking back, the Patriots roster was a sweater, the injuries were a loose thread, and each injury pulled little by little until eventually the whole thing came unraveled. The injuries began before the 2015 season even started, when fullback James Develin landed on injured reserve in the preseason. LaFell began the season on the physically unable to perform list, and center Bryan Stork began the season on the short-term injured reserve. Both LaFell and Stork would come back, but the Patriots had to start without them. Then, in Week 4 against the Cowboys, left tackle Nate Solder suffered a torn left bicep that ended his 2015 season. The injury forced right tackle Sebastian Vollmer to play on the left and forced backup Marcus Cannon into the starting lineup.

Despite the myriad injuries, the Patriots continued their winning ways with a 34–27 victory against the Indianapolis Colts in a Deflategate rematch, but this was their first taste of adversity on the season. The Colts held a four-point lead in the first half and took a one-point lead into the locker room. The adversity continued the next week against the New York Jets, when the Patriots faced a four-point fourth-quarter deficit before Brady led two touchdown drives against new Jets head coach Todd Bowles' defense to help clinch a 30–23 win.

LaFell made his return in Week 7, but it was far from triumphant as the receiver dropped three passes in his first outing. But just in time for LaFell's return, more injuries cropped up. That's when backup tackle Marcus Cannon went down with a toe injury, which forced backup Cameron Fleming into a starting spot. Despite the injuries, the Patriots beat the Miami Dolphins 36–7 and lost rookie guard Tre' Jackson to a knee injury. Their depth at offensive tackle took yet another hit when Vollmer suffered a concussion that left the Patriots with Cameron Fleming and former starting center Stork as their two starting offensive tackles.

For those of you keeping score at home, that's three injured tackles, which means the Patriots were on their fourth and fifth options at the position. But the Patriots could deal with all those injuries; it was in Week 10 that the Patriots suffered a near-fatal blow. The timing and quick pace of the passing game had been the saving grace for the Patriots offense through their strife on the offensive line, but when Julian Edelmen suffered a foot injury against the New York Giants, the Patriots finally hit their threshold. They escaped New York with a 27–26 win and their undefeated season intact, but the aforementioned "sweater" that had been unraveling? It now looked more like a halter top.

Thankfully for the Patriots, by this time players began making their return to the lineup. Cannon returned in Week 11 against the Buffalo Bills, but another week brought another injury, as Amendola went down with a knee injury while working in an expanded role in Edelman's absence. Again, the Patriots escaped with a 20–13 win against the Bills, but more bad injury luck brought the Patriots their first loss of the season.

The Patriots headed into a Week 12 matchup with the Denver Broncos without Edelman, Amendola, and several others. And during the course of the game, they lost two of the most important players on the roster: Gronkowski and linebacker Dont'a Hightower. Losing Gronkowski raided the Patriots of their best offensive weapon and losing Hightower removed their best run-stopping linebacker.

So it wasn't a huge surprise when the Patriots' offense went into the tank against the Broncos and when the defense became a sieve against the run. Scott Chandler subbed in for Gronkowski and finished the game with five catches on 11 targets for 58 yards and a touchdown. Jonathan Freeny was Hightower's replacement, but the Patriots' run defense took a huge hit, and the Broncos ran the ball down the Patriots' throats 32 times for 179 yards and three touchdowns. The 30–24 loss was the first hiccup in the Patriots' 2015 season and it was quickly followed by the second hiccup.

The very next week, the Philadelphia Eagles laid a 35–28 beating on the Patriots—and yes, a seven-point loss doesn't look much like a beatdown, but that's because it started out as a 14-point Patriots lead in the first half and turned into a 21-point deficit in the space of roughly 30 minutes of football. The Eagles' 35-point scoring flurry began with a poorly timed dropkick, which gave the Eagles a short field for a touchdown. It included a blocked punt returned for a touchdown, a punt returned for a touchdown, an interception returned for a touchdown, and ended with a 12-play, 80-yard touchdown drive.

It was just the 10th losing streak of Belichick's Patriots career, but it wouldn't even be the last time that year. The only good news out of that game was the return of Jamie Collins—after a four-week absence with an undisclosed illness—and that Gronkowski would make his return to the lineup against the Houston Texans.

Belichick had his first meeting with former Patriots offensive coordinator Bill O'Brien, who had taken a job with the Texans two years after joining Penn State as the successor to Joe Paterno. It was a reunion of massive proportions with former and current Patriots matched up against one another. Bill O'Brien, Vince Wilfork, quarterback Brian Hoyer, and former Patriots defensive coordinator

Romeo Crennel were all former Patriots who were now part of the Texans organization. All that familiarity didn't help the Texans, as the Patriots picked up a 27–6 win while picking up yet another loss at running back. LeGarrette Blount went down for the season, leaving the Patriots with only the inexperienced James White and special teams ace Brandon Bolden in their backfield.

White proved to be an explosive play-maker in the passing game, but neither White nor Bolden gave the Patriots a consistent threat on the ground. Despite their lack of a talented pure runner, the Patriots followed up their win against the Texans with a 33–16 win against the Tennessee Titans, in which Brady was once again the life force of the offense, completing 23-of-35 passes for 267 yards and two touchdowns.

The Patriots strung those two wins together before hitting one last snag on their way toward the playoffs: two more losses to close out the season. With no running game to speak of, Belichick began looking in the scrap heap for anyone with two legs who could run the ball and happened upon veteran Steven Jackson, an unsigned free agent and former Pro Bowler who had been out of the league for the entire year up to that point. The Patriots were in a dire situation at running back, though, and needed a warm body. Jackson didn't offer much of an immediate return on investment against a stout Jets defensive front seven (seven carries for 15 yards), and his contributions never amounted to much for the Patriots, but his signing is a shining example of the crippling toll the injuries took on the team.

The Jets had already come close to beating the Patriots earlier in the season, so it wasn't a huge shock when they gave New England a tight game the second time around. Bowles learned his lesson from the first meeting and opted not to blitz Brady. The first time around, the Jets sent extra pressure at Brady on 28 of his 60 dropbacks. In the rematch the Jets only went after Brady with a blitz on eight out of 33 dropbacks.

They didn't need to. Brady didn't have his security outlets on short passes in Edelman and Amendola, so the pressure could take its time getting home. The offense took another blow when Vollmer injured his leg, forcing backup LaAdrian Waddle into the starting lineup. Despite just eight blitzes, the Jets got pressure 16 times (nearly 50 percent), and Brady finished 22-of-31 passing for 231 yards, one touchdown, and one interception.

But more than any of that, this game was notorious for a Belichick coaching decision that turned into a blunder. The Patriots won the coin toss and elected to kick instead of receive on the opening overtime kickoff, allowing the Jets to have the first crack on offense. That decision meant that if the Jets scored a touchdown, the game was over. Five plays, 80 yards, and 2:37 later, exactly that happened. Eric Decker caught the game-winning touchdown over Butler.

The Patriots made another curious coaching decision with their gameplan the next week against the Dolphins. At 12–3 the Patriots still had a chance to clinch the AFC's No. 1 seed; all they needed was a win. Instead, their gameplan consisted of a run-heavy approach aimed at running the clock out and retaining what little health remained on the roster. There were 21 rush attempts against five pass attempts in the first half, though the Patriots finished the game with 27 rush attempts and 25 pass attempts after they fell behind by a touchdown headed into the locker room.

On one hand the decision made sense based on the Dolphins' inability to stop the run (fifth worst run defense in 2015). On the other hand, even with the Patriots limping into the playoffs, they needed the win in this game to get the No. 1 seed. It was too important of a game to put in the hands of Jackson and Bolden over Brady. But that's what they did, and Belichick closed out the season with back-to-back losses, marking the first time in Belichick's Patriots career that his team failed to win at least one of its last two games and the 11th overall losing streak of his Patriots career.

★ ★ ★

When the Kansas City Chiefs dominated the Texans 30–0 in the opening round of the playoffs, it felt like a warning shot to their next opponent, which happened to be the Patriots. Of course, people immediately began to wonder if the Patriots would suffer the same fate to the Chiefs that they had suffered in 2014 on *Monday Night Football*. And the way the Patriots had played in the final six games of the season, the Patriots looked like a vulnerable team.

That just so happens to line up with Julian Edelman's injury. Before that, Brady had an outlet to get rid of the ball to if the pressure was closing in. The Patriots dealt with injury after injury, thanks in large part to the quick passing attack. When Edelman was injured, though, it exposed the other fatal flaws with the team—namely, the lack of a running game and the porous pass protection.

As mentioned earlier, in the first nine games (with Edelman on the field), Brady spent an average of 2.21 seconds in the pocket, the shortest in the NFL. In the final seven games, that average jumped to 2.55 seconds, still among the quickest, but knocked down to seventh in the league.

So, with Edelman set to return just in the nick of time, there was a lot of pressure on him to help elevate the offense to its original state and to return the quick element to the passing game. He and Brady delivered. Edelman had 10 receptions

Bill Belichick embraces Denver Broncos quarterback Peyton Manning, following the AFC Championship Game in 2016. That game represented the 20ᵗʰ and final time Manning would face one of Belichick's teams; Belichick won 12 of them.
(USA TODAY Sports Images)

for 100 yards. It was as if Edelman had been there all along. Brady looked comfortable in the pocket, going 28-of-42 passing for 302 yards and two touchdowns, while facing pressure on just seven out of his 43 dropbacks and delivering the ball in an average of 2.19 seconds.

Still, the Patriots had no semblance of a running game and finished with 14 carries for 38 yards and a touchdown on a Brady sneak. And the competition was about to get a lot tougher and a lot more familiar as well.

For the first time in his career, an aging and injured Peyton Manning played poorly on a week-in, week-out basis. He completed less than 60 percent of his passes and had nine touchdowns and 17 interceptions before an injury forced him out of the lineup and made way for Brock Osweiler, just in time for the Broncos' regular-season encounter with the Patriots. In the final game of the season, though, Osweiler's play took a turn for the worse, and Manning was given another chance to lead the team into the postseason.

So, it was Brady-Manning XVII (Brady was up 11–5) and Belichick-Manning XX (Belichick was up 12–7), but of all those games, this might be the game where Manning's performance meant the least. He completed 17 of his 32 passes (53.1 percent) for 176 yards (5.5 yards per attempt) and two touchdowns. Thanks to the presence of Hightower, the Patriots did a much better job of keeping the Broncos' running game in check this time around with just 30 rushes for 99 yards (3.3 yards per carry).

It was one of the Patriots' best defensive performances of the year. It was also one of their worst offensive performances of the year. The Broncos' No. 1-ranked defense held the Patriots in check. Brady completed just 27-of-56 passes (48.2 percent) for 310 yards (5.5 yards per pass), one touchdown, and two interceptions. Even with such a high concentration of passes, it still felt like the Patriots tried too hard to run the ball. That's because they only gained 44 yards on the ground (2.6 yards per carry) and one touchdown on their 17 carries. The Broncos did a good job on Edelman, holding the shifty receiver to seven catches for 53 yards.

Yet, despite all of that, the Patriots might have won were it not for a few key plays in the game. The first was a missed point-after by Stephen Gostkowski and the first since his rookie year. The bigger problem was a pair of empty possessions in the fourth quarter, when Belichick decided to go for a fourth-down conversion instead of kicking an easy field goal, and even bigger than that was the failed two-point conversion with 12 seconds left in the game that could have sent it to overtime.

It is probably of no consolation to Belichick, but the 2015 Patriots were better than anyone could have expected given the severity and number of injuries on their roster. If the Patriots had somehow won Super Bowl L against the Carolina Panthers, the 2015 season might have represented the finest coaching performance of Belichick's career.

CHAPTER 31

★ ★ ★

Bill Belichick vs. Paul Brown

Pick a current NFL head coach. You have 32 choices. Once you've chosen one, write his name down. There's a better than 50 percent chance that the coach's name you just wrote down is a descendent from some branch of the Paul Brown coaching tree. And if you happened to write down the name of the subject of this book, there's a 100 percent chance he's connected to Brown's coaching tree.

There are currently 21 active head coaches who are connected with Brown in some way. Granted, in some cases we're talking about coaches who are a part of a tree that sprouted out of Brown's coaching tree, but the connection can still be made. It's like the NFL coaching version of Six Degrees of Separation.

Take Jeff Fisher, for example. The St. Louis Rams head coach was the Philadelphia Eagles defensive coordinator under Buddy Ryan from 1989 to 1990. Ryan was a defensive line coach for the New York Jets from 1968 to 1975, where Charley Winner was head coach from 1974 to 1975, where Winner had joined Weeb Ewbank's staff with the New York Jets and became Ewbank's successor. Ewbank was an assistant under Brown with the Cleveland Browns from 1949 to 1953.

If you thought that was hard to follow, it gets even more complicated with the current Patriots head coach. Bill Belichick was a defensive assistant and an assistant special teams coach under Red Miller with the Denver Broncos in 1978. Miller was the offensive line coach for the St. Louis Cardinals from 1966 to 1970, when Winner was the head coach. Wrap it up with the Winner-Ewbank and Ewbank-Brown connections, and you find that Belichick's entire coaching tree is technically just one sprout off of Paul Brown's coaching tree.

If you go back through history, you'll also find many of the coaches listed in this book were descendants of the Brown coaching tree. Take Bill Walsh, for example. Walsh has his own lengthy, winding tree from his time as the Cincinnati Bengals offensive coordinator and the San Francisco 49ers head coach. It's a tree that includes former Green Bay Packers head coach Mike Holmgren, former Baltimore Ravens head coach Brian Billick, and current Seattle Seahawks head coach Pete Carroll and Cleveland Browns head coach Hue Jackson. Other former head coaches, from Don Shula to Chuck Noll to Tony Dungy to Tom Coughlin, are also a part of the tree.

But as indicated in the earlier chapter about Walsh, Brown's impact spreads further than just the names on his tree. It also goes to the ideas and philosophies he helped popularize, many of which are still felt today. And Walsh's story presents a great illustration of trust, one of the elements that makes a great coach. If Brown had never given Walsh the freedom to tinker the offense as he saw fit, his Bengals likely would not have enjoyed their run of wild

Active Coaches Associated with Brown's Coaching Tree

Head Coach	Current Team
Bruce Arians	Arizona Cardinals
Bill Belichick	New England Patriots
Jim Caldwell	Detroit Lions
Pete Carroll	Seattle Seahawks
Jack Del Rio	Oakland Raiders
Jeff Fisher	St. Louis Rams
John Fox	Chicago Bears
John Harbaugh	Baltimore Ravens
Hue Jackson	Cleveland Browns
Chip Kelly	San Francisco 49ers
Gary Kubiak	Denver Broncos
Mike McCarthy	Green Bay Packers
Mike McCoy	San Diego Chargers
Mike Mularkey	Tennessee Titans
Bill O'Brien	Houston Texans
Chuck Pagano	Indianapolis Colts
Sean Payton	New Orleans Saints
Andy Reid	Kansas City Chiefs
Ron Rivera	Carolina Panthers
Rex Ryan	Buffalo Bills
Mike Tomlin	Pittsburgh Steelers

success, and we might not have one of the most central offensive philosophies of modern football. That, in turn, would have dried up a large stem of that coaching tree. It's difficult to imagine what modern coaching and football would look like without Brown's heavy influence.

If Brown's legacy were just the sum of the legacy of the coaches he's touched and influenced, it would be mighty impressive. As it stands, however, he already has his own formidable legacy with more league championships than any other coach in history. He has won seven championships—four in the All-America Football Conference in the Browns' first four years of existence from 1946 to 1949. He won three more NFL championships following the AAFC's merger with the NFL in 1950.

Brown's early success was in a weak league/conference, but that success carried over to the NFL when the Browns were up against more formidable competition. They ranked first or second on offense and defense from 1946 to 1949 and continued that streak on defense from 1950 to 1957. Most importantly, the Browns won every single playoff game they participated in for the first five years of Brown's head coaching career. And how did they respond when they lost three straight NFL championships from 1951 to 1953? By winning two more in 1954–55.

The first decade of Brown's illustrious career was filled with success and accounted for all seven of his NFL championships. He didn't recapture that glory in his last seven years with the Browns from 1956 to 1962 or in his eight-year stint with the Cincinnati Bengals from 1968 to 1975, but through it all, he proved he could coach any team to success.

When the Browns had Jim Brown and a dominant running game, Paul Brown made the ground attack the center of his offense, and the Browns ranked in the top 10 in rushing each of Brown's first 10 years as head coach. When he had Walsh drawing up a brilliant offensive gameplan and quarterback Ken Anderson slinging the ball all over the yard, Brown dialed up the passing game significantly. Those Bengals teams were among the top 10 passing offenses in the league in five of Brown's eight years as coach.

It's hard to imagine any coach having a bigger impact than Brown, but Belichick might make it close. If Belichick wins three more Super Bowls, there would still be those who would not put him past Brown in the pantheon of the

Tale of the Tape

Coach	Bill Belichick	Paul Brown
Years as a head coach	21	25
Career W–L	223–113	213–104–9
Ratio	.664	.672
Playoff trips	14	15
Playoff W–L	23–10	9–8
Division championships	13	14
NFL/AAFC championships/Super Bowl wins	4	7

greatest head coaches of all time, simply for the influence Brown had on the game as a whole.

Of course, in a few decades, we could be looking back at some aspects of Belichick's career as turning points in the way people think about the strategies of the game of football. We're already seeing his scheme-versatile approach taking hold across the NFL.

But Belichick has influenced coaching in other ways, too. His approach to free agency and the draft has changed the way personnel evaluators think about building a team. In the current age of parity in the NFL, Belichick's impact could be felt in a different manner but on a similar level to Brown's.

CHAPTER 32

★ ★ ★

Spygate and Deflategate

If you played word association with Bill Belichick's name in New England, your responses would mostly go something like this: greatness, success, dynasty, and a litany of other words that connote Belichick's winning history. If you played that same game with that same name anywhere else in the country, your responses would be much different: cheater, Spygate, Deflategate, and other words to connote the ignominy from the other 31 fanbases across the NFL.

In the eyes of the latter group, the accusations represent sound reasoning to discredit Belichick's entire career. Their question is whether the Patriots would have been a dynasty without the videotaping or whether they would have made it to Super Bowl XLIX with properly inflated footballs. In the former group, the accusations that surround the Patriots in these scandals are seen as sour grapes from bitter rivals and less accomplished teams. Their question lies with whether those scandals had any impact on the outcome of games, and in some cases, whether it's even valid to call them scandals.

Most of Belichick's most ardent detractors either don't know or fail to acknowledge two very important details when discussing Spygate. The first detail: the problem wasn't *that* the Patriots filmed their opponent's signals—there never was and there still is not a rule against it. The problem was *the location from which* they filmed the signals. Teams were allowed to film signals from the press box but not from the field. At times, a team could not see the opposing coaches from the press box, so it was at these times that the team would send someone onto the field.

The second detail: the punishment wasn't based on the rule, but on a memo sent out by the league. Article 9.1 (C) (14) of the Constitution and Bylaws of the NFL reads: "Any use by any club at any time, from the start to the finish of any game in which such club is a participant, of any communications or information-gathering equipment, other than Polaroid-type cameras or field telephones, shall be prohibited, including without limitation, videotape machines, telephone tapping, or bugging devices, or any other form of electronic devices that might aid a team during the playing of a game."

However, then-NFL head of football operations Ray Anderson sent out a memo to all 32 teams that read as follows: "Videotaping of any type, including but not limited to taping of an opponent's offensive or defensive signals, is pro-hibited on the sidelines, in the coaches' booth, in the locker room, or at any other locations accessible to club staff members during the game."

The memo mentions signals, but the rule does not. The memo mentions video-taping from locations that are accessible to club staff members; the rule does not. It might be more apropos to call it "Memogate," or "SidelineNotPressBoxgate." But the story of Memogate/SidelineNotPressBoxgate/Spygate didn't end after Week 1 of the 2007 season.

The Patriots image was tarnished further by what turned out to be a false report the day before Super Bowl XLII, claiming that an assistant by the name of Matt Walsh had filmed the St. Louis Rams' walkthrough in advance of Super Bowl XXXVI against the St. Louis Rams. The report was proven inaccurate, and *The Boston Herald* issued a retraction, but to this day, the false story is perpetuated by media and fans who are unaware, willfully or otherwise, that the report was retracted.

How much of an advantage did the Patriots gain from filming their oppo-nents' hand signals? There's no way to quantify it, but it's safe to say that *some* benefit was drawn. Otherwise, why carry it out?

It's also worth noting that other teams might have been videotaping signals, too. "I think all teams do that. That's been going on forever," former Dallas Cowboys coach Jimmy Johnson said. "This is exactly how I was told to do it 18 years ago by a Kansas City Chiefs scout. I tried it, but I didn't think it helped us. Bill Belichick was wrong because he videotaped signals after a memo was sent out to all teams saying not to do it. But what irritates me is hearing some reactions from players and coaches. These players don't know what their coaches are doing, and some of the coaches have selective amnesia because I know for a fact there were various teams doing this. That's why the memo was sent to everybody. That doesn't make Belichick right, but a lot of teams are doing this."

★ ★ ★

Deflategate could not have happened at a worse time. Not only were the Patriots in the throes of preparing for a sixth appearance in the Super Bowl, but they were also looking for their first Super Bowl win since Spygate. The Patriots' lack of Super Bowl hardware was good enough for anyone looking for evidence that Belichick's legacy was built on a bed of lies and cheats.

And now the Patriots were chasing that fourth Super Bowl trophy while running from the shadow of another scandal. The Patriots were being investigated for using footballs that were outside of the league-mandated range of 12.5 to 13.5 pounds per square inch (psi) during the 2014 AFC Championship Game against the Indianapolis Colts. This time it wasn't a misinterpretation of a rule that led to an unnecessary tidal wave of controversy around the Patriots. Instead, it seems they were ignoring the laws of chemistry.

The NFL hired an attorney named Ted Wells to investigate. The league had hired Wells in the past, most notably to investigate the Miami Dolphins' 2013 locker room bullying incidents involving Jonathan Martin and Richie Incognito. The Wells Report tells one story: that it was "more probable than not" that Tom Brady was "generally aware" that two equipment staffers, John Jastremski and Jim McNally, intentionally released air from the footballs after their inspection by officials and before they had been brought to the field prior to the AFC Championship Game. It said that Brady knew about this based on the context of text messages sent between the two staffers and some sent between Jastremski and Brady after the story became national news.

According to *The New York Times*, an examination of science could lead to another narrative: the temperature and rain-soaked conditions on the field provided the perfect conditions for natural football deflation. The Ideal Gas Law says that the product of pressure inside the ball and the volume of the ball is proportional to the amount of air and other gases inside the ball multiplied by the temperature. All of those different factors are at play when determining the exact inflation level of the ball.

The Wells Report acknowledges the Ideal Gas Law through the research of an independent science firm Exponent (a firm that has also developed research denying the impact of second-hand smoke in causing cancer and has also developed a reputation as a "hired gun" in conducting scientific experiments with desired outcomes).

Never mind all the details about whether McNally walked directly past a group of gameday officials while carrying the footballs they were supposed to be supervising. Never mind details of whether Walt Anderson should be believed for his claim that he used a logo gauge to measure footballs before the game to his best recollection. (The logo gauge has a Wilson logo and a long, crooked needle and reads higher PSI; the other has no logo and a short, straight needle and can read lower PSI readings than its logo-bearing counterpart.) It's an easy distinction to make given that logo gauges are twice as long as their non-logo counterparts.

In some cases, those details break in favor of the Patriots, but they are not part and parcel to the argument. "The mere fact that Wells needed such detail and nuance to reach a conclusion shows that the results of the air pressure testing and analysis should have been deemed inconclusive for proof of cheating. Instead, Wells and Exponent massaged and tinkered and assumed and disregarded the best recollection of referee Walt Anderson just enough to find that the Patriots cheated," Mike Florio of ProFootballTalk wrote.

Is it possible that McNally was able to deflate 12 footballs in 100 seconds while he made a trip to the bathroom? Yes, though one would imagine that process to be highly inexact in an incredibly short window. Is it possible that the footballs became underinflated due to the conditions in New England on a cold January night? It *is* called the Ideal Gas Law, not the Ideal Gas Theory.

So, it makes sense that nearly each of the Patriots' 12 footballs were found to be underinflated when checked at halftime. According to ProFootballTalk, each of the Patriots' balls were checked twice and then each re-inflated to 12.5 psi before the Colts' balls were measured. And even then, three of the four Colts balls that were measured—that's all they had time to measure at halftime—were found to be inflated below 12.5 psi.

Belichick's legacy likely will be tainted in the eyes of his biggest detractors by the *perception* of Spygate and Deflategate, not the reality of Spygate and Deflategate. Once you cut through all the fat, you find that there's not much meat left. Putting aside team biases, any feelings on Spygate should be determined by whether you feel the league has a right to punish teams based on memos, not written rules that need to be voted on by all 32 teams.

CHAPTER 33

★ ★ ★

Bill Belichick and Tom Brady: The Definition of Synergy

Tom Brady wasn't supposed to be the starting quarterback of the New England Patriots.

That job was supposed to be occupied by Drew Bledsoe, presumably until the year 2011. The 6'5", 238-pound quarterback signed a record setting 10-year, $103 million contract on March 8, 2001.

Brady, on the other hand, was a beanpole at 6'4" and 211 pounds. The 199th overall pick of the 2001 draft, selected less than two months after Bledsoe's mega-contract, he waited until the sixth round to hear his name called, which means just about every other team had as many as five opportunities to take him. Usually, when you're taken that late in the draft, you're a long shot to even make the roster—much less to start at your position in the span of a little over a year.

But even before September 23, 2001, when Bledsoe headed to the locker room and Brady took the field, there was a changing of the tide taking place at quarterback. Brady was (and still is) Bill Belichick's style of quarterback. He's extremely cerebral, detailed, and prepared. Of course, Belichick had no way of knowing that Brady would become one of the best quarterbacks of all time, but all Belichick wanted was a quarterback to fit his offense, and Brady was exactly the kind of quarterback Belichick needed to carry out his versatile, interchangeable gameplan that can attack offenses' weaknesses each week.

Maybe that's why Belichick made the unusual call to keep four quarterbacks on his roster in 2001. Even with a below-average skillset in some areas, Brady had the work ethic and the mind-set to become the ideal Patriots quarterback with time. Not only did Brady become the ideal Patriots quarterback, but he and Belichick grew together to the point where they have now become inseparable.

The Belichick-Brady relationship is mutually beneficial. One without the other is like peanut butter without jelly—or jelly without peanut butter. Good on its own, much better when paired with the other. "There's no quarterback I'd rather have than Tom Brady," Belichick said after the team's 23–20 nail-biter win against the Baltimore Ravens in the 2011 AFC Championship Game. "He's the best. He does so much for us in so many ways, on so many different levels. I'm really fortunate that he's our quarterback and for what he's able to do for this team. It's good to win with him and all the rest of our players."

In that game against the Ravens, Brady was a paltry 22-of-36 for 239 yards and two interceptions. But those comments weren't about what Brady meant to the team in that game; they were about what Brady has meant to Belichick throughout his career. Without Brady, Belichick wouldn't have had a quarterback who could run the several different variations of the Patriots offense. Without Belichick, Brady wouldn't have had a coach who could so capably shift his offense from season to season—and even from week to week—based on the best players available on the roster.

Take the '06 and '07 teams, for example. One year, they were a run-first offense where Brady and a lackluster set of pass catchers were taking a backseat as the Patriots tried to manage games. The next year, Brady and the receivers were flying high and setting records as the Patriots chose to dictate the tempo by piling on the points. Brady was not only versatile enough to execute these two styles of offense, which could only be described as polar opposites, but Belichick was also savvy enough to know how to tailor the offense to his players through scheme, concepts, and play calls.

The juxtaposition between '06 and '07 serves as the best illustration of how this relationship worked and why it worked. It works because Brady covers a lot of the Patriots' deficiencies. He can take a cast of average receivers and make them look good, a cast of good receivers and make them great, and a cast of great receivers and make them the best offense in NFL history. Belichick, on the other hand, can take any skill level of players and build an offense that works.

But it runs deeper than that. The defense, rightly so, gets a lot of credit for the Patriots' success from 2001 to 2004. The offense is credited for much of the

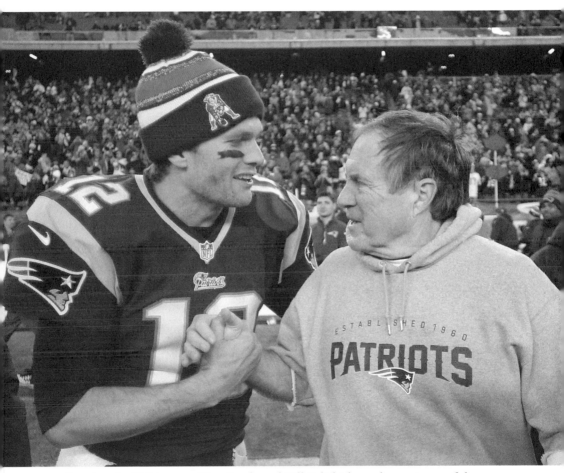

Entering the 2016 season, Tom Brady and Bill Belichick are the most successful quarterback/head coach combination in NFL history with 172 regular-season and 22 postseason wins. (USA TODAY Sports Images)

team's success from 2007 to 2013. All the while, the Patriots offense kept evolving from a controlled passing attack and a run-first approach, to a more explosive downfield threat, back to a more run-heavy approach and reeled-in passing game, to a record-setting vertical passing attack, to a two-tight end offense, to a spread offense with no downfield threat at wide receiver. Brady and 10 other players on offense have executed it all, and Belichick and his staff have drawn it all up.

Neither one has been dramatically more responsible for the team's success than the other. You could argue that from 2001 to 2004 Belichick and the defense had more of the spotlight, while Brady took a majority of the spotlight in 2007, 2010, and some of the other years of record-setting offensive fireworks shows. Even in those years, though, Belichick was adjusting in other areas to ensure the Patriots kept winning. Each man is a major reason why the other is one of the all-time greats.

Belichick's accomplishments are also Brady's; Brady's are also Belichick's. Together, they are one of a kind. Dan Marino and Don Shula, Joe Montana and Bill Walsh, Troy Aikman and Jimmy Johnson, and Vince Lombardi and Bart Starr are quarterback/head coach combinations that accomplished great things in the NFL, but the accomplishments of these dynamic quarterback/head coach duos don't approach the accomplishments of Belichick and Brady.

They are the winningest combination in NFL history with 172 regular-season wins and 22 postseason wins. They are the only duo to win three Super Bowls in a four-year span, advance to six Super Bowls, reach 10 championship games, and one of only two combinations to win four Super Bowls (along with Chuck Noll and Terry Bradshaw with the Pittsburgh Steelers). They're also the only ones that boast a 16–0 regular season and a 21-game consecutive win streak.

They've done it all while enduring constant changes within the organization, both on the field and on the sidelines. From Randy Moss to Rob Gronkowski, from Kevin Faulk to Danny Woodhead to Shane Vereen, it's never a question of whether the Patriots offense will be successful—just how. And it's because of Brady and Belichick together.

APPENDIX

★ ★ ★

Bill Belichick by the Numbers

(Stats recorded through Super Bowl 50)

Career numbers
Regular-season win-loss: 223–113 (.664)
Postseason win-loss: 23–10 (.697)
Overall win-loss: 246–123 (.666)
Challenges won: 41
Super Bowl championships: 4
Conference championships: 6
Division championships: 13

Seasons leading NFL
Offense, scoring: 3
Offense, yards: 2
Offense, turnovers: 5
Offense, pass yards: 1
Defense, scoring: 2
Point differential: 5
Yardage differential: 1
Turnover differential: 2

Single-season bests
Offense, scoring: 589 (2007)
Offense, yards: 6,848 (2011)
Offense, turnovers: 10 (2010)
Offense, pass yards: 5,084 (2011)
Offense, rush yards: 2,278 (2008)
Defense, scoring: 237 (2006)
Defense, yards: 4,613 (2007)
Defense, turnovers: 41 (2012, 2003)
Defense, pass yards: 3,041 (2007)
Defense, rush yards: 1,434 (2003)
Point differential: 315 (2007)
Yardage differential: 1,967 (2007)
Turnover differential: 28 (2010)

Significant NFL records
Most consecutive wins: 21 (2003–04)
Most consecutive regular-season home games won: 31 (2006–11)
Most consecutive postseason wins: 10 (2001–05)
Single-season point differential: 315 (2007)
Most career conference championship appearances: 10
Most career playoff wins: 23

Ranking on all-time leaderboard
Wins: Fifth, 223
Win percentage: 13th, .664
Games above .500: Third, 110
Years in the playoffs: Fourth, 14
Playoff games: Third, 33
Playoff wins: First, 23
Playoff win percentage: 11th, .697
Super Bowl wins: First, 4 (tied with Chuck Noll)
Conference championship victories: First, 6 (tied with Don Shula)

★ ★ ★
Acknowledgments

One of the reasons I took on this assignment was to write an acknowledgments section. I've always wanted the perfect forum to thank every person who ever helped me become who I am today. Now, as I sit down to write it, my biggest fear is realized: there are too many people to thank.

I'll start with my mom and dad, married 37 years as I type this, and my sister. Mom for teaching me compassion and understanding; Dad for teaching me football and how to be an adult; my sister for being my confidante, for always giving me something to laugh about, and for never quite letting me be the most sports-obsessed person in our family. You've all three been an amazing support system.

I want to thank Mike Reiss, without whom this opportunity would probably have never come my way. Mike, you had a huge impact on me in my early years as a sportswriter and you continue to have an impact on me today. When I heard you had recommended me for this book, I was flattered beyond words. I'm so privileged to know you and so grateful to have your support.

I'd also like to thank my English professors at University of Southern Maine, namely Rick Swartz, Lorrayne Carroll, Jane Kuenz, and Shelton Waldrep, who all provided great guidance to me and always created fantastic discussion that made me think. I would also need to thank my high school English teachers, namely Stu Palmer, for sparking my appreciation for English. While I'm at it, I might as well thank every teacher I've ever had.

I would also like to thank my editors, but particularly Matt Pepin, who has been one of the staunchest supporters I've had in my career. Matt, you put my career on a strong path by offering me an opportunity at Boston.com. You put a lot of faith in me based only off what you'd read and what other people had said. I'm forever grateful.

The Triumph Books editors helped tremendously with this book, especially Jeff Fedotin and Tom Bast. Tom, you gave me a huge opportunity to write this book. Jeff, you were a huge help throughout the process as a sounding board for my ideas, thoughts, and concerns. I owe you both big time.

There are also a lot of people who helped writing this book, like Bob Hyldburg, Patriots historian and author of *Total Patriots*; the magazine clips you gave me were pure gold, and your book was a huge help.

I would also like to thank people who contributed or whose thoughts and opinions helped shape some of the content you read. Those people include Christopher Price (WEEI.com), Mike Dussault (PatsPropaganda.com), Javier Gorriti and Russ Thompson (The Big Jab 96.3FM in Maine), John Rooke (Patriots.com radio and Gillette Stadium announcer), Field Yates (ESPN), Greg Bedard (*Sports Illustrated*), and countless other Patriots writers, fans, and media personalities who all do a tremendous job covering the team in a highly competitive market.

I'd like to thank every person and Patriots fan who follows my work, especially Jay Kelleher and Nick Stevens. Your support is why I'm still doing this. Your feedback is what keeps me thinking and what keeps me honest.

I would also like to thank Mike Mayock for writing the foreword. I'm honored to have you involved in this project.

But as much as I'd like to individually thank every friend, acquaintance, colleague, peer, boss, and anyone who has helped me in any way from childhood to adulthood, there just isn't the space. I owe you a beverage for not making enough room.

Sources

Altavilla, John. "Rams Not Surprised by Pats' Rise." *Hartford Courant*, January 29, 2002. http://articles.courant.com/2002-01-29/sports/0201291000_1_rams-linebacker-london-fletcher-patriots-mike-martz.

Banks, Don. "The Worst Play Call in NFL History Will Haunt Seahawks in 2015." *Sports Illustrated*, July 21, 2015. http://www.si.com/nfl/2015/07/21/nfl-worst-play-call-seahawks-patriots-super-bowl-xlix-pete-carroll-marshawn-lynch.

Battista, Judy. "Patriots Hire Belichick, and Everyone's Happy." *The New York Times*, January 28, 2000. http://www.nytimes.com/2000/01/28/sports/pro-football-patriots-hire-belichick-and-everyone-s-happy.html.

Bedard, Greg A. "A Meeting of the Minds." *TheMMQB.com* (Sports Illustrated), December 3, 2014. http://mmqb.si.com/2014/12/01/mike-mccarthy-green-bay-packers.

Bedard, Greg A. "With 1 Word, Patriots' No-Huddle an NFL Marvel." *The Boston Globe*, October 9, 2012. https://www.bostonglobe.com/sports/2012/10/08/patriots-huddle-relies-power-one/nHTapuVnBOwfFlffwTrN6J/story.html.

Bensinger, Ken and Ralph Vartabedian. "Toyota Calls in Exponent Inc. As Hired Gun." *Los Angeles Times*, February 18, 2010. http://articles.latimes.com/2010/feb/18/business/la-fi-toyota exponent18-2010feb18.

Bishop, Greg. "Darrelle Revis Is Ready His Return to the Jets." *TheMMQB.com* , August 6, 2015. http://mmqb.si.com/mmqb/2015/07/28/darrelle-revis-new-york-jets-return.

Borges, Ron. "NFL Will Crack down on Pass Interference." *The Boston Globe*, March 31, 2004. http://www.boston.com/sports/football/patriots/articles/2004/03/31/nfl_will_crack_down_on_pass_interference/?page=2.

Britton, Tim. "For Belichick and Pats, Cutdown Day Is More Complicated Than You Think." *Providence Journal*, August 30, 2012. http://www.providencejournal.com/sports/patriots/content/20120830-for-belichick-and-pats-cutdown-day-is-more-complicated-than-you-think.ece?template=printart.

Burke, Brian. "Defending Belichick's Fourth-down Decision." *The Fifth Down*. November 16, 2009. http://fifthdown.blogs.nytimes.com/2009/11/16/defending-belichicks-fourth-down-decision/.

Byrne, Kerry. "The Steel Curtain's Great Statistical Secret." *FootballNation.com*. December 2, 2009. http://www.footballnation.com/content/the-steel-curtains-great-statistical-secret/6893/.

CBS News. *Eye to Eye: Bill Belichick*. May 16, 2008. Posted April 29, 2016.

Clayton, John. "Patriots Release Milloy; Bills Interested." *ESPN*, September 3, 2003. http://espn.go.com/nfl/columns/story?id=1607519&columnist=clayton_john.

Czarniak, Lindsay. "Gronk! The Interview." *ESPN: The Magazine* December 10, 2014,. Accessed April 29, 2016. http://espn.go.com/nfl/story/_/id/11981326/patriots-rob-gronkowski-interview.

Florio, Mike. "AEI's Debunking Reportedly Gets Debunked." *ProFootballTalk.com*. June 29, 2010. http://profootballtalk.nbcsports.com/2015/06/29/aeis-debunking-reportedly-gets-debunked/.

— "Belichick Blames Welker Injury on Reliant Stadium Turf." *ProFootballTalk.com*. January 4, 2010. http://profootballtalk.nbcsports.com/2010/01/04/belichick-blames-welker-injury-on-reliant-stadium-turf/.

Forbes, Gordon. "Walsh, Like His West Coast Offense, Was All out." *USA TODAY*, February 4, 2008. http://usatoday30.usatoday.com/sports/football/nfl/2008-02-03-forbes-walsh_N.htm.

Freeman, Mike. "Belichick Has Patriots' Ears; Now the Hard Part." *New York Times*, July 26, 2000. http://www.nytimes.com/2000/07/26/sports/pro-football-belichick-has-patriots-ears-now-the-hard-part.html.

Gasper, Christopher. "Why Didn't the Patriots Want Wes Welker?" *The Boston Globe*, March 14, 2013. https://www.bostonglobe.com/sports/2013/03/13/wes-welker-didn-leave-patriots-was-pushed-away/aRnqiEVUVJDGIdZKakxjjJ/story.html.

Goldberg, David. (May 15, 2015). accessed April 29, 2016. http://wellsreportcontext.com/.

SOURCES

Greenberg, Alan. "Bledsoe's Record Deal: 10 Years, $103 Million." *Hartford Courant*, March 8, 2001. http://articles.courant.com/2001-03-08/sports/0103082886_1_bledsoe-s-record-deal-patriots-salary-cap.

— "With Bledsoe, Belichick Fumbles." *Hartford Courant*, November 22, 2001. http://articles.courant.com/2001-11-22/sports/0111221552_1_belichick-fumbles-brady-s-performance-bill-belichick.

Harris, David. *The Genius: How Bill Walsh Reinvented Football and Created an NFL Dynasty*. Manhattan, NY: Random House LLC, 2008.

Hill, Rich. "New England Patriots Have a History of Paying Record Contracts for Players." *PatsPulpit.com*. July 16, 2015. http://www.patspulpit.com/2015/7/16/8976261/new-england-patriots-have-a-history-of-paying-record-contracts-for-players.

Howe, Jeff. "Bill Belichick Reflects on His Father's Impact on His Career, Says Football 'was my life as a kid.'" *NESN.com*, January 30, 2012. http://nesn.com/2012/01/bill-belichick-reflects-on-his-fathers-impact-on-his-career-says-football-was-my-life-as-a-kid/.

Hurley, Michael. "Harbaugh Says Belichick's Formations 'clearly deception'; Brady Says 'figure it out.'" *CBS Boston*, January 10, 2015. http://boston.cbslocal.com/2015/01/10/harbaugh-says-belichicks-formations-clearly-deception-brady-says-figure-it-out/.

Hyde, Dave. "Hyde: The School of Jimmy Johnson Open to Sports' Top Minds." *Sun-Sentinel*, July 15, 2015. http://www.sun-sentinel.com/sports/fl-hyde-column-0716-20150715-column.html.

Jaworski, Ron, David Plaut, and Greg Cosell. *Games That Changed the Game, the: The Evolution of the NFL in Seven Sundays*. United States: ESPN Video, 2010.

King, Peter. "Master and Commander: With Football Principles Learned Under His Dad, a Coach at Navy, Brainy Bill Belichick Has Turned New England into the NFL's Mightiest Vessel." August 9, 2004. Accessed April 29, 2016. http://www.si.com/vault/2004/08/09/8213489/master--and--commander-with-football-principles-learned-under-his-dad-a-coach-at-navy-brainy-bill-belichick-has-turned-new-england-into-the-nfls-mightiest-vessel.

Layden, Tim. *Blood, Sweat & Chalk: Inside Football's Playbook: How the Great Coaches Built Today's Game*. United States: Time, Incorporated Home Entertainment, 2010.

Marvez, Alex. "Dumbest Call in Super Bowl History Could Be Beginning of the End for Seattle Seahawks." *FoxSports.com*, February 2, 2015. http://www.foxsports.com/nfl/story/super-bowl-seattle-seahawks-pete-carroll-darrell-bevell-russell-wilson-dumbest-call-ever-020215.

Maske, Mark. "'Worst play-call in Super Bowl History' Will Forever Alter Perception of Seahawks, Patriots." *The Washington Post*, February 2, 2015. https://www.washingtonpost.com/news/sports/wp/2015/02/02/worst-play-call-in-super-bowl-history-will-forever-alter-perception-of-seahawks-patriots/.

— "Broncos Penalized Again for Salary Cap Violations." *Washington Post*, September 17, 2004. http://www.washingtonpost.com/wp-dyn/articles/A28969-2004Sep17.html.

— "Tuck Rule Hard to Grasp." *The Washington Post*, October 15, 2005. http://www.washingtonpost.com/wp-dyn/content/article/2005/10/14/AR2005101401828.html.

Musick, Phil. "The General Is Private." *Pro! Magazine*.

NFL Films. *A Football Life—Bill Belichick*.

—*America's Game—2001 New England Patriots*.

—*America's Game—2003 New England Patriots*.

—*America's Game—2004 New England Patriots*.

—*America's Game—2014 New England Patriots*.

O'Boyle, Tom. "'Hail to the Redskins': What Coach Joe Gibbs Did to Make a Bad Team Great." *Pittsburgh Post-Gazette*, December 27, 2015. http://www.post-gazette.com/ae/books/2015/12/27/Hail-to-the-Redskins-What-coach-Joe-Gibbs-did-to-make-a-bad-team-great/stories/201512270023.

O'Connor, Ian. "The Man Who Made Belichick Great." *ESPN*, February 4, 2015. http://espn.go.com/nfl/playoffs/2014/story/_/id/12270179/ian-oconnor-how-bill-belichick-father-inspired-an-nfl-great.

Ozanian, Mike. "The NFL Will Conclude Belichick and Brady Did Not Cheat." *Forbes*, January 25, 2015. http://www.forbes.com/sites/mikeozanian/2015/01/25/the-nfl-will-conclude-belichick-and-brady-did-not-cheat/#234edbdc4694.

Petraglia, Mike. "Of Ice Picks, Tablets and the Bill Belichick Teaching Method." *WEEI.com*, September 19, 2014. http://www.weei.com/sports/boston/football/patriots/mike-petraglia/2014/09/19/ice-picks-tablets-and-bill-belichick-teach.

Rapoport, Ian R. "Vikings and Patriots in Talks: Randy Moss Asked for Trade." *Boston Herald*, October 6, 2010. http://www.bostonherald.com/sports/patriots_nfl/new_england_patriots/2010/10/vikings_and_patriots_talks_randy_moss_asked_trade.

Reiss, Mike. "Patriots Humbled as Jets Deliver a Beating." *The Boston Globe*, November 13, 2006. https://www.bostonglobe.com/sports/2006/11/13/patriots-humbled-jets-deliver-beating/SQfyJmii7Lz9vyrhjm78TN/story.html.

SOURCES

— "Patriots Won't Be Hit Harder." *The Boston Globe*, September 21, 2007. http://www.boston.com/sports/football/patriots/articles/2007/09/21/patriots_wont_be_hit_harder/

—"Pats Quickly Shifted from Welker to Amendola." March 14, 2013. Accessed April 29, 2016. http://espn.go.com/boston/nfl/story/_/id/9050742/2013-nfl-free-agency-new-england-patriots-quickly-shifted-wes-welker-danny-amendola.

— "Seau Signed." *The Boston Globe*, August 18, 2006. http://www.boston.com/sports/football/patriots/extra_points/2006/08/seau_signed.html.

Robinson, Alan. "Steelers' Smith Guarantees Upset of Pats."*Associated Press*, December 5, 2007. http://www.washingtonpost.com/wp-dyn/content/article/2007/12/05/AR2007120503087_pf.html.

Rosenthal, Gregg. "Buccaneers Trade Aqib Talib to Patriots for Draft Pick." *Around The NFL*. November 1, 2012. http://www.nfl.com/news/story/0ap1000000088693/article/buccaneers-trade-aqib-talib-to-patriots-for-draft-pick.

Sachs, Marty. "Cowboys Reflect Johnson's Football Philosophy."*Post-Bulletin*, January 27, 1993. http://www.postbulletin.com/cowboys-reflect-johnson-s-football-philosophy/article_5d380147-386d-5fd1-a307-79ec136e8fd9.html.

Seifert, Kevin. "George Halas—There From The Start." *ESPN*, June 8, 2013. http://espn.go.com/nfl/story/_/page/greatestcoach4/greatest-coaches-nfl-history-george-halas.

Shaughnessy, Dan. "Belichick Gaffe Unrivaled." *The Boston Globe*, November 16, 2009. http://www.boston.com/sports/football/patriots/articles/2009/11/16/belichick_gaffe_unrivaled/.

Sheaffer, Scott. "The Truth About Spygate: Punishing Success and Promoting Parity." *Bleacher Report*. June 14, 2009. http://bleacherreport.com/articles/199345-the-truth-about-spygate-punishing-success-and-promoting parity.

Smith, Michael. "Patriots Outlast Titans in Frigid Playoff Test." *The Boston Globe*, January 11, 2004. https://www.bostonglobe.com/sports/2004/01/11/patriots-outlast-titans-frigid-playoff-test/8EhwV4QK6OZspiprfurliKJ/story.html.

Smith, Michael David. "Peyton Manning Calls Bill Belichick 'greatest NFL coach of all time.'" *ProFootballTalk.com*. January 15, 2010. http://profootballtalk.nbcsports.com/2014/01/15/peyton-manning-calls-bill-belichick-greatest-nfl-coach-of-all-time/.

Stewart, Larry. "'Very disappointed,' Hackett Gets the Ax." *Los Angeles Times*, November 28, 2000. http://articles.latimes.com/2000/nov/28/sports/sp-58380.

Toomay, Pat. "Understanding Madden, Part 1." *ESPN*, February 11, 2005. http://espn.go.com/page2/s/toomay/021105.html.

Wells, Theodore, Brad Karp, and Lorin Reisner. *Investigative Report Concerning Footballs Used During the AFC Championship Game On January 18, 2015*. n.p.: Paul, Weiss, Rifkind, Wharton & Garrison LLP, 2015. https://www.documentcloud.org/documents/2073728-ted-wells-report-deflategate.html.

Wilson, Philip. "Temp Job with Colts Taught Young Belichick Valuable Lessons." *USA TODAY*, January 20, 2007. http://usatoday30.usatoday.com/sports/football/nfl/patriots/2007-01-20-belichick-start_x.htm.

Wojciechowski, Gene. "Look to Cleveland to Understand Belichick." January 28, 2008. Accessed April 29, 2016. http://espn.go.com/espn/columns/story?id=3217121&columnist=wojciechowski_gene&sportCat=nfl.

Websites

www.ProFootballFocus.com
www.Pro-Football-Reference.com
www.NFL.com
www.ESPN.com